I0575748

Studies in Judaism

Dedication

This volumeof Marvin Fox's Essays is dedicated to our dear children, Avrom and Debra; Daniel and Barbara, Sherry and Laurence; and our beloved grandchildren, Jeremy, Aliza, Roniel, Emunah, Eytan, Amy, Naomi, Aaron, David, Joshua, Michael and Jonathon.

All of them join me in expressing our profound gratitude to Marvin's esteemed colleague and devoted friend, Professor Jacob Neusner, whose remarkable efforts have brought about the publication of this work.

June Fox

TABLE OF CONTENTS

VOLUME TWO

III

SOME PHILOSOPHERS

VOLUME ONE

GREEK PHILOSOPHY, MAIMONIDES

PREFACE

MEMOIR

BIBLIOGRAPHY OF MARVIN FOX

I

GREEK PHILOSOPHY

1. THE TRIALS OF SOCRATES. AN INTERPRETATION OF THE FIRST TETRALOGY

2. THE DOCTRINE OF THE MEAN IN ARISTOTLE AND MAIMONIDES: A COMPARATIVE STUDY

3. A HISTORY OF THE DOCTRINE OF THE MEAN IN EARLY GREEK THOUGHT: FROM HOMER THROUGH PLATO

II

MAIMONIDES

4. A NEW VIEW OF MAIMONIDES' METHOD OF CONTRADICTIONS

5. PROLEGOMENON TO *THE TEACHINGS OF MAIMONIDES* BY A. COHEN

6. REVIEW: JULIUS GUTTMANN, *THE GUIDE OF THE PERPLEXED BY MOSES MAIMONIDES*

7. REVIEW: SHLOMO PINES, *THE GUIDE OF THE PERPLEXED BY MOSES MAIMONIDES*

8. MAIMONIDES AND AQUINAS ON NATURAL LAW

David Shatz, PhD

Review Essay

REMEMBERING MARVIN FOX:
ONE MAN'S LEGACY TO JEWISH THOUGHT

Collected Essays on Philosophy and on Judaism, by MARVIN FOX.

Edited by JACOB NEUSNER.

Volume one: *Greek Philosophy, Maimonides.*

Volume two: *Some Philosophers.*

Volume three: *Ethics, Reflections.*

Academic Studies in the History of Judaism, Binghamton, New York: Global Publications, Binghamton University, 2001.

This essay by Professor David Shatz of Yeshiva University is an abridged version of one published in *Tradition*, volume 36, No. 1, Spring 2002. It is reprinted here by permission of *Tradition* and The Rabbinical Council of America.

INTRODUCTION

Marvin Fox was a leading contributor to Jewish thought for nearly half a century and enjoyed an unusually fulfilling career before cancer claimed his life in 1996 at the age of 73. A *musmakh* of Hebrew Theological College in Chicago (1942) and chaplain in the Air Force during World War II, Fox trained in philosophy at the University of Chicago, where he received his doctorate in 1950 on the subject of methodology in ethical theory. Defying the odds against a Jewish professor earning a high post in academia at the time, he dreamt in the late 1930's and early '40's of becoming a professor of philosophy in a major university—and a scholar of Jewish studies to boot. (So his wife, Dr. June Fox, discloses in a moving prefatory memoir.) Thanks to a combination of natural talent and the post-war need for professors who would teach returning G. I.'s, Fox earned an academic appointment. He taught philosophy at Ohio State University for twenty-six years, during which he also performed rabbinic functions in Columbus, albeit without an official position. A substantial number of his publications were of a Jewish nature, but aside from visiting professorships in Israel, he did not teach a Jewish studies course until he changed institutions in 1974. In that year, Fox came to Brandeis University as a professor and then chair of the school's distinguished Department of Near Eastern and Judaic Studies. Later he was appointed Director of the Lown School of Jewish Studies. After retiring from Brandeis in 1994, he taught in the departments of religion and philosophy at Boston University.[1]

Fox's academic honors included many awards and distinguished editorial positions, and he was a vital force in the founding and dramatic growth of academic Jewish Studies programs in the United States and Israel. A caring, beloved, and diligent mentor, he guided many students to degrees, helped them find jobs in a tight market, and raised money to assist their scholarly endeavors. A measure of the esteem in which colleagues held him is that the *Festschrift* for him comprised four volumes (!) and, like the book being reviewed now, was edited by no less an academic force than Jacob Neusner.[2] The respect Fox earned in the scholarly world owed to both his intellect and his integrity, personal traits which made his career in academia a *Kiddush ha-Shem*, especially given the love and respect for Orthodoxy that he openly conveyed to the academic community. He was a consummate *mentsch*, ever gracious and elegant even in receiving criticism, and was blessed with a sparkling wit. Fox also dedicated himself to challenges facing the Jewish community, particularly day school education. He was a leading figure in Torah Umesorah as well as a contributor to the magazine *The Jewish Parent* and anthologies on Jewish education. He also had an impact on adult education.

Fox was a master communicator and teacher, both orally and in writing. Whereas much of philosophy today is riddled with jargon and formulas and is totally inaccessible to non-specialists, Fox's essays display a stunningly consistent clarity, flow, eloquence and accessibility. Seldom does a sentence or paragraph need to be reread to be understood. In addition, his range is remarkable. I confess to not having had a full measure of his versatility until I paused to reflect holistically on the thirty-four scholarly works in these volumes and to scan the full listing of Fox's 148 works contained in volume one of the collection.[3] He was at home and prolific in both Jewish and general philosophy, writing with equal acuity about, on the one hand, Socrates, Aristotle, David Hume, Immanuel Kant,[4] Paul Tillich, F. H. Bradley, and John Dewey, and, on the other, Halevi, Maimonides, Maharal, Rav Kook, Martin Buber, Abraham Joshua Heschel, and Eliezer Berkovits. Thus, one essay proposes an edifying understanding of the progression among the four Platonic dialogues that center on Socrates' trial and death, while another elucidates the Holocaust experience as it emerges in Yiddish stories by Zvi Kolitz ("Yossel Rakover Speaks to God") and Chaim Grade ("My Quarrel With Hersh Rasseyner"). One essay traces the history of the doctrine of the mean from Homer to Plato, while another analyzes the presuppositions and implications of *hespedim* delivered by Rabbi Joseph B. Soloveitchik, *z.t.l.* One essay deftly critiques the ethical theologies of Bradley and Dewey, another formulates a novel theory of the *Perplexed*. One paper explores Hume's views on human nature, while another presents a stimulating account of Jewish ethics....

Fox offered a plausible reason for philosophy's importance. To understand his argument, it is imperative to distinguish between philosophy as a body of teachings—Plato's philosophy, Kant's philosophy, Rambam's philosophy, and so forth—and philosophy as a *method*. As a method, philosophy is, in William James' phrase "an unusually stubborn attempt to think things through." Or, as Fox puts it, "critical thinking about the theoretical foundations of whatever subject or text is being analyzed." "Philosophy thus defined," he tells us, "is a universal and inescapable human activity which can be applied to any subject. It is not the exclusive claim of the professional philosopher but an ongoing task of every man"(3:98).[5] Fox states:

> The very nature of philosophic thinking is such that it can and should be applied without exception to the entire corpus of Jewish literature, Bible, Talmud, and other major Jewish works are not systematic philosophic treatises, but they will never be fully understood if we do not approach them with the concerns and techniques of philosophy... The texts which seem least philosophical are often the ones which demand philosophical analysis....[6]

Fox gives a variety of examples (see vol. 3, pp. 95-112). Proper analysis of any text requires a (philosophical) theory of interpretation. Unpacking a phrase like *en ruah hakhamin noha hemenu*, or understanding a *mishna* which rules that we issue a *mi she-para* (a curse) against someone even though he has acted in accordance with the technical law (*Bava Metsia* 4:2), requires an approach to the (philosophical) question of how law relates to morality.[7] Philosophical tools must be used to explicate biblical thought and also *Hazal's* pronouncements on freedom, divine law, justice and other topics. Rashi, who is often characterized as anti-philosophical, "demands no less philosophical insight and sophistication" than do biblical commentaries by Spanish *parshanim*, because he has a theory of interpretation, holds views on anthropomorphism, and so on. Likewise, "serious literature that deals with the human condition has some philosophical and religious dimensions.... Even purely historical or documentary treatments of the Holocaust are permeated with philosophical and religious questions" (3:207). If philosophical questions surface in literature and history, then presumably mastery of philosophic method will deepen one's study of literature. I do not think Fox means that to develop a philosophy is merely to *raise* these questions about texts using the method of analytical reasoning. Rather, to "do" philosophy well is to raise them and answer them—to use constructively the method Fox describes, to provide a theory of law and morality, of interpretation, or of freedom, or to argue that there can be no such theories. What we call Jewish philosophy must be developed by analytical tools....

II. PHILOSOPHY, THE HISTORY OF PHILOSOPHY, AND THE PHILOSOPHY OF HISTORY

Fox's vision of how philosophy can illuminate many areas of Judaism becomes still clearer when we examine his attitude toward purely historical studies of philosophical figures, which seek only to trace influences and set context. Fox, recall, earned his philosophy doctorate in America. Unlike European-trained scholars of Jewish thought, therefore, he was trained to focus on philosophical problems and to regard figures and movements as important objects of study mainly insofar as they had something to contribute to addressing those problems.[8] This point is illustrated as well by his studies of Plato, Aristotle, David Hume, F. H. Bradley and John Dewey. Those essays are certainly directed beyond the historical, engaging large philosophical issues such as the foundations of ethics. Even though philosophy journals and publishers of books in analytic philosophy have over the past twenty-five years showed a marked turn to the history of philosophy, their objective is to pursue history in the service of developing philosophical ideas. The sparseness of footnotes in Fox's writings reflects a predilection for original thought and for elucidating ideas in contemporary terms, as opposed to extensive citation of influences and relationships in the European style.

Regarding an exclusively historical approach to Jewish philosophy, Fox offers gentle but unmistakable criticism:

> [W]e must recognize how severely and needlessly we limit philosophy if we restrict it to the study of the history of Jewish philosophy... (3:97) As scholars continue to pursue these and similar [historical] studies, they should not lose sight of the philosophic purpose of the enterprise. ...The kind of philosophic approach which we take for granted when we study Plato or Aristotle, Descartes or Spinoza, Whitehead or Wittgenstein, should be adopted in our studies of Jewish philosophy. To do anything less is to transform great philosophic works into textbooks for linguistic and historical studies. We can only claim to understand a serious Jewish philosopher when we are able to provide a systematic formulation of his philosophy of Judaism (3:110-11).

Students inform me that in his classes Fox would always stress the ongoing resonance and relevance of an idea.[9] To be sure, rendering history of philosophy secondary has drawbacks and pitfalls. An idea's meaning can be skewed when isolated from its historical context: and a figure could be unfairly criticized for not thinking like a philosopher. Fox is aware of these dangers and does not belittle the need for genuine sensitivity to historical context and to a thinker's goals.[10] Historians might feel that his analyses of classic figures need more historical contextualization. But on the whole, his encouraging the search for a thinker's potentially enduring idea or underlying method, which must then be assessed philosophically, can be of great help in forming our attitudes to many problems. Interestingly, some scholars made the move from scholarly studies of medieval historical figures to articulation of their own theology (Emil Fackenheim, Abraham Joshua Heschel, Eliezer Schweid). In Israel today, despite a somewhat rigid compartmentalization of academic departments, a significant number of people trained in philosophy engage in both historical studies and the articulation of theological stances and ethical or political philosophies. This suggests the possibility of productively using the history of ideas to form new viewpoints, exactly as Fox urged.

In recent years Orthodoxy (across its various "wings") has displayed a turn to history; a look at Orthodox journals and the scholar-in-residence circuit confirms this. But Fox, I think, might have wanted to see a more philosophical approach to historiography than has been common.

Here is an example. Centrist Orthodoxy highlights the phenomenon of change in Jewish history—changes in ideologies and practices, for example; by contrast, right wing Orthodoxy tends to present everything as a seamless continuity. Centrists therefore confront a problem. If Judaism changes so much, why battle any particular deviational phenomenon? Why not just say "Well, the religion changes"? How can we reconcile commitment to a particular version of Judaism with knowledge of historical fluctuations? This is simply the philosophical thicket known as the problem of historicism.[11] It strikes me that if such philosophical questions were part of centrist Orthodoxy's agenda, it would lead to a deeper understanding of what religious commitment entails and how the study of history should proceed.

Likewise consider the question of whether Jewish history affords us normative precedents. To take an example, thanks to the researches of such scholars as Moshe Idel, Ephraim Kanarfogel, and Elliot Wolfson (and of course, ultimately Gershom Scholem), we now know that mysticism has been widespread in Jewish history, infiltrating, as Kanarfogel shows, even ranks of the *Ba'alei ha-Tosafot*.[12] Now there would seem to be important and difficult tensions between mysticism and the worldview of "madda." What are we to infer from the persistent historical presence of mysticism vis-à-vis what Orthodox Jews today must pursue? Must we more actively cultivate mysticism because of what history teaches about Judaism?[13] This is another question of the sort Fox might have asked. I suggest, then, that his conception of philosophy as a method to be applied across many domains can lead to fruitful—and pressing—lines of inquiry.[14]

III. FOX ON THE LIMITS OF REASON

The essays in this collection vary greatly in their objectives. Some are purely expository; others put familiar sources into a large framework. Some are purely critical; others contain constructive theorizing. Fox seems always to have carefully thought through his goals and to have varied the balance of exposition and criticism, as well of criticism and theory-building, from assignment to assignment. In fact Fox (in a book chapter not included in the volume[15]) once wrote a kind of "Rashi," a line-by-line commentary to Rambam's treatment of the *Gan Eden* narrative. This testifies to his creativity in finding the right genre in which to explore a text or issue. In the remainder of this essay I will concentrate on the essays in which Fox stakes out his own philosophy or finds a congenial philosophy in a particular author.

In particular, I focus on one theme that runs through Fox's writings: the limits of human reason. From studying philosophy, he learned that we cannot rationally prove there is an external world, or that nature's workings in the future will resemble its past operations. He also internalized the problems involved in establishing objective ethical values. This theme of skepticism shapes Fox's views on faith, on morality, and then finally on the philosophy of Maimonides.

Faith

Let us begin with the grounding of faith. In an essay on David Hume, the great eighteenth century Scottish philosopher, Fox quotes Hume's intriguing remark that "A person, seasoned with a just sense of the imperfections of natural reason, will fly to revealed truth with the greatest avidity."[16] As Fox points out, Hume may have intended this remark tongue in cheek, but the serious point is that philosophy shows us that our most precious beliefs about the world are not sufficiently warranted on the basis of evidence. Once people realize the limited powers of the human intellect, once they face up to our inability to secure certainty in knowledge, religious faith can be upheld.

Fox's faith draws support, as I said, from his philosophical training, which taught him skepticism concerning the powers of the mind. Perhaps the clearest statement of this view is in an essay that appeared in *Commentary* in 1966 in a symposium on "The Condition of Jewish Belief." Fox wrote then:

> I believe, because I cannot afford not to believe. I believe, as a Jew, in the divinity of Torah, because without God's Torah I have lost the ground for making my own life intelligible and purposeful. To believe because life demands it is not peculiar to religious men. It is something that reasonable men do as a matter of course in other areas. For example, most men in Western society believe that there is some necessary relationship between reason and reality, though no decisive evidence can be offered for this conviction. They hold to it because if the world does not conform to human reason then it is unintelligible, and we find that an unbearable state of affairs. Rather than face the pain of an unintelligible world we affirm, as an act of faith, that it must be rationally ordered. We insist that whatever reason finds necessary must be the case in reality and whatever reason finds impossible can never be the case in reality. And we do so rightly, for with anything less our lives would become a hopeless chaos. The same holds true of the Jew who believes in the Torah as divine, even while acknowledging that he has and can have no decisive evidence. He believes because the order, structure, direction, and meaning of his life are at stake, because the alternative is personal and moral chaos.[17]

Another way to put this might be to say, with apologies to Socrates, that the overexamined life is not worth living. A worthwhile life will involve logical leaps, or else purpose and meaning will be lost. This argument is not *anti*-philosophical. Rather, it represents a type of philosophical argument that enjoys currency among philosophers today.[18] Fox's familiarity with the problem of skepticism and with the pragmatist tradition in philosophy, which stresses the practical consequences—for example, the emotional benefits—of believing in certain cases,[19] is evident in the line of thought he endorses.

While I accept this basic approach, its limitations should be noted. Most obviously, Fox's reasoning places no constraints on what people might find meaningful, what might give order, structure, and purpose to their lives. For all he has said, extremists of all kinds can use the same argument to defend their beliefs and actions; thus his position courts relativism and a legitimation of wrongful worldviews and practices.[20] Atheists can claim that to attribute the real power in the universe to a single being who lies beyond nature is a thought they psychologically cannot endure. In addition, whereas there is no serious evidence that our reason is *not* reliable, there are *prima facie* difficulties with religious belief, such as the problem of evil and the fact that God does not provide greater evidence for His existence and the divinity of His revelation. Fox needs a reply to these challenges to faith.[21] That said, it strikes me that as a *strategy* for defending faith, Fox's approach is an instructive caution against imposing on religious believers standards for knowledge that are not imposed on other beliefs, and that he ultimately charts a fruitful path.[22]

Halakha and Morality

The Orthodox community has been deeply exercised over whether Judaism recognizes a valid standard of ethics that is independent of halakha, and if so, whether this standard, which presumably is reflected in intuitions about what is moral and immoral, is operative and influential in *pesak*. Sometimes the question is framed as whether Judaism believes in natural law (a standard of morality that reason can discover independently of religion) or as whether general ethical intuitions have an impact on halakhic decision making. For the most part, the centrist community stresses both the validity of ethical intuitions and their vitality in *pesak*.

Fox, by contrast, held a deep skepticism about the ability of human beings to discover general ethical norms, and for this reason rejected the idea that Judaism believes in a valid ethical standard that can be known without God's commands. The *Commentary* essay cited above argues this point explicitly: "Those who think that moral principles are self-validating would do well to study the history of ethical theory. Contemporary moral philosophers are still struggling—with notably little success—to find independent foundations for their ethical principles."[23] Fox deploys skepticism in critiquing Thomas Aquinas's views on "natural law" and maintains that Maimonides, in contrast to Aquinas, rejected natural law teaching (1:183-208). The difficulty of grounding ethics objectively also is salient in his writing on Dewey. At times, at least, Fox went so far as to deny that any significant Jewish thinker ever believed in natural law; so, for example, even though Sa'adya Gaon separated *mitsvot* into *sikhliyyot* (rational) and *shim'iyyot* (revelational) and thus ostensibly believed in a rational ethics, Fox held that this is a misleading characterization of Sa'adya's position.[24]

The best sources for his views are an essay I regard as a gem, a 1979 work entitled "The Philosophical Foundations of Jewish Ethics: Some Initial Reflections" (3:51-74), originally published as a pamphlet by the University of Cincinnati, and an essay titled "The Mishnah As A Source for Jewish Ethics" (3:75-93). In "Philosophical Foundations," Fox argues against the widespread idea that the Noahide laws represent laws discoverable by human reason. He maintains that the very language of *"mitsvot"benei Noah* implies heteronomously imposed laws (laws imposed by an authority from without, i.e. other than oneself), and that certain details of the Talmud's discussion in *Sanhedrin* 56a-b militate against the natural law conception: the *gemara's* appeal to *Genesis* 2:17-18, where God commands Adam concerning trees in Gan Eden, as the text for a *midrash halakha* from which the laws are derived; the inclusion of *ever min ha-hai* (flesh cut from a living animal); and the proposal of additional or alternative items such as prohibitions against castration and sorcery, which are not universally held moral principles. Besides contesting others' appeal to Noahide laws as a proof of an independent morality, he rejects arguments based on Nahmanides' famous glosses on "you shall be holy" (*Leviticus* 19:2) and "do the straight and the good" (*Deuteronomy* 6:18). Fox observes that these commands are just that, a divine imperative. His idea here is that it is odd to say that ethics has a value independent of halakha when the reason one accepts ethics is that halakha (or God) tells us to do so! Jewish ethics, therefore, is ultimately heteronomous.

In talmudic and later halakhic texts it often *appears* that a legal rule is overridden by values that are derived from an external standard of morality. Fox maintains that in all such cases the value that is invoked is *internal* to Judaism, not external. Take, for example, the mishna *Bava Metsia* 4:2: a person who has paid the money for an object, but has not yet taken formal possession through *meshikha*, may technically renege, but is administered a curse for doing so. Fox maintains that since the value of keeping one's word is a Jewish value, one need not turn to external ethical values in order to explain why *Hazal* imposed the curse. Similarly, if Rabbi Akiva and Rabbi Tarfon opposed capital punishment (*Makkot* 7a), this need not reflect the influence of external values but rather of the "internal" value of human life. If a priest does not examine a *nega* that erupts during a festival until after the festival, and does not examine a groom's eruption until after the seven days, then "even if we conjecture that the decision is based on humane moral considerations, we should remember that these considerations are not imposed from without, but reflect a choice between competing values in the Torah itself." (3:87-88). Likewise, laws based on *tikkun olam, darkhei shalom* or *takkanat ha-shavim* are based on certain *Jewish* values; "Concern for the general welfare, fairness, and compassion, are all an established part of the system" (Ibid., 89). Citing the existence of harsh-sounding rulings in cases of *mamzerut*, Fox insists that "it is not an independent morality or axiology which motivates the Sages of the Mishna. They teach the law as they understand it, even when it seems to run contrary to our (perhaps even their own) moral tastes" (3:83). Finally: "There seems to be very little evidence that the Mishna entertains any conception of a realm of the ethical which is independent of the law" (3:93).[25]

Fox's arguments should give pause to anyone who invokes the "usual suspects," that is, commonly cited texts, to vindicate claims of natural law in Judaism. He is right that given what seems to be a moral hesitation to apply a certain halakha, be it *ben sorer u-moreh*,[26] be it capital punishment, be it strict *din* as opposed to *peshara*, we cannot blithely assume that the morality is derived from without as opposed to from within. Even Nahmanides' famous comments on "be holy" and "do the straight and the good" refer to a standard that is inferred from *other laws of the Torah*. This is especially evident when Ramban draws a parallel between "be holy" and "do the straight and the good" and the general law "*tishbot*" on Shabbat. The applications of *tishbot* are extrapolated from other laws of the Shabbat and clearly do not come from an independent ethic.

Nonetheless, despite the formidable strength of Fox's challenge to the usual proof texts, his denial of the validity of general ethical intuitions faces serious difficulties. I further believe that his attempt to make all values that are invoked in halakhic decision making to be "internal" eventually will encounter serious obstacles and possibly failure. (In what follows I assume he did not mean for his claim about the values being internal to apply *only* to *Hazal*, but rather to halakha generally.)

I shall assume for our purposes that Fox is not advocating the notoriously difficult view that there is no valid standard of ethics outside of God's will, that, in Dostoevsky's phrase, "if there is no God, everything is permitted."[27] Instead I take him as believing that such a standard exists, while denying our ability to *know* the correct standard. (Hence the necessity for our using halakha as the source of "ethical" knowledge.) Now if we cannot know a correct ethical standard, we cannot form the intuition that we owe gratitude to a creator by reference to gratitude as an "external" value dictated by our moral sense; we cannot assert, on the basis of independent moral intuitions, that we must keep promises—for example the one we made at Sinai—or that we must tell the truth;[28] we cannot praise God for what He has done using an external standard;[29] we cannot see evil as a problem by invoking an "external" standard by which Nazi atrocities are wrong. Fox could well assert *"in hakhi nammi."* But aside from the counterintuitiveness of these assertions, Fox's critique of Eliezer Berkovits' attempt to explain God's allowing Nazi atrocities (in Berkovits' *Faith After the Holocaust*) reveals that he, Fox, is not a total skeptic about validating "external" values. "It is monstrous to suggest that, in the last analysis, we have no possibility of sound moral judgment.... Happily [philosophers who may say this] are better than their theories, and they continue to affirm the classical distinctions between good and evil even though they cannot provide any ultimate sanction for the values which they cherish" (2:96). It is difficult to see how this impassioned trust in our moral perceptions of the Nazi atrocity can sit together easily with the notion that moral judgments cannot be known independently.

Suppose we put aside this concern; suppose we allow that the judgments about gratitude and about evil are all "internally" based. Can all cases really be codified using only rules together with intuitions that are extrapolated from Jewish sources? At times the legal precedents would seem to be too meager, and the underlying value system too unclear. Sometimes, when we extrapolate values from the system, we end up with irreconcilable but ostensibly equally weighty values. Arguably, in order to rule in such cases, one must appeal to an external value to decide which internal value deserves greater weight.

Furthermore, consider Orthodox attitudes to slavery, polygamy, *kiddushei ketanna* and various inequalities (e. g., in the distribution of an inheritance). If Fox were right, "externally derived" ethical objections to these practices, today or long ago, would not be admissible in the halakhic process. Those who portray the halakha as insulated from "external" values typically state that halakhic positions taken in these areas may coincide with, for example, democratic values, but those values are not *appropriated* unless they are judged to be also internal Torah values.[30] What then can justify changed attitudes to the practices I named? How could we claim that authorities who oppose such practices do so on the basis of an "internal" value, when it is clear that the Torah long allowed the practice *despite* its (presumed) knowledge of the opposing internal value?[31] Unfortunately, Fox did not get to write a major book on Jewish ethics as he had planned. I am certain he would have delved into these problems.[32]

Maimonides

In light of his stress on skepticism, it is not surprising that Fox's work on Maimonides concentrates on the question of how much scope Maimonides gives to human reason. He staunchly opposes scholarly interpretations that portray Maimonides as an arch rationalist who thought that reason provides answers to all questions, even to the point of (on some interpretations) according no significant epistemological status to either divine revelation or rabbinic tradition.[33]

Fox also cogently rejects a widely adopted hermeneutic that portrays Rambam as a closet heretic. Much of the "esotericist" case rests on Maimonides' statement in the introduction to the *Guide of the Perplexed* that he has deliberately inserted contradictions into the work, some of which are of the "seventh" kind (which I will not bother to explain here). Medievel esotericists (e.g., Samuel ibn Tibbon, Joseph ibn Kaspi, Moses Narboni), as well as Leo Strauss and Shlomo Pines of the twentieth century, construe Maimonides as implying that his true view is to be found in the more radical statement in a contradictory pair. Against this trend, Fox wrote a witty, incisive review of Pines' translation of the *Guide of the Perplexed*, the standard English version of the work (I:165-81). The review included a zestful and amusing application of Strauss' methods (as used in his preface to Pines' translation) to Strauss' own words. By questioning the conventional wisdom (Strauss' view), Fox—again, impressively—was a pioneer of a novel approach to the contradictions in the *Guide*, an approach that seems to be catching on in the scholarly world.[34] Basically, the approach maintains that the "contradictions due to the seventh cause" are not contradictions that Maimonides inserts to hide his own radical opinions. Rather, the contradictions reflect the inability of human reason to decide certain issues.[35] His portrait of Maimonides reflects Fox's own awareness of uncertainty.

For all his recognition of reason's limitations, Fox believed that philosophical inquiry must continue. In this he was, I think, emulating his own description of Socrates. In the dialogue *Phaedo*, Socrates speaks of the "misologists," those who despise logic because of its perceived inability to arrive at definite conclusions. Plato's Socrates knew both the dangers of dogmatism and the pitfalls of misology. Hence he concluded, in Fox's words, "the best way is the middle way, that of continuing inquiry without stop, neither hoping for cheaply won certainties, nor hating inquiry because it rarely justifies such certainties" ("The Trials of Socrates," 1:19).

IV. CONCLUSION

What, in particular, can we learn from Marvin Fox? Many things, I have suggested: that philosophy is important for the study of all Jewish texts; that it can provide meaning to our lives as Jews; that it need not be perceived as a nemesis of faith but on the contrary can be utilized as a constructive support. Openness to the study of culture not only is compatible with a deep commitment to religious life, but it nurtures such a commitment....

Fox's philosophical writing, so clear and engaging, is an excellent place to begin the serious study of *mahashava*, whether in high schools, universities, or adult education groups. That readers will challenge his words and will want to go beyond his writings is a tribute to his capacity to stimulate. Perhaps by recalling Marvin Fox and his historical context, we can recapture and even recreate those good old days when *mahashava* mattered.

I close this lengthy review essay with Fox's own words. In one essay Fox explicates a principle that he suggests guided the Rav [Rabbi Joseph B. Soloveitchik] in his eulogies. He calls attention to a Yiddish *derasha* in which the Rav compares a person to a *Sefer Torah*.[36] Fox deduces that:

> If a Jew is a *Sefer Torah*, then to know an individual Jew requires the same kind of intellectual effort, the same kind of conceptual formulation and elucidation, as does every other topic in the study of Torah. The more eminent the person, the greater and deeper his learning, the more exemplary his virtue, the more creative and sound his leadership, the more sensitive his piety, the greater the intellectual challenge to understanding the departed personality. ("The Rav as Mapsid," 2:157)

Many sided, virtuous, and profound, Marvin Fox, his life and thought, deserves to be studied and expounded.

NOTES

[1] The information in this paragraph is taken from the prefaces by editor Jacob Neusner and by June Fox.

[2] Jacob Neusner (ed.), From Ancient Israel to Modern Judaism: Intellect in Quest of Understanding: Essays in Honor of Marvin Fox (Atlanta: Scholars Press for Brown Judaic Studies, 1989).

[3] The bibliographic information on the last five items is incomplete, but three of those items appear in the volumes.

[4] Many a philosophy student has been raised on the popular Thomas K. Abbott translation of Kant's *Fundamental Principles of the Metaphysics of Morals*, published in 1949 as part of the Bobbs-Merrill "Library of Liberal Arts" series. Fox wrote the introduction to that volume.

[5] Similarly, Mark Steiner has argued that the study of, say, intention or causation as these are utilized in a Talmudic *sugya* is an instance of philosophy. By this criterion, the writing of Rabbi Israel Salanter on subjects like weakness of will and humility is itself philosophy—of a high caliber—even though the author is to all appearances a foe of philosophy. See Steiner's interesting analysis in "Rabbi Israel Salanter As a Jewish Philosopher," *The Torah u-Madda Journal* 9(2001): 42-57, esp. 42-46.

[6] The essay from which I am quoting, "The Role of Philosophy in Jewish Studies" (essay #27, 3:95-111), actually attempts to show philosophy's relevance to *academic* Jewish studies. But if cogent, Fox's argument would affect even non-academic study of *Tanakh*, Talmud or Midrash, so I feel comfortable applying it to the non-academic sphere. Fox's approach dovetails nicely with the Rav's view that Jewish philosophy can (and must) be constructed out of the Bible and halakhic sources. See Yitzhak Twersky, "The Rov," *Tradition* 30:4 (1996): 28-36, for an explanation of the role that philosophy plays for the Rav in explicating Jewish texts.

Fox has other remarks about philosophy: e. g., that it utilizes arguments (3:123-32), and that it "is not an intellectual chess game which uses concepts in place of rooks and pawns.... Only when human thought reaches the level of deepest earnestness does it become philosophical. Only when a thinker addresses himself to the deepest human questions can he become a philosopher" (2:45). I will not try to integrate these comments into the one I focus on, but I do think that in the end his view is a cohesive one.

[7] Like most writers who deal with this topic, Fox does not make use of the vast literature on philosophy of law, especially on natural law vs. positivistic theories of law. I think this trend is unfortunate, but will not say more on that subject even though I later take up Fox's views on the place of moral intuitions in halakha.

[8] The relevance of the contrast between European universities and the University of Chicago was pointed out to me by my colleague Charles Raffel, who studied with Fox. I recall serving on an orals committee with Fox, questioning a doctoral candidate whose chosen area was medieval theories of prophecy. Some professors

appropriately quizzed the student on the origins of the theory of the Active Intellect, which plays a major part in medieval theories. But Fox, likewise appropriately, wanted to know, "how would you identify a prophet if someone claimed to be one today?" (The issue is discussed in the Torah, but Fox wanted an epistemological account.)

[9] I am reminded here of Yosef Hayyim Yerushalmi's contentions that studying history for history's sake may fail to provide "meaning." See *Zakhor*, pp. 94-100. However (as Dr. Benny Kraut noted to me) Yerushalmi is saying that to find meaning one might have to *replace* history with memory, which rejects historical method, while Fox is saying that one can find meaning in the ideas that the history of Jewish Philosophy uncovers—the history need not be *rejected*. Likewise, one may be tempted to draw an analogy to opposition in yeshivot to historical studies of talmudic *sugyot*. By contrast Fox values the history of philosophy and indeed it provides the fund of ideas that the philosopher evaluates.

[10] For example, he prefaces his attempt to systematize and analyze Maharal's ideas, which are spread across different writings, with this caveat: "Our task is to construct the system which is lacking in the writings of MaHaRaL, and to do so without imposing upon him thought-forms and structures which are alien and which distort or misrepresent his intentions." ("The Moral Philosophy of MaHaRaL," 2:105). Elsewhere, Fox says that the absence of arguments and evidence in Rav Kook's writing shows he was not a philosopher, but adds that it is "no derogation of his stature" to say this, and that "It is not a service to his thought to try to force it into artificially constructed systematic forms since this is certain to distort its inner meaning and to rob it of its force." ("Rav Kook: Neither Philosopher Nor Kabbalist," 2:123; in Fox's view, Rav Kook is best described as a poet.). He adds: "It may well be that he can speak to the quest for Jewish spirituality in our time more effectively than those thinkers who follow a classical model." (Ibid., 131).

[11] David Berger relates that some academic historians have responded to his critique of Lubavitch messianism by invoking the historicist argument "that beliefs change, that religions evolve. Hasidism itself was an innovation. Religious Zionism was an innovation." See Berger, *The Rebbe, The Messiah, and the Scandal of Orthodox Indifference*, 142. If such criticisms were accepted, it seems to me, that would result in no one ever standing up for any view in science, politics, ethics, economics, or anything else, since views and realia in all these areas change. "Let history tell" is hardly sound advice when history might tell different things depending upon whether one acts. As I once heard Sidney Morgenbesser, the renowned Columbia University philosopher, put it, when you make decisions in a given time and place, you must make them as an agent, not a spectator.

[12] Karnafogel, *Peering Through the Lattices: Mystical, Magical, and Pietistic Dimensions in the Tosafist Period* (Detroit, 2001).

[13] I thank Mr. Lippman Bodoff for posing such questions about the normativity of history vis-à-vis research into Kabbala.

[14] Another example is the current division between "history" and "memory," the former generally advocated by the centrist Orthodox and the latter by the "Orthodox right." I believe that each side confronts certain tensions in its approach that so far have gone unacknowledged.

[15] See his *Interpreting Maimonides* (Chicago: University of Chicago Press, 1990), 152-98.

[16] Hume, *Dialogues Concerning Natural Religion*, ed. Norman Kemp Smith (2nd ed., London, 1947), p. 227, quoted by Fox at 2:14.

[17] The quotation is from the book version of the *Commentary* symposium, *The Condition of Jewish Belief* (New York and London, 1966), pp. 59-60. The essay is not included in the present collection, which reprints articles of a more scholarly nature.

[18] See the selections in Paul Helm (ed.), *Faith and Reason* (Oxford, 1999); see also Stephen T. Davis, *Faith Skepticism and Evidence* (Lewisburg, PA, 1978); William J. Wainwright, *Reason and the Heart: A Critique of Passional Reason* (Ithaca, NY and London: Cornell University Press, 1995); and my "The Overexamined Life Is Not Worth Living" in *God and the Philosophers*, ed. Thomas V. Morris (New York: Oxford, 1994), 263-84, esp. pp. 267-69, 277-84. In defense of religious belief, I argue there (p. 268) that "Hume taught us, in effect, that it is a *vice* to be too rational, to hold out for rigorous arguments in *all* walks of life. Only a mad person would want to conduct his or her life with complete, Spock-like logicality." That is not to say that Hume would endorse my or Fox's use of his philosophy.

[19] See especially William James' classic, "The Will to Believe" (1896), deservedly reprinted seemingly everywhere.

[20] Ironically, Fox raises this point against Abraham Joshua Heschel's attempt to ground religion in intuition: "Must we not admit the equal validity of every religious doctrine which bases itself on intuition? Can we reject all but our own? Surely we, as Jews, are bound to insist on the truth of our own position and to reject any religious view that contradicts our teachings…. But [according to Heschel] on what ground do we make such a selection?" (2:56).

[21] Cf. the essays "Berkovits' Treatment of the Problem of Evil? (2:93-104) and "Theodicy and Anti-theodicy in Biblical and Rabbinic Literature" (3:173-85).

[22] See the readings in note 18.

[23] The Condition of Jewish Belief, p. 62.

[24] See "Maimonides and Aquinas on Natural Law," in vol. 1, at pp. 186-88. Fox's claim is that *mitsvot* are *useful* according to Sa'adya, but not *ipso facto* "rational,"

[25] In light of Fox's position that we can discover the *usefulness* of *mitsvot*, it is difficult to block the appeal to an external standard, since after all we can access the standard of *usefulness*. That is, once *mitsvot* are acknowledged to be "useful," why shouldn't intuitions about "usefulness" enter into the halakhic process? Here he would respond that the usefulness of *mitsvot* is discovered only after the fact (this is how he understands *mishpat* as used in *Yoma* 67a). But I don't see why we can't form reliable independent judgments of usefulness and desirability.

[26] Judy Heicklen long ago convinced me, however, that a celebrated statement of R. Shimon at *Sanhedrin* 71a is not an instance of ethical scruples affecting halakha. R. Shimon states: "because he ate a *tartemar* of meat and drank half a log of *Italki* wine, his father and mother take him out to be stoned? Rather, [the *ben sorer u-moreh*] never was and never will be. Why was it written? Study and receive reward." This, Ms. Heicklen argued, should not be understood to be voicing an *ethical* scruple about *ben sorer u-moreh*. Such a reading would make R. Yonatan's response (that he saw such a case) particularly insensitive to the moral issue (as if the moral problem were met by saying "it happened!"). Also, there would then be only a tenuous parallel between *ben sorer u-moreh* and the immediately ensuing cases of the condemned city and the leprous house. In those instances the reason the case "never was and never will be" is presented as practical, not ethical. Hence, a better reading of the text is that instead of voicing an ethical concern, R. Shimon is asking whether *practically speaking* a case could arise in which both parents choose to have their son executed for such an offense. (The *mishna* requires both parents to consent.) R. Yonatan retorts that he saw such a case, so parents could indeed go through with the process. If this reading is correct, the thesis that *Hazal* had "ethical scruples" about *ben sorer u-moreh* will have to be based on other rabbinic positions in the Talmud about this law, not R. Shimon's.

[27] Plato's *Euthyphro* 9e-11b provides the classic objection to this view: if there are no ethical standards outside of God's will, God is arbitrary. Another objection is that "God is good" would be a tautology. The best examination I know of the various forms of "divine command morality" is Avi Sagi and Daniel Statman, *Religion and Morality* (Amsterdam and Atlanta, GA, 1995).

[28] That promises are binding and truth telling obligatory even independently of Sinai is maintained by R. Yitzhak Hunter in *Pahad Ytshak, Rosh Hashana* (Brooklyn, 5734), *ma'amar* 15, 117-23, esp. 119-22, elaborating on a statement of Rabbenu Yona. (I thank Rabbi Dov Linzer for this reference.)

[29] Gottfried Wilhelm Leibniz, *Discourse on Metaphysics* (1686), sect. 2, argues that our praising God for the kind of world He made requires praising Him by an external standard: "…why praise him for what he has done if he would be equally praiseworthy in doing the contrary?" (The translation is from *Philosophical Essays*, trans. and ed. Roger Ariew and Daniel Garber [Indianapolis: Hackett Publishing, 1989].)

[30] Notice that I do not here saddle an "internalist" with denying any causal role to external ethical standards in the halakhic decision making process. In particular, the internalist need not take the implausible position that it is a *coincidence* that major *posekim* today (as opposed to eighty years ago) do not oppose women voting. Rather, I attribute to the internalist the much more nuanced position that exposure to external values may lead someone to think about and come to appreciate a previously neglected or underappreciated internal Torah value, and eventually to make this value decisive in *pesak*. In such cases the external value is found to

accord with the deeper values of the Torah itself. (I thank David Berger for suggesting this formulation.) If we allow the internalist to frame his position this way, the argument that "it can't be a coincidence" becomes ineffectual. Of course, the internalist still has the task of identifying the relevant "internal Torah values."

[31] The usual way of understanding slavery, polygamy and *kiddushei ketana* is to say that in allowing these practices the Torah made concessions to the moral sense and societal structure prevalent at a particular time in history. When society and the moral sense change, the concession is withdrawn and a more ideal norm is implemented. However, whereas one can easily say that the practices I named are merely once-exercised options that there can be no moral objection to *not* exercising, in the case of drawing up a will to distribute an inheritance equally among heirs one is going against a Torah *mandate*, it seems. The fact we would frown on someone who used the *Torah* method of distribution is difficult to account for without acknowledging that moral sense or society may evolve to the point of making a Torah *requirement* unacceptable. Even here, however, one may use technical legal devices to write halakhically valid wills that distribute an inheritance equally. For an internalist, while the motivation for using the legal devices might appear to be conformity to societal norms, the person is not violating a Torah mandate, and one could say that use of the new forms conforms to deeper values of the Torah.

[32] Admittedly, the "internalist" could say that the decisor is using an "intuitive" weighing of values based on intimate and unverbalizable knowledge of Torah. But what someone "could" say and what someone *should* say are two different things. Much more needs to be explained about how this unberbalizable intuition is formed. The decisor must explain what is "intuitive" about the judgment that *the weight of Torah "values"* lies in a particular direction.

[33] See his book, *Interpreting Maimonides* (Chicago: University of Chicago Press, 1990).

[34] See especially the important article by Yair Lorberbaum, "The 'Seventh Cause': On Contradictions in Maimonides' *Guide of the Perplexed*" (Heb.), *Tarbiz* 69, 2(5769): 211-37. Also see Alfred Ivry, "Islamic and Greek Influences on Maimonides' Philosophy," in *Maimonides and Philosophy*, ed. Shlomo Pines and Yirmiyahu Yovel (Dordrecht: Marinus Nijhoff, 1985), 139-56, esp. pp. 151-2, and Kenneth Seeskin, *Searching for a Distant God: The Legacy of Maimonides* (New York: Oxford University Press, 2000), 177-88. Lorberbaum mentions Fox's anticipation of his own view, but he disputes Fox's argumentation and the details of his thesis (Lorberbaum, 218).

[35] For a critical evaluation of Fox's *Interpreting Maimonides*, see my review in *Speculum* 68, 3 (July 1993): 770-72. I have borrowed some of my wording here from the earlier review.

[36] The *derasha* was translated from Yiddish into Hebrew by Shalom Carmy as "*Adam Mashul le-Sefer Torah*," in *Bet Yosef Shaul* (New York, 5754) pp. 68-100.

Preface

Professor Marvin Fox was born October 17, 1922 in Chicago, Illinois and died in Newton, Massachusetts, on February 8, 1996. Professor Marvin Fox received his B. A. in philosophy in 1942 from Northwestern University, the M. A. in the same field in 1946, and the Ph. D. at the University of Chicago in 1950 in that field as well. His education in Judaic texts was certified by rabbinical ordination as Rabbi by the Hebrew Theological College of Chicago in 1942. He served as a Jewish Chaplain in the U.S. Army Air Force during World War II in 1942-1946. He taught at Ohio State University from 1948 through 1974, rising from Instructor to Professor of Philosophy. During those years he served also as Visiting Professor of Philosophy at the Hebrew Theological College of Chicago (1955) and also at the Hebrew University of Jerusalem and Bar Ilan University (1970-1971). In 1974 he came to Brandeis University as Appleman Professor of Jewish Thought, and from 1976 onward he has held the Lown Professorship. In 1975-1982 and from 1984-1987 he was Chairman of the Department of Near Eastern and Judaic Studies at Brandeis, and from 1976 he has also served as Director of the Lown School of Near Eastern and Judaic Studies. In 1980-1981 he was Visiting Scholar in Jewish Philosophy at the Center for Jewish Studies of nearby Harvard University.

He has received numerous academic awards, a selected list of which includes the following: 1956-1957: Elizabeth Clay Howald Post-Doctoral Scholarship; 1962-1963, Fellow of the American Council of Learned Societies; 1975-1978, Director of the Association for Jewish Studies regional conferences, funded by the National Endowment for the Humanities; 1977-1980, Director of the project, "For the Strengthening of Judaic Studies at Brandeis and their Links to the General Humanities," also funded by the National Endowment for the Humanities. From 1979 he has been Fellow of the Academy of Jewish Philosophy; 1980-1981, Senior Faculty Fellow, National Endowment for the Humanities. He has served on the editorial boards of *the AJS Review, Daat, Judaism, Tradition, Journal for the History of Philosophy*, and other journals. He has lectured widely at universities and at national and international academic conferences and served as

Member of the National Endowment for the Humanities National Board of Consultants for new programs at colleges and universities. Over the years he has counseled various universities and academic publishers as well.

His ties to institutions of Jewish learning under Jewish sponsorship are strong. He has served on the Advisory Committee of the Jewish Studies Adaptation Program of the International Center for University Teaching of Jewish Civilization (Israel), since 1982; International Planning Committee of the Institute for Contemporary Jewry of the Hebrew University since that same year; member of the governing council of the World Union of Jewish Studies since 1975; secretary, 1971-1972, vice president, from 1973-1975, and then president, from 1975-1978, of the Association for Jewish Studies; and he has been on the board of directors of that organization since 1970. From 1964 through 1968 he served on the Executive Committee of the Conference on Jewish Philosophy; from 1970 until his death on the Executive Committee of the Institute of Judaism and Contemporary Thought of Bar Ilan University; from 1972 as Member of the Academic Board of the Melton Research Center of the Jewish Theological Seminary of America; Member of the board of directors of the Institute for Jewish Life from 1972 through 1975; member of the board of directors of the Library of Living Philosophers, Inc., from 1948; Associate of the Columbia University Seminar on Israel and Jewish Studies from 1968 through 1974; and many other organizations.

His committee service at Brandeis University has covered these committees: Graduate School Council; Philosophy Department Advisory Committee and Reappointment and Promotions Committee; University Tenure Panels; Academic Planning Committee (Chairman, 1982-1984); Faculty Committee for the Hiatt Institute; Tauber Institute Faculty Advisory Committee and its academic policy sub-committee; Committee on University Studies in the Humanities; Faculty representative on the Brandeis University Board of Trustees (1978-1980). His professional memberships include the American Philosophical Association, the Metaphysical Society of America, the Medieval Academy of America, as well as the Association for Jewish Studies, Conference on Jewish Philosophy, and American Academy for Jewish Research.

When I taught at Brown, I called upon Professor Fox for counsel in the fifteen years after Professor Fox came to Brandeis University. And he responded, always giving his best judgment and his wisest counsel. Professor Fox was a good neighbor, a constant counselor, and valued friend.

In the sequence of eight academic conferences that I presented annually at Brown Universixty in the 1970s, Professor Fox played a leading role in the planning of the programs and in scholarly interchange. At that time, also, Brown and Brandeis Universities held a conference at which graduate students in the respective graduate programs met and engaged in shared discussion of common interests. Professor Fox moreover has taken a position on numerous dissertation committees in Brown's graduate program in the History of Judaism. His conscientious and careful reading of these dissertations give to the students the benefit not only of his learning but also of his distinct and rich perspective upon the problem of the dissertation.

I organized and edited the *festschrift* published in his honor in my series at Scholars Press, as follows:

From Ancient Israel to Modern Judaism. Intellect in Quest of Understanding. Essays in Honor of Marvin Fox. Atlanta, 1989: Scholars Press for Brown Judaic Studies. I-IV.

I. *What Is at Stake in the Judaic Quest for Understanding? Judaic Learning and the Locus of Education. Ancient Israel. Formative Christianity. Judaism in the Formative Age: Religion.*

II. *Judaism in the Formative Age: Theology and Literature. Judaism in the Middle Ages: The Encounter with Christianity. The Encounter with Scripture. Philosophy and Theology.*

III. *Judaism in the Middle Ages: Philosophers. Hasidism. Messianism in Modern Times. The Modern Age: Philosophy.*

IV. *The Modern Age: Theology, Literature, History.*

I also organized the celebration in Professor Fox's honor held by President Evelyn Handler of Brandeis University in connection with the publication of the festschrift.

This volume of his essays offers to a new generation of scholars of Jewish thought and philosophy a selection of his more important writings.

Their original publication is indicated in the bibliography of Marvin Fox that follows.

The essays collected and presented here represent the selections of Dr. June Fox in consultation with the editor.

Jacob Neusner

Research Professor of Religion and Theology
Program in Religion and Institute of Advanced Theology
Bard College
Annandale-on-Hudson, New York 12504

neusner@webjogger.net

Marvin Fox - A Memoir

Memoirs have a tendency to be less than faithful to the truth. The writer may romanticize, or rely on anecdotes, or fill in spaces when she was not present at times being recollected in the life of the memorialized. This memoir is different from most, I believe. I knew Marvin all my life—when he was a child, a teenager, a young man, and as my husband of fifty-two years, until his death. I believe that the words, which follow, faithfully describe him, the events of his life, and the goals, and aspirations which animated him, since I was privileged to observe and share them with him for so many decades.

Marvin's parents and his older brother emigrated to the United States from Russia, to escape the persecution of Jews and the turmoil of the Russian Revolution. They came to Chicago (where a number of relatives resided) in October of 1922. Marvin was born within a few days after their arrival. The early years in America were a time of great poverty for his family, which, in truth, was not alleviated for two decades. But his parents knew that a better life for their children depended upon education and study, and they inspired him to read and learn, both the culture of their new society and Jewish texts and sources, which they revered and he came to revere as well.

At a very early age, in the late 1930's, while studying at the Hebrew Theological College, he became a student at Northwestern University, and became fascinated by philosophy. I recall, vividly, listening to him formulate his dream for our future. He wanted to become a professor of philosophy, in a major secular university, and a Jewish scholar as well. It was a hopeless dream, as we well knew, at least the professor part. There were virtually no universities which employed Jews as academics, and few which welcomed them even as students. Although he was extraordinarily gifted, a kind professor in the Philosophy Department spoke to him, and told that such an aspiration for a young Jewish man was virtually impossible, and that he needed to face reality.

It took World War II to create a new reality. Marvin joined the United States Army Air Force, after his graduation from Northwestern and the end of his rabbinical studies at the Yeshiva. He served as a Jewish Chaplain for almost four years, which provided extraordinarily important insights into the many facets of America, which he had never experienced. We were married in the middle of the war. When we returned to Chicago, hundreds of thousands of young men who had served their country were descending upon the universities, subsidized by the G.I. Bill. This influx of ordinary Americans into higher education did more to undermine elitism in American society than, perhaps, any legislative action before or since in the history of our country.

The universities needed professors to teach their students, and though it may not have been their preference, they were obliged to hire as faculty, anyone qualified to teach. During the late 40's, and forward to this day, Jewish men and later women entered academia in large numbers. Marvin started and completed his Ph.D. at the University of Chicago, and in 1948 was appointed to the faculty of Philosophy at the Ohio State University, in Columbus. Here he spent twenty-six years, teaching with great distinction, writing, assuming a leadership role in faculty affairs, engaging actively as a community leader, both locally and nationally, raising our family, and achieving the first part of his dream for his future.

The second part—becoming a Jewish scholar—became a "private" occupation. Marvin wrote, published, and lectured extensively in the field of Jewish thought, at the same time as he studied and published in general philosophy. His good friends and colleagues in philosophy and the humanities at Ohio State good-naturedly referred to the "Jewish thing" as his "hobby." Judaic studies were not considered, by scholars, as worthy of inclusion in the academic curricula of the universities in America. With the exception of Harvard and Columbia, which had a few scholars of Judaica on their faculties, serious Jewish study was confined to the Seminaries, Dropsie College, and Brandeis University, which was founded in 1948.

By the 1960's, this landscape also began to change. Marvin played a significant role in bringing about the change. In the early 60's, a wonderful philanthropic member of the Columbus Jewish community, Samuel Melton, who was very interested in promoting Jewish study at Ohio State, came to Marvin to discuss the possibility of endowing a chair in Judaic studies. Marvin served as negotiator with the University administration, which was receptive to the idea. It was determined that it would be a chair in Jewish History. It was necessary to convince the members of the History Department that Jewish history was a legitimate area of study—the history of the Jews at most merited one chapter or one part of a lecture in a World History class. Marvin found an ideal candidate for the chair: a professor from the Hebrew University who had studied and taught with Salo Baron at Columbia. He was a noted scholar and a charismatic teacher. Upon meeting him, the history department was convinced that Jewish history was indeed a worthy subject for study, and Jewish Studies was instituted at Ohio State. The administration, at Marvin's urging, brought in a professor of Hebrew, acquired a Judaic library collection, employed a Judaic librarian, and a new discipline found its way in to the University in the heartland of our country.

At the same time, a small group of faculty of Judaica at seminaries, at an occasional university, and men and women who were interested in developing Jewish studies in higher education gathered at Brandeis University and founded the Association of Jewish Studies. Marvin was among the group, which grew larger with each passing year, until its membership has surpassed one thousand. More and more universities introduced Jewish Studies, following the Ohio State model or creating alternative models. Marvin served as president of the Association, helped launch its academic journal, and acted as consultant to numerous university administrations as they planned and adopted Judaic Studies in their institutions.

In 1974, Marvin was invited to join the Department of Near Eastern and Judaic Studies at Brandeis University, as a Professor of Jewish Philosophy. He had never taught a course in Jewish studies in his entire career as a professor of philosophy in America. (He had done so only as a visiting professor at the Hebrew University of Jerusalem in 1970.) The second part of his dream then became a reality. He joined a faculty of scholars distinguished in every aspect of Jewish study. He became and served as Chairman of the Department for many years. He was appointed Director of the Lown School of Jewish Studies, which included contemporary as well as classical Jewish Studies. He had, for the first time in his life, many doctoral students in Jewish Studies, whom he guided to degrees and saw them placed in teaching positions in universities all over the world. No longer pursuing a "hobby", he devoted his writing primarily to topics related to Jewish thought. He remained at Brandeis until his retirement in 1994, having experienced the most rewarding professional years of his life.

A final culminating experience came his way after he left Brandeis. Boston University, which occasionally appointed distinguished emeritus professors to its faculty, invited him to join the departments of Religion and Philosophy in that capacity. He enjoyed a wonderfully satisfying year with interesting new colleagues and new students, a pattern which he hoped would continue on into the future. Alas, he became mortally ill at that point and died in a matter of months.

Marvin Fox was a very large, imposing man, with a deep and sonorous voice which he could project in an auditorium filled with one thousand students, using no microphone. He had an infectious laugh and an extraordinary wit. He was more than a teacher—he was constantly involved in solving problems, which he did with consummate skill. He found jobs for students and supported them in obtaining tenure. He raised money for countless needy scholars, and helped them publish their books. He was an advocate for academic freedom and freedom to speak out for professors and students. He mediated disputes, and promoted academic harmony. He lived as an observant Jew among colleagues and friends who had never known an observant Jew and gained their respect. He knew well some of the greatest scholars of his day. He saw the creation of the State of Israel and had the great satisfaction of teaching there. He was the father of three dearly loved children, of whom, together with their spouses, he was inordinately proud. And he lived to see and know his eleven grandchildren, who were perhaps, the greatest joy of his life.

Shortly before he became ill with his last illness, he told me, one day, "I have lived the most richly rewarding life any man could have hoped for. How many of us can say that all the dreams of their youth have come true? I can—and I have been truly blessed."

His life was a blessing for us, as is his memory.

June T. Fox, PhD
Chicago, Illinois
March, 2001

10

RELIGION AND HUMAN NATURE
IN THE PHILOSOPHY
OF DAVID HUME

Of the many ambiguities that characterize Hume's philosophy none is so deep or so puzzling as his treatment of religion. We find statements in Hume's writings that would do credit to the most reverent orthodoxy and other statements that criticize religious beliefs with such excessive violence that they go beyond the boundaries of good taste. Perhaps his own attitude is best expressed at the end of his *Natural History of Religion* where he says that, "the whole is a riddle, an aenigma, an inexplicable mystery."[1] But a careful study of Hume's works give us some clues for resolving at least that part of the riddle which has to do with his own views about religion. In this essay I shall try to show that the commentators have largely failed to grasp the main point of Hume's anti-religious polemic. In placing the emphasis on his refutations of the proofs for the existence of God, or on his skeptical doubts concerning miracles, students of Hume have overlooked his most powerful anti-religious weapon. As a result they have been unclear about Hume's own theory of religion.

Hume had both generous and bitter things to say about traditional religion. There are passages in which he speaks with seeming reverence about "our most holy religion"[2] and in which he advises us to "fly to revealed truth with the greatest avidity."[3] These are opposed by passages in which he asserts that most religious principles must be viewed as nothing but "sick men's dreams... or the playsome whimsies of monkeys in human shape."[4] The interpretation of these passages has posed a problem for students of Hume and has led most of them to conclude that whenever he says anything appreciative about religion it is either sarcastic or else in

1

deference to the social utility of religion. But in leaving the matter there they overlook what is most important.

Religion posed problems that occupied Hume deeply. In the introduction to his *Treatise* he expresses the hope that human knowledge in its various branches will be much advanced by his investigations, but he is especially confident that "The improvements are the more to be hoped for in natural religion."[5] This initial concern was sustained throughout his life. Not only did he take elaborate care to insure the posthumous publication of his *Dialogues Concerning Natural Religion,* but he even made revisions in the manuscript during the last year of his life.[6] For more than twenty-five years he had kept the manuscript of this work and returned to work on it on more than one occasion. How shall we explain Hume's life-long, preoccupation with religion? What were the improvements for which he hoped? Why, if he was convinced that religion was little more than "sick men's dreams," did he continue to devote intense thought to the subject?

The answer, I believe, lies in another area that concerned Hume deeply, namely human nature. We concentrate so much on Hume's epistemology and his criticism of metaphysics that we tend to forget that the title of his first and largest book is *A Treatise of Human Nature.* E. C. Mossner, in his *Life of David Hume,* brings the crucial issue to our attention with a most effective rhetorical device. Mossner opens his book with a dedication, "To a young David in the hope that he, too, will never lose faith in the dignity of human nature." He concludes the biography with a chapter entitled, "The Dignity, of Human Nature." What is eminently clear is that we are being told that the preservation of human dignity was the profoundest interest of Hume's life. I believe that Mossner is correct and that Hume's struggles with religion stem largely from his desire to maintain the dignity of human nature.

In the Western world claims about human dignity have traditionally grown out of a religious foundation.[7] The biblical description of man as created in the divine image was the ground for belief in the intrinsic worth of each man, as such, and in the superiority of men over all other creatures. Even when religious writers denigrated man it was primarily because they saw him as fallen away from his ideal possibilities. Both Judaism and Christianity depend on a view of man as unique and superior to all other earthly creatures. These religions view man as God's special concern. Divine revelation is addressed only to man; the hope of final redemption is held out only to man; and in Christian teaching God saves man by assuming a human form. Explicitly or implicitly Western morality is closely tied to this way of thinking about man. All earthly existence is in the service of man. The best animal may be sacrificed, if necessary, to preserve the life of the most unsavory man.

So long as man is understood to be but "little less than God"[8] because he is God's special creature it is easy to maintain the usual claims about the dignity of man. Hume, however, faced an aggravated problem. He rejected Christian orthodoxy, but wanted to maintain the moral attitudes and the reverence for man which had for centuries been based on that orthodoxy. It is a credit to his rigorous intellectual honesty that he did not make the task easier for himself by closing his eyes to the proper conclusions of his own naturalism. As we shall show, he pursued his line of argument relentlessly, even when it forced him to conclusions that were not to his taste.

In his thinking about human nature Hume was far more deeply influenced by certain of his non-religious predecessors than by the religious tradition. There is a long line of thinkers, stretching from antiquity to Hume's own time, who deny all superiority to man. Hume had close acquaintance with many of these thinkers and was deeply influenced by them. The most famous ancient source is in Plutarch's *Moralia* in the section "Beasts are Rational." Odysseus has been given an opportunity to speak with Gryllus, formerly a man now transformed into a swine. If Odysseus can persuade Gryllus that the human state is superior, Circe will change him back into a man. But Odysseus fails. Gryllus argues most impressively in defense of the superiority of beasts, showing that "The soul of beasts has a greater natural capacity and perfection for the generation of virtue"[9] than the souls of men and also that "animals have a natural endowment of reason and intellect."[10] This work of Plutarch's and the opening of Book VII of Pliny's *Natural History* are the most familiar standard sources in classical antiquity which argue for the superiority of animals.[11]

As a student of classical literature Hume certainly knew these passages, but there were closer and more immediate influences. While early Renaissance humanism had stressed the superiority of man, by the late sixteenth century Montaigne and other writers had again reduced man to the beasts or even less.[12] And in the eighteenth century Pierre Bayle marshaled arguments and evidence against the superiority of man. In the article "Rorarius" in his *Dictionary,* Bayle gives us the sources and grounds for the view of Rorarius who "undertook to shew... not only that beasts are rational creatures, but that they make better use of their reason than man."[13] Hume had read Montaigne and Bayle carefully. From them, as from Plutarch and Pliny, he learned to think of man as nothing more than an animal.[14]

It is this view of man which constitutes Hume's most powerful anti-religious weapon. Christianity and Judaism are not seriously threatened by refutations of proofs for the existence of God. In their lack of demonstrative evidence for the existence of God men of religious faith are not in worse condition than are philosophers who believe in the existence of bodies or in the uniformity of nature without sufficient evidence. "Thus the sceptic still continues to reason and believe, even tho' he asserts, that he cannot defend his reason by reason; and by the same rule he must assent to the principle concerning the existence of body, tho' he cannot pretend by any arguments of philosophy to maintain its veracity."[15] If Hume's attack on religion depended only on invalidating the proofs for the existence of God it would have been trivial. And it would have come with poor grace from a man who was driven to admit that though almost all of our supposed knowledge goes beyond what is justified by the evidence, we nevertheless continue to believe.

The real danger to religion is to be found in those relatively unnoticed sections of Hume's works in which he considers the nature of man in comparison with animals. In his essay "Of the Dignity or Meanness of Human Nature" Hume has given us a valuable key to understanding his position properly. He begins by commenting on the widely varied views that have been advanced concerning the dignity of man, and then suggests that authors should decide whether to argue in behalf of man's dignity or his meanness only on the basis of which view best fits their rhetorical talents. In this essay his own qualified argument in behalf of human dignity must also be seen as a rhetorical exercise, for he tells us explicitly that society is better served when man is exalted. "The sentiments of those who are inclined to think favourably of mankind, are more advantageous to virtue, than the contrary principles which give us a mean opinion of our nature. When a man is prepossessed with a high notion of his rank and character in the creation, he will naturally endeavour to act up to it, and will scorn to do a base or vicious action, which might sink him below that figure which he makes in his own imagination."[16] The same motivation which causes him at times to speak kindly of religion is operating here. "In one respect only does he recognize Christianity as standing by itself, namely, that for him and his contemporaries in Britain the Reformed Church teaching stood officially for religion, and that the good citizen was therefore in duty bound to pay it outward deference... while yet none the less reserving his right to criticize it freely in his own thoughts, and subject to certain recognized conventions also in his own writings."[17] When speaking about human dignity in a popular essay Hume must exalt man for the sake of preserving public morality. But when he considers man in his serious philosophic works he attacks without restraint. In the *Treatise* man is reduced to being nothing more than any animal. This reduction, as we shall show, is neither accidental nor casual. It is carefully planned and worked out in meticulous detail and is given such a strategic place in the ordering of the parts of the *Treatise* that it cannot escape the attention of any careful reader of that book. By way of this reduction of man to animal Hume deals the severest of all blows to religion.

The religious position depends on the belief that man is essentially different from animals, that the difference is not one of degree but of kind. It is this very claim that Hume denies. In his view, we cannot know the essence of human nature, "and any hypothesis that pretends to discover the ultimate original qualities of human nature, ought at first to be rejected as presumptuous and chimerical."[18] Since we cannot have any direct knowledge of human nature we can only study it by way of analogy. In religious thought man is analogized to God, and the human ideal is expressed as *imitatio dei*. The same is true of those classical philosophers who see man as unique and superior to all other creatures. Plato, for example, speaks of man's soul as being like the unseen, the unchanging, and, above all, the divine.[19] Hume finds the analogy with God useless, since we know nothing about God. This is perhaps the strongest point that is made in the *Dialogues Concerning Natural Religion*—that we find neither justification nor meaning in attempts to analogize man and God. In the *Treatise* Hume does not even attempt such an analogy, but tries instead to understand man on the model of animals.

Of all the claims to man's uniqueness none has persisted more than the belief that man is the only rational animal. Yet Hume begins his discussion of reason in animals by saying that "no truth appears to me more evident than that beasts are endowed with thought and reason as well as men."[20] In fact, human reason can only be understood, according to Hume, on the model of animal reason. "Reason is nothing but a wonderful and unintelligible instinct in our soul,"[21] an instinct exactly like the instincts of animals. At the end of the *Treatise* Hume concedes a limited natural superiority to man, but this is only a superiority of degree. "Men are superior to beasts principally by the superiority of their reason; and they are the degrees of the same faculty, which set such an infinite difference betwixt one man and another."[22] It is worth noting that this admission of limited superiority occurs in Hume's discussion of morals, a fact the significance of which we shall explain later. But when he is comparing human and animal reason under the rubric "Of Knowledge and Probability," men seem to come out second best. Reason is an instinct, and no man can act instinctively in complex matters with the unerringly elaborate and delicate skill with which, for example, a bird builds its nest. In his fumbling efforts to adapt means to ends man is far inferior to many animals, rarely rising to the level of "those more extraordinary instances of sagacity" which occur among animals. Hume destroys the belief in human rational superiority, and with it one of the firmest foundations of the religious view of man's nature. To make his argument especially effective he sets it at the end of Part III, "Of Knowledge and Probability." He seems to want to make certain that his readers will carry away as their final thought a conception of human reason which cannot be used to exalt man in any way above the animals.

Near the end of Book I of the *Treatise* Hume strikes another blow against the religious conception of man. The substantial identity of the individual person is an important element in orthodox religious doctrine, without which the belief in the immortality of the soul and the hope for reward and the fear of punishment make no sense. That Hume had great trouble with the problem of personal identity is well known. What we need to take note of in the present discussion is the fact that he explains human identity by analogy with animal identity and denies any significant distinction between them. "The identity," he says, "which we ascribe to the mind of man, is only a fictitious one, and of a like kind with that which we ascribe to vegetables and animal bodies. It cannot, therefore, have a different origin, but must proceed from a like operation of the imagination upon like objects."[23] Again we see Hume eliminating a traditional distinction and thus denying man's uniqueness and superiority.

Lest it be thought that these views may not have been consciously anti-religious on Hume's part it might be well to provide unmistakable evidence that he knew exactly what he was doing. In his discussion of vice and virtue he concludes that virtue is closely connected with pride and vice with humility. This seems so blatantly opposed to Christian morality that Hume cannot let the matter pass in silence. He reveals his hand unambiguously when he says that, "There may, perhaps, be some, who being accustomed to the style of the schools and the pulpit, and having never considered human nature in any other light, than that in which they place it, may here be sure."[24] Hume explicitly announces that he views human nature in a light significantly different from that "of the schools and the pulpit." This instance is characteristic of his treatment of human nature, a treatment which is consistently and consciously opposed to the views "of the schools and the pulpit."

In Book I of the *Treatise* Hume reduced human knowledge to a set of idiosyncratic psychological processes shared by men and animals. It might be thought, however, that as a feeling passional creature man may be different from animals and that this is the ground of his claims to uniqueness. But in Book II Hume turns vigorously against this view as well. His elaborate analysis of the human passions is punctuated by the regular identification of human and animal emotions. Part I, "Of Pride and Humility," concludes with a section on pride and humility in animals. Part II, "Of Love and Hatred," ends with a section on the love and hatred of animals. Part III ends in a similar though somewhat less obvious way. In all these sections Hume stresses two points. First, that man is to be understood only by analogy with animals. Second, that there are no essential differences between animal and human psychology.

At the end of the discussion of pride and humility Hume argues that "all the internal principles, that are necessary in us to produce either pride or humility, are common to all creatures; and since the causes, which excite these passions, are likewise the same, we may justly conclude, that these causes operate after the same manner through the whole animal creation."[25] Love and hatred, the subject of Part II, offers a more revealing instance of Hume's reduction of man to an animal. He begins by asserting that "The object of love and hatred is evidently some *thinking Person.*" In the next sentence, speaking of the cause of these passions he broadens his category and speaks of them as "always related to a *thinking being.*" That "thinking person" and "thinking being" are not synonymous becomes clear in the next sentence when he says that "The cause of love and hatred must be related to a person or thinking being."[26] Lest we have any doubt as to what these "thinking beings" may be, Hume clarifies the matter a little later in the discussion when he asks us "to observe the force of sympathy through the whole animal creation, and the easy communications of sentiments from one thinking being to another."[27]

Here we see clearly that animals are thinking beings for Hume, and the logic of his position causes him to eliminate the supposed differences between "thinking persons" and animals. At the end of the exposition of love and hatred his view is stated explicitly. "But to pass front the passions of love and hatred... as they appear in man, to the same affections as they display themselves in brutes; we may observe... that love and hatred are common to the whole sensitive creation... Every thing is conducted by springs and principles, which are not peculiar to man, or any one species of animals."[28]

Part III of Book II of the *Treatise* is entitled "Of the Will and Direct Passions." Hume allows no distinction between men and animals in his treatment of this topic. Instead he is so convinced of their similarities that he does not even find it necessary to discuss them. He concludes his exposition by saying, "I waive the examination of the will and direct passions, as they appear in animals; since nothing is more evident, than that they are of the same nature, and excited by the same causes as in human creatures."[29] Men and animals are essentially alike in their passional life as in their rational life. In this way Hume concludes the book on the passions, leaving us with a final note that underscores his systematic elimination of the differences between men and animals. In each case he has set the crucial passage at the end of a section, thus seeking to make sure that it would be noted and that it would leave a lasting final impression.

There is, however, an oddity that needs to be explained and integrated into our analysis. A final section is added to the end of Book II which deals with "Curiosity or the Love of Truth." Though this discussion does not fit into the ordered pattern of the *Treatise* Hume, nevertheless, feels that it would be strange if in a philosophic analysis of the passions he ignored the love of truth completely. However, he acknowledges that, "'Tis an affection of so peculiar a kind, that would have been impossible to have treated of it under any of those heads, which we have examined, without danger of obscurity and confusion."[30] How does this section fit into the scheme of our analysis?

At first glance Hume seems here to want to save a bit of face for man. After having told us repeatedly that human psychology is only one instance of animal psychology, he seems to be saying to his worried readers, "Fear not! At least man has his love of truth, and this is not shared by animals." Love of truth is equated with philosophy, and it might heal our wounded pride a bit to remind us that philosophy is a peculiarly human activity. This is the impression that one might get from a quick and cursory reading of the section. However, a closer and more careful reading will show that, in a subtle way, Hume is only strengthening his case against the uniqueness of man.

To begin, we should note that philosophy or love of truth is reduced by Hume to a passion—a most undignified state for what is normally supposed to be the highest activity of human reason. Hume adds an even more severe blow when he proclaims that "There cannot be two passions more nearly resembling each other, than those of hunting and philosophy, whatever disproportion may at first sight appear betwixt them."[31] The only other analogy he offers is between philosophy and gambling (which has the same motive drive as hunting). In effect, while seeming on the surface to exalt man because he alone philosophizes, Hume has actually brought man down from all his claims to eminence. It is true that in this section he makes no explicit comparison between men and animals. But the comparison is not made because it is not necessary. Hunting is very much an animal activity. If man's love of truth is understood as nothing more than a variety of hunting, then philosophy has lost all claim to special status. Man, the philosopher, is only carrying on another animal activity. Good taste may have prevented Hume from saying directly that philosophers are animals. It did not prevent him from suggesting that an animal stalking his prey and a philosopher pursuing truth are engaged in essentially similar activities.

The strongest traditional fortress of human uniqueness and superiority is man's moral nature. Even those theologians who refuse to place their trust in the uniqueness of man's reason affirm that man is unique in his moral capacity. It is as a moral agent that we see in man reflections of the divine. As the serpent puts it to Eve, when tempting her to eat the forbidden fruit, "You will become like God, knowing good and evil." If it can be maintained that morality distinguishes man essentially from all creatures we can still preserve our belief in man as a special being. However, Hume does not allow us even this ego-saving comfort.

As might be expected, when he deals with morals Hume is more circumspect than when dealing with reason or the passions. There are distinct social advantages in maintaining the dignity of man as a moral agent, advantages which Hume wants to preserve. He is not ready, however, to preserve them at the cost of intellectual dishonesty. "When any opinion leads us into absurdities, this certainly false; but 'tis not certain an opinion is false, because 'tis of dangerous consequence."[32] Hume is anxious to reduce the dangerous consequences, so far as he can, but he will not restrict the development of his inquiry because he fears that his conclusions may be dangerous. Thus, in Book III of the *Treatise* he makes no explicit statement that reduces human morality to an animal activity. Such a statement would be needlessly hazardous. Yet, a careful reading of his treatment of morals leads inevitably to just such a reduction.

Early in his discussion he seems even to deny that there is animal morality. In arguing that morality does not consist in relations he makes his point by showing that though animals and men exhibit the same relations these relations do not evoke identical moral judgments. For example, "incest in the human species is criminal... and the same relations in animals have not the smallest moral turpitude and deformity."[33] To many readers Hume seems to be saying here that morality is a peculiarly human phenomenon. All he actually says is that those who conceive of morality as consisting in relations will be forced to admit "That every animal must be susceptible of all the same virtues and vices for which we ascribe praise and blame to human creatures."[34] This extreme proposition Hume will not grant. However, his denial is not based on the principle that animals have no morality, but only on the conviction that it is a mistake to conceive of virtue and vice as relations. An analysis of Hume's theory of morals will show that it offers us no ground for the claim that there are any essential distinctions between human and animal nature.

In Hume's view moral distinctions are derived from a moral sense. "To have the sense of virtue, is nothing but to *feel* a satisfaction of a particular kind from the contemplation of a character. The very feeling constitutes our praise or admiration. We go no further; nor do we enquire into the cause of the satisfaction."[35] If this is all there is to man's moral awareness it is hardly a ground for asserting that man is either unique or superior. The moral sense may be peculiar to man, but various other animals have peculiar senses of their own. Possession of any given sense cannot be taken as evidence that a creature is more than a mere animal. No one would argue that a dog is a being of special status and value merely because dogs are able to hear sounds that men cannot hear or to smell odors that men cannot smell. Moreover, the moral sense involves certain feelings of approval and disapproval, and Hume admits without hesitation that animals also have such feelings. In some cases, the causes or the objects of the feelings may be unique to man. But this does not confer on him any special status.

When we follow the development of Hume's analysis of morals we are left with no doubt that he meant to eliminate the presumed distinctions between men and animals even in the moral sphere. There are two kinds of virtues, natural and artificial. The prototype of the artificial virtues is justice, and it is under the rubric "Of justice and Injustice" that the artificial virtues are dealt with. That animals do not exhibit the artificial virtues is not a defect on their part. Quite the contrary, justice and the other artificial virtues result from man's inferiority. "Here then is a proposition, which, I think, may be regarded as certain, *that 'tis only from the selfishness and confined generosity of men, along with the scanty provision that nature has made for his wants, that justice derives its* origin."[36] Justice and the other artificial virtues that are concerned with property are no indication of man's superior God-like nature. They seem, rather, to make man lower than the animals. For the animals are both better favored by nature and better able to provide for their wants without the elaborately contrived artificiality of human morality. The artificial virtues are a mark of man's degradation, not of his exaltation.

Defenders of man may quickly rise to the challenge by pointing out, quite correctly, that, according to Hume, justice and the other artificial virtues arise not merely from man's self-concern, but also from his sympathy with other men. "Thus self-interest is the original motive to the *establishment* of justice: but a *sympathy* with public interest is the source of the moral *approbation* which attends that virtue."[37] "Thus it appears, that sympathy is a very powerful principle in human nature, that it has a great influence on our taste of beauty, and that it produces our sentiment of morals in all the artificial virtues."[38] If sympathy constitutes the real ground of human morality, is it not here that we see the significant superiority of man over the animals? This hope is quickly shattered when we recall that Hume explicitly finds sympathy among animals, and, moreover, that he understands human sympathy on the model of animal sympathy. All we need do is to "take a general survey of the universe, and observe the force of sympathy through the whole animal creation."[39] Sympathy in man is not a high-minded piece of altruism, divine in nature, but an animal response common to all the members of the animal kingdom.

If man is not guaranteed his superiority by possession of the artificial virtues, then he will certainly not be helped by the natural virtues. For these virtues depend on pleasure and pain and are expanded through sympathy. But animals respond to pleasure and pain, and, as we have shown, they, too, exhibit sympathy.[40] Human nature is animal nature, and natural virtue in man is nothing but an elaboration of responses that are part of man's animal nature. In a fitting conclusion to this attack on the superiority of man Hume rejects the common distinction between natural abilities and moral virtues.[41] In so doing he removes the last possibility of separating man from the animals. If moral virtues and natural abilities are essentially the same, if the attempts to distinguish them turn out to be "merely a dispute of words,"[42] then nothing of moral significance that is possessed by man can be denied to animals. Hume has set his views down in an unmistakable way here at the end of his *Treatise.* He leaves no room for doubt that he believes that man is nothing more than an animal. As knower, as passionate being, and as moral agent, man is basically like other animals. When theologians and philosophers ascribe special status to man, when they compare him to God, they render a false and misleading account of human nature.

Much as he wanted to support a belief in the dignity of man Hume was unable to find any evidence for man's natural and intrinsic superiority.[43] If, nevertheless, he continued to affirm human dignity it was not on any sound theoretical grounds. All he could do, as he admitted in the essay on "The Dignity or Meanness of Human Nature," was to employ his rhetorical skills in praise of man, knowing that in human society the strategies of rhetoric are generally more effective than the intricacies of philosophical argument. At the start of his philosophical career, in his Introduction to the *Treatise,* he reminds us that in most cases " 'tis not reason, which carries the prize, but eloquence; and no man needs ever despair of gaining proselytes to the most extravagant hypothesis, who has art enough to represent it in any favourable colors. The victory is not gained by the men at arms, who manage the pike and the sword; but by the trumpeters, drummers, and musicians of the army."[44] As a man of humane social concern Hume was ready to employ his eloquence to preserve decency in human society. As a philosopher he followed out his inquiries to their most unpleasant and most dangerous conclusions.

In developing this view of human nature Hume has rejected the most fundamental claims of the religious tradition. If he can salvage anything at all, it can only be a thin and attenuated natural religion. Among the most fundamental beliefs of Judaism and Christianity is the doctrine that man is a special creature, specially endowed by God, and of special concern to God. It is this creature that receives God's revelation, and it is to this creature that the hope of salvation is extended. The God of Western religion is not only the Lord of nature, but also the Lord of history, concerned with the affairs of men. This relationship presupposes a conception of human nature such as was developed in the religious tradition. Clearly these doctrines are impossible for Hume. In fact, he not only reduces man to an animal, but suggests in his *Dialogues* that we might do the same to God. If man is only an organism, and if all we claim to know of God is that he is analogous to man, then why not conceive of God as an animal as well?[45]

Revealed religion depends on the existence of a direct relationship between man and God. The strongest anti-theistic arguments in the *Dialogues* are those that deny any such relationship. The main reason for introducing the discussion of the problem of evil in the Di*alogues* is to show how little ground there is for asserting that God has a special concern for man and his world. But this is only an extension of the conception of man that Hume had arrived at in the *Treatise*. Even orthodox theologians puzzle over the problem of evil. What gives power to Hume's posing of the problem is that he does so on a base which has already made it impossible to take seriously any notion of God's providential concern for man. All that can remain for Hume is the highly attenuated natural religion which is devoid of all religious substance. If, as Hume asserts, "The dispute concerning theism... is merely verbal,"[46] it is because he has purged rational theism of its traditional doctrinal content. In its place he has left us with a single conclusion which is "the whole of natural theology. That the cause or causes of order in the universe probably bear some remote analogy to human intelligence."[47] He goes on to say that if this proposition is not thought of as having any significance for human life or human action, then everyone should be able to assent to it. That is to say, even natural religion can command assent only when it is reduced to a single trivial proposition.

One wonders if this was the great improvement in natural religion that Hume hoped for in his early years. One wonders whether he was willing to rest here. There is no decisive evidence, but merely the conjectures of the commentators—conjectures which more often reveal their own attitudes than those of Hume. This much is certain-that he could find no philosophical grounds for believing in the preeminence of either the God or the man of traditional religion. It is equally clear that he wanted very much to strengthen the fabric of civilized society and to preserve our belief in human dignity. What we cannot know with certainty is how he viewed the strategic situation. The appeal to faith at the end of the *Dialogues,* and elsewhere in his works, may have been written with an ironic tongue in Hume's cheek.[48] It may also be that Hume saw how deeply his naturalistic conclusions threatened the humane values which he cherished, and that he was serious when he wrote that, "A person, seasoned with a just sense of the imperfections of natural reason, will fly to revealed truth with the greatest avidity."[49] Whatever his intention he made the issues and the choices clear and the need for decision inescapable.

MARVIN FOX
OHIO STATE UNIVERSITY

NOTES

[1] David Hume, *The Natural History of Religion* (Stanford: Stanford University Press, 1957), p. 76.
[2] David Hume, Enquiry Concerning *Human* Understanding (Selby-Biggs edition; Oxford, 1902), p. 130. Cf. *Treatise of Human Nature,* p. 250.
[3] David Hume, *Dialogues Concerning Natural Religion,* ed. Norman Kemp Smith (2d ed.; London, 1947) p. 227.
[4] *Natural History of Religion,* p. 75.
[5] David Hume, *A Treatise of Human Nature* (Selby-Biggs ed.; Oxford, 1951). p. XIX.
[6] *Dialogues,* p. 5 of Kemp Smith's Introduction.
[7] Hendel maintains this point when he says of Hume, "We have seen him showing reverence for persons. Where reverence dwells in human nature, there religion has its roots." Charles W. Hendel, *Studies in the Philosophy of David Hume* (Princeton: Princeton University Press, 1925), P. 14.
[8] Psalms, 8:6. This is a literal translation.
[9] Plutarch, *Moralia* (Loeb edition), P. 501 = 987B.
[10] *Ibid.,* P. 531 = 992C.
[11] For additional sources see A. 0. Lovejoy and George Boas, *Primitivism and Related Ideas in Antiquity* (Baltimore: Johns Hopkins University), Ch. XIII.
[12] Montaigne, *Essays,* trans. E. J. Trechmann (Oxford: Oxford University Press, 1927), "Apology for Raymond Sebond," *passim.*
[13] Pierre Bayle, *Dictionary, Historical and Critical,* 8 (London, 1739), 757; cf. the entire article, "Rorarius."
[14] In his *Philosophy of David Hume* Norman Kemp Smith writes: "We know that Hume read extensively in Bayle's Dictionary ... Bayle, too, is often simply the mouthpiece of Montaigne—one of the few modem writers to whom Hume makes explicit reference." (P. 325).
We also know that Hume had studied Cicero and other ancients who make man superior to animals. But on this point they did not persuade him.
[15] *Treatise,* p. 187.
[16] "Of the Dignity or Meanness of Human Nature," in *Essays Moral, Political, and Literary by David Hume,* eds. T. H. Green and T. H. Grose 1 (New York, 1898), 151. Hume speaks of various "sects" in the opening paragraph of his essay and makes the following observation: "The most remarkable... are the sects, founded on the different sentiments with regard to the *dignity of human* nature; which is a point that seems to have divided philosophers and poets, as well as divines, from the beginning of the world to this day. Some exalt our species to the skies, and represent man as a kind of human demigod, who derives his origin from heaven, and retains evident marks of his lineage and descent. Others insist upon the blind sides of human nature, and can discover nothing, except vanity, in which man surpasses the other animals, whom he affects so much to despise. If an author possess the talent of rhetoric and declamation, he commonly takes part with the former: If his turn lies towards irony and ridicule, he naturally throws himself into the other extreme."
[17] *Dialogues,* p.10 of Kemp Smith's Introduction. Cf. *Enquiry Concerning Human Understanding,* p. 147: "Men... draw many consequences from the belief of a divine existence, and suppose that the deity will inflict punishment on vice, and bestow rewards on virtue ... Whether this reasoning of theirs be just or not, is no matter. Its influence on their life and

conduct must still be the same. And, those, who attempt to disabuse them of such prejudices, may, for aught I know, be good reasoners, but I cannot allow them to be good citizens and politicians; since they free men from one restraint on their passions, and make the infringement of the laws of Society, in one respect, more easy and secure."

[18] *Treatise*, p. xxi.

[19] Phaedo, 78b-81a. Norman Kemp Smith in his Commentary *on Kant's Critique of pure Reason* makes the observation that Kant approached these problems "from the point of view of the difference rather than of the kinship between man and the animals." This approach "leaves him free from that desire which exercises so constant, and frequently so deleterious an influence, upon many workers in the field of psychology, namely to maintain at all costs, in anticipation of conclusions not yet by any means established, the fundamental identity of human and animal intelligence." (p. xlviii)

[20] *Treatise*, p. 176.

[21] *Treatise*, p. 179.

[22] *Treatise*, p. 610; cf. *Enquiry Concerning Human Understanding*, p. 107, note 1. in the *Dialogues* he speaks with contempt of "This little agitation of the brain which we call thought." (p. 148) See also Norman Kemp Smith, "The Naturalism of Hume," Mind, N. S., 14, 1905, 155.

[23] *Treatise*, p. 259; cf. pp. 253ff.

[24] *Treatise*, p. 297.

[25] *Treatise*, p. 328.

[26] *Treatise*, p. 331, my italics.

[27] *Treatise*, p. 363.

[28] *Treatise*, p. 398.

[29] *Treatise*, p 448.

[30] *Ibid.*

[31] *Treatise*, p, 451.

[32] *Treatise*, p. 409.

[33] *Treatise*, p. 467.

[34] *Treatise*, p. 468, my italics.

[35] *Treatise*, p. 471.

[36] *Treatise*, p. 495.

[37] *Treatise*, pp. 499-500.

[38] *Treatise*, pp. 577-8.

[39] *Treatise*, p. 363.

[40] Cf. *Treatise*, pp. 574-6.

[41] Cf. *Treatise*, pp. 606ff.

[42] *Treatise*, p. 606.

[43] Cf. Hendel, *op. cit.*, p. 328: "Hume seems to have been increasingly alive to the reality, and even the mystery of human personality. Despite his inability to show any warrant for our idea of a person he had continued to employ it, and had even emphasized it, in his later studies of sentiment and morality."

[44] *Treatise*, p. xviii.

[45] *Dialogues*, p. 161.

[46] *Dialogues*, p. 218.

[47] *Dialogues*, p. 227.

[48] Kemp Smith contends that Hume learned from Bayle "That there is no surer method of rendering religion doubtful than to subject it to the tests of reason and evidence, and at the same time to speak of it as resting solely on revelation." (Introduction to the *Dialogues*, p. 41.)

[49] *Dialogues*, p. 227.

11

TILLICH'S ONTOLOGY AND GOD

In spite of the fact that Paul Tillich is often spoken of as a distinguished philosopher, serious study of his work leads to the conclusion that he is, at best, an important Christian theologian, but that he forfeits every usual claim to the title "philosopher." Though philosophers have differed widely in their doctrines and methods, they have as a matter of principle been committed to genuine inquiry, to the open and free search for answers to our most serious questions. By this standard Tillich must be excluded from the philosophic circle.

He describes his work as occurring within the limits of a "theological circle." It is a circle which not only establishes the limits of inquiry but also dictates in advance the answers to basic questions. Though Tillich claims to respect the philosophic way he explicitly says of the Christian theologian (i.e., himself) that, "He is certain that nothing he sees can change the substance of his answer, because this substance is the *logos* of being, manifest in Jesus as the Christ."[1] This makes it clear that, however wide Tillich's scholarship and however subtle his insight, his work is to be seen, not as a philosophy, but as an explication of Christian doctrine from his special perspective. Theology is defined by Tillich as "the methodical interpretation of the contents of the Christian faith,"[2] and he says that the criterion to be applied to each theologian is "his acceptance of the Christian message as his ultimate concern."[3]

Though Tillich has usually been clear and explicit about Christian commitment as the foundation of all his thought, many of his admirers forget this limitation. They tend to speak of Tillich's work as if it had independent philosophic significance. Often one reads analyses of Tillich which ignore, at their peril, the Christian framework which he imposes on every important question arid presupposes in all his answers. It would not be fair, however, to blame the eager Tillichians for their uncritical enthusiasms, since Tillich is himself primarily responsible for fostering the view that his work transcends the parochial limits of Christianity. He does this in two ways. The first is his repeated insistence that the Christian revelation is the absolute and final revelation which must be seen as the criterion by which to judge every other claim to revelation. It is even more than the criterion of every revelation. Tillich insists that Christian revelation is the ground for judging and evaluating every significant aspect of human existence. He expresses this conviction in a clear and uncompromising way:

> The final revelation, the revelation in Jesus as the Christ, is universally valid, because it includes the criterion of every revelation and the *finis or telos* (intrinsic aim) of all of them. The final revelation is the criterion of every revelation which precedes or follows. It is the criterion of every religion and of every culture, not only of the culture and religion in and through which it has appeared. It is valid for the social existence of every human group and for the personal existence of every human individual. It is valid for mankind as much, and, in an indescribable way, it has meaning for the universe also. Nothing less than this should be asserted by Christian theology.[4]

Tillich holds further that each genuine philosophic quest senses its own incompleteness and presses beyond its own limits to search for the truth of revelation. "Reason does not resist revelation. It asks for revelation, for revelation means the reintegration of reason."[5] Tillich bases this claim on the conviction that "the answers to the questions implied in Man's predicament are religious, whether open or hidden."[6] Now if philosophy, at least when it is serious, finds its fulfillment in revelation, and if revelation means the Christian revelation (in Tillich's version), then it is clearly the case that even when he is explicating specifically Christian doctrine Tillich must believe that he is setting down universal philosophic principles, or at least pointing to the conclusions which all philosophic inquiry must reach.

Were Tillich satisfied to restrict his claims severely we might have no quarrel with him. If he were merely saying that he has found in Christianity a way to give meaning to his own existence, or that *he* has been grasped by Christian revelation and is forced to affirm it, his position would be unassailable. The fact that many other people fail to find the ground of their own being in Tillich's version of Christianity would only point to differences in their background, temperament, sensitivity and personal orientation. No one can seriously argue against Christianity as a way which can bring meaning and direction into human life. But when Tillich, with all his supposed liberalism, insists that Christianity is *the* way for all men, and that even philosophy cannot escape the magnetic attraction of the Christian revelation, he becomes obligated to offer some persuasive evidence. This is his minimal duty as a theologian who thinks that he has united kerygmatic and apologetic tendencies in a single system.

When we ask, "Is Tillich a theist?" we are asking something more serious than the question suggests at first glance. We are not asking the question which Tillich has answered countless times, namely whether he believes in God. His denial of theism in any usual sense and his claim that God can be understood only as the ground-of-being but not as a being are too well-known to require repetition. Even the problem as to whether this view is meaningful and defensible need not concern us here. In the Tillich literature the question has been explored widely and from many points of view. We must ask ourselves whether philosophy does actually find its fulfillment in revelation, whether Tillich has given us any reason to believe that the Christian revelation is the one criterion of all revelation and of all culture, and finally, whether Tillich's doctrine is even sound Christianity. Within the brief space that remains to me I should like to show that all three questions should be answered negatively.

Tillich's conviction that philosophy is ultimately driven to quest for revelation is based on a particular understanding of both the human and the philosophic situations. Tillich sees man as living in a state of existential anxiety. Human existence is burdened by its estrangement from the ground of all being. Man is the victim of his own creativeness. He finds himself totally unacceptable and is thus alienated from God and even from himself. Every man is fallen Adam, forcibly separated from his source, estranged from God and overcome by his own meaninglessness. In this state man searches with desperation or to restore his wholeness, but. says Tillich, he discovers his "inability... to break through his estrangement. In spite of the power of his finite freedom, he is unable to achieve the reunion with God."[7] Under these conditions, if he is favored, man will be seized by the power of Jesus as the Christ, and he will be transformed through his participation in the New Being. In the Christ he finds the perfect instance of a man who, though limited by his humanity, attained wholeness and reunion with God. This classic instance has been revealed to us, and through participation in this revelation we may find meaning. It is this revelation which makes our existence bearable. It is through this revelation alone that we gain the "courage to be." If this is truly man's situation, then every man is driven to quest for revelation as a condition for enduring his own humanity. Philosophy is, then, in the nature of the case, unable to redeem man; it has no choice but to press beyond its own boundaries and to seek its own final realization in the Christian revelation.

Tillich's picture of the human situation has the strategic advantage of being currently popular. He holds "that today man experiences his present situation in terms of disruption, conflict, self-destruction, meaninglessness, and despair in all realms of life. This experience is expressed in the arts and in literature, conceptualized in existential philosophy, actualized in political cleavages of all kinds, and analyzed in the psychology of the unconscious."[8] Though this is a widely accepted picture it is only partially accurate. In our time, as in every other period of man's history, there are also men who experience their situation in terms of wholeness and integrity, self-affirmation and meaningfulness. Existential philosophy is not the whole of contemporary philosophy, nor is existential literature the whole of contemporary literature. There are even respectable alternatives to Freudian psychology.

It is undeniable that the tendencies which Tillich has noted are very prominent, but there is no evidence that they are inherent in the human situation. History and the contemporary world have produced too many instances of lives that were not torn by despair for its to believe that man, as such, is condemned to the self-torturing anxieties which Tillich presents as inevitable. It may be Christian doctrine that man is hopelessly lost and that he can only be saved by divine grace. Certainly one has no right to impose such a view indiscriminately on all mankind. Even the Bible can be read (and has been read) quite differently. In the Hebrew Bible as it was understood by the spiritual heirs of those who first gave it to the world man is seen as having his own substantial worth and claim. Man is understood as sharing in God's work, and this means that he has within himself the elements of his own fulfillment. The same view of man can be found, *mutates mutandis*, in much of western philosophic thought as well. Jews will be astonished to learn from Tillich that in their heart of hearts they can see themselves as incapable of achieving salvation without the Christian revelation. Most of the philosophers whose names are enshrined in the textbooks of the history of philosophy would be equally astonished to learn that, willy nilly, they, too, were searching for the Christian revelation. It will not do to dismiss casually every man who is free of a feeling of estrangement by saying that he is obtuse and insensitive, or else blind to his own inner struggle. Alongside the men, in every age, who experience their "present situation in terms of disruption, conflict, self-destruction, meaninglessness, and despair," there are equally sensitive and perceptive men who experience their situation in opposite terms. It is the sheerest arbitrariness on Tillich's part to present his own experience of the human situation and his own very idiosyncratic reading of the history of philosophy as if they were universal. Only if one approaches philosophy with Tillich's kind of Christian conviction already in hand can one arrive at the conclusion that philosophy fulfills itself in revelation. Tillich claims that all philosophy is concerned to know only so that it may finally believe. This is a distortion of most of the history of western philosophy.

Our second question has almost answered itself. There seems to be no ground, except his own faith, for Tillich's view that the Christian revelation is the criterion of all revelation and all culture. Even if we accept *his* picture of the human situation, overcoming estrangement does not depend on the Christian revelation. Many non-Christian philosophers and theologians claim for their own doctrines the power of making man whole, which is what Tillich understands by salvation. Tillich knows perfectly, well that there are Jews, and Moslems and free-thinkers, all of them affirming doctrines for which they claim validity and which explicitly reject the Christian revelation. Where, then, is the supposed universality and finality of this revelation?

Tillich deals with this problem in a wholly unacceptable way. He interprets almost every creative human effort as "preparation for the final revelation." Included in this "universal preparatory revelation" are "Xenophanes' and Heraclitus' criticism of the Homeric Gods and Plato's philosophical interpretation of the Appolonian-Dionysian substance of Greek culture."[9] One hardly needs to comment on this tactic, which, having initially committed itself to the view that Jesus as the Christ is the center of history, is then unable to see history except as leading to and fulfilling itself in Christianity. It is surely possible to deal soundly with Xenophanes, Heraclitus and Plato without seeing their work as a series of unknowing efforts to prepare mankind for the advent of the Christ. Similarly, when Tillich asserts that, "the history of Israel shows that no group can be the bearer of the final revelation, that the break-through and the perfect self-surrender must happen in a personal life,"[10] i.e. in the life of Jesus, he is expressing a parochial Christian view not a self-evident truth which must be acknowledged by every reasonable man. Tillich struggles to keep from arrogating universal claims to particular forms of historical Christianity and to the individual churches. But this does not affect his unwavering insistence that "the eternal criterion of truth... is manifest in the picture of Jesus as the Christ."[11] This insistence is based on a faith which seems to hold Tillich firmly in its grasp. So long as his aims are kerygmatic he need only proclaim the message, but when he turns to apologetics repeated proclamation is not enough.

Tillich's efforts to mediate between ontology and Christianity are hampered by other difficulties as well. His purely philosophic statements are open to much critical questioning, particularly, his denial that God is a being and his affirmation that God is the ground-of-being. But these philosophic statements are especially, troubling, when they are made into the foundations of a Christian theology. Seeking to build a bridge across the abyss. Tillich is sometimes thought to separate Christianity from philosophy, Tillich bravely proclaims: "*Against* Pascal I say; the God of Abraham, Isaac, and Jacob and the God of the philosophers is the same God. He is a person and the negation of himself is a person."[12]

In order to achieve this union Tillich employs a dialectical scheme in which he moves between philosophy and theology. He tries to demonstrate that each requires the other, and then concludes that they must rest on a common foundation. We have already tried to show that, contrary to Tillich, philosophy need not be seen as moving toward revelation. It can also be shown that when he conceives of religion as moving toward philosophy Tillich is distorting some of the most essential elements of religion. The God of Abraham, Isaac, and Jacob is *not* the God of the philosophers, and when he is transformed into the latter he ceasès to be the former. As Tillich himself acknowledges, the central issue is the conception of God as person, a conception which is alien to the philosophers but a necessary condition of biblical religion. "According to every word of the Bible," Tillich correctly informs us, "God reveals himself as personal. The encounter with him and the concepts describing this encounter, are thoroughly personal." He goes on to admit that the central question is, "How can these concepts be brought into a synthesis with the search for ultimate reality?"[13]

Tillich's problems are especially aggravated by his denial of a transcendent God. Such a being might possibly be personalized, but Tillich's God, i.e., the ground-of-being, cannot be personalized. As a result, Tillich shifts all the usual personalistic Christian conceptions to the point where they are unrecognizable. Prayer, for example, is spoken of in these terms:

> It is the presence of the mystery of being and an actualization of our- ultimate concern. If it is brought to the level of a conversation between two beings, it is blasphemous and ridiculous. If. however, it is understood as the 'elevation of the heart,' namely, the center of the personality, to God, it is a revelatory event.[14]

How far removed this is from ordinary conceptions of prayer is obvious. But it seems likely that even such sophisticated Christians as St. Augustine and St. Thomas had notions of prayer which, by Tillich's, standards, are "blasphemous and ridiculous."

In similar fashion Tillich has taken most of the articles of Christian faith and so adjusted them to the demands of ontology (as he understands it) that they lose their personalistic character. Thus, in contrast with established tradition, he holds that "the doctrine of creation does not describe an event. [But that] it points to the situation of creatureliness and to its correlate, the divine creativity."[15] What is astonishing is that at the same time he claims as his own the doctrine of *creatio ex nihilo*. He also affirms that the doctrine of God's omnipotence "is magic and an absurdity if it is understood as the quality of a highest being who is able to do what he wants." Instead, in Tillich's version "When the invocation 'Almighty God' is seriously pronounced, a victory over the threat of nonbeing is experienced, and an ultimate courageous affirmation of existence is expressed."[16] He speaks of the virgin birth as "an obviously legendary story,"[17] and holds that the Resurrection, if understood as having to do with the physical body of Jesus, is an absurdity which "becomes compounded into blasphemy."[18] These, and many similar instances, raise serious doubts as to whether Tillich's views are in any significant respects continuous with historical Christian teaching concerning God as personal. Christianity seems to have given way to ontology.

In an admiring statement Reinhold Niebuhr describes Tillich as walking along a narrow fence. Such a road, says Niebuhr, "is not negotiated without the peril of losing one's balance and falling over on one side or the other," but, Niebuhr adds, in spite of an occasional fall, Tillich "performs on [the fence] with the greatest virtuosity."[19] I would suggest a different description. Tillich seems to me to be striving mightily to walk on two fences at once. One fence is named "ontology" and the other "Christianity."

Unhappily, while these fences are occasionally at a close and manageable distance, they are more often far apart and even turn in opposite directions. Tillich, with all his ability, cannot help falling in between. He struggles with desperation to hold on to both fences, at least with his finger-tips. But having failed, he tries to build a new fence which will be easier to walk along I am not sure what this new fence should be named. I know only that none of the old names fit.

NOTES

[1] *Systematic Theology,* Vol. I, p,. 64.
[2] *Ibid., p).*15.
[3] *Ibid., p.* 11.
[4] *Ibid.,* p. 137; cf. pp. 9, 15,16,28,46; also Vol. II, pp. 89, 151, 166-8; also *Biblical Religion and the Search for Ultimate Reality.* Pp. 21-2.
[5] *Ibid.,* p. 04.
[6] *Ibid.,* Vol. II, p. 26.
[7] *Ibid.,* p. 79.
[8] *Ibid.,* Vol. I, P. 49.
[9] *Ibid.,* p. 141
[10] *Ibid.,* p.143, cf. pp. 227f.
[11] *The Protestant Era.* P. xiii.
[12] *Biblical Religion, etc.,* p. 85.
[13] *Ibid.,* p. 22.
[14] *Systematic Theology.* Vol. I, p. 127.
[15] *Ibid.,* p. 253.
[16] *Ibid.,* pp. 273-4.
[17] *Theology of Culture,* p. 66.
[18] *Systematic Theology,* Vol. II, p. 156.
[19] *The Theology of Paul Tillich,* pp. 226-7

12

KIERKEGAARD AND RABBINIC JUDAISM

I

The religious thought of Kierkegaard is clearly among the dominant religious philosophies of our time. Its influence has been strongly felt in Christian circles and has also penetrated through various routes into contemporary Jewish thought. Numbers of Jewish thinkers, some eminent names among them, have discovered religion anew through the influence of Kierkegaardian existentialism. They have rejected the rabbinic tradition, or in some cases have been ignorant of it, and are determined to cast Judaism into a Kierkegaardian mold. Whatever the merits of Kierkegaard's work, and they are many, I think it can be shown effectively that his doctrines are, on the whole, antithetical to traditional Jewish beliefs. Any man has the right to follow Kierkegaard if this is the direction in which his thought and experience lead him. But no man has the right to ascribe to Judaism ideas and attitudes which violate the very spirit of the Jewish tradition. Yet, such violations have occurred with increasing frequency in recent years. Kierkegaard and the crisis theologies, more than the Bible and the Talmud, are supplying both the impulse and the direction of much contemporary Jewish thought. Under these influences such attitudes as despair, dread, pessimism, anxiety are being championed as the necessary consequences of religious maturity. As a result, the usual Jewish optimism is rejected as naive, and the concept of salvation in history through good works is abandoned in favor of a doctrine of divine grace whose workings no man can grasp. While I would admit quite readily that this side of the religious life has a legitimate place in Judaism or in any mature religion, I would deny categorically that these doctrines are the whole of Judaism or even that, so far as they go, they are normative Judaism.

In what follows, I shall attempt to show how far the rabbinic tradition, which is after all, apart from the Bible, the most fundamental source of Jewish doctrine, differs from Kierkegaard's views. If we examine the interpretation of the *akedah,* the story of the offering of Isaac, as it occurs in the Talmud and the various Midrashim and contrast it with Kierkegaard's treatment of the same event in *Fear and Trembling* we shall discover a very different religious world from that in which Kierkegaard moved. It is not the primary purpose of this essay to argue for the Rabbis and against Kierkegaard. It is its purpose to show how the Rabbis' understanding of the *akedah* differs from Kierkegaard's, and to insist that a properly *Jewish* theology must follow the rabbinic teachings and reject the views of Kierkegaard. Jewish thinkers should learn readily from every source of instruction. But they must take heed lest they be overwhelmed by doctrines which are at best directive, but can never be normative for Judaism.

II

The few recent efforts to analyze the *akedah* through the understanding and insights of Jewish sources have been commendable but partial.[1] They tend to be polemical and their polemic centers on the problem of the relationship between the ethical and the religious. Kierkegaard understands the *akedah* as involving a teleological suspension of the ethical. Though our ordinary moral norms would make the murder of one's own child one of the most repellent of all crimes, in the *akedah* Abraham's readiness to perform such an act is transformed into a perfect expression of love of God and of faith in God. To Kierkegaard this means that the "knight of faith" when he confronts God directly may have to abandon even his deepest moral commitments, and an act which, in other circumstances is ugly and wicked becomes sublime when it is an act of perfect faith. The religious, as thus conceived, is beyond the ethical, is absolutely distinct from the ethical, and even requires a suspension of the ethical. A man of true faith must be ready to violate the universal moral law when God requires it of him.

The main burden of argument in the first of the articles to which reference was made above, is merely that Judaism makes no such break between the ethical and the religious. As its author, Rabbi Gumbiner, understands the matter, the ethical and the religious are identical. There can be no conflict between the moral law and the life of faith. God does not permit, and certainly He does not require, the violation of ethical obligations. For Rabbi Gumbiner the prime significance of the *akedah* lies in the fact that it "is a prophetic tract designed to show that God does not demand and will not accept the sacrifice of a child... The story had been told to demonstrate the fact that God did not demand the sacrifice, that men should understand that ethical conduct was the mode of worship demanded by God."[2] He concludes that Kierkegaard's doctrine of the teleological suspension of the ethical is a "Christian doctrine historically unfounded, dialectically unnecessary, and, from the Jewish standpoint ethically and religiously impossible."[3] Dr. Baumgardt, in his article, does not deny the essential correctness of Gumbiner's strictures. But he adds a caution, namely that we must not forget that Kierkegaard also emphasizes an important point when he stresses the "truly paradoxical nature of the divine command in the Abraham and Isaac story... the 'absurdity' of the moral conflict involved, and the torment, the fear and trembling endured."[4]

III

One of Kierkegaard's most deeply held convictions is that religious faith is not rational in character. With some of the early Church Fathers he believes that a genuine religious commitment is one which says, *"Credo quia absurdum est."* Man's reason is not adequate to an understanding of God, nor is reason sufficient to bring man into proper relationship with God. On the contrary, if man had to rely on his intelligence alone, then faith would be impossible, according to Kierkegaard. Faith transcends intelligence and even violates intelligence. "A man can become a tragic hero by his own powers—but not a knight of faith... To him who follows the narrow way of faith no one can give counsel, him no one can understand. Faith is a miracle...."[5]

It is from this point of view that Kierkegaard understands Abraham's part in the *akedah*. Abraham's faith was a belief by virtue of the absurd. Human reason, presumably, could never understand or justify God's ways with Abraham. The biblical version of the episode is terse and cryptic and, therefore, is open to interpretation. God demands the sacrifice of Isaac, while He acknowledges that he is "thy son, thine only son, whom thou dost love." God demands the sacrifice of a child whom he brought into the world through His own personal intervention, a child who, He had previously promised, would carry on Abraham's work and his teaching. But for this most incomprehensible demand God gives no reasons and Abraham requires no reasons. Instead "Abraham arose early in the morning", hastening to fulfill the divine command. This is all that we are told in the Bible, and with this text before him Kierkegaard does a brilliant job of exhibiting the absurdity of God's demand and the perfect quality of Abraham's faith. No human intelligence can understand God's demand for the sacrifice of Isaac. Intelligence would see here only a violation of God's own promises and purposes, and, even worse, a violation both of the most elementary rules of moral decency and of natural sentiment. But Abraham's faith, his love of God, was so complete that he hastened to comply with the commandment, asking no questions and raising no objections. Such faith is truly a miracle; it is a true instance of belief by virtue of the absurd. Kierkegaard gives his readers the feeling that Abraham believed, not in spite of the absurdity, but precisely because of the absurdity. As a distinguished Kierkegaard scholar has expressed it, "The various determinants of faith are by Kierkegaard concentrated in the single category of the *absurd,* since the movement of faith seems paradoxical to the ordinary consciousness from which faith emerges."[6]

Such a view is appropriate within the framework of the Christian tradition, since many of the articles of Christian faith are mysteries. The very foundations of Christian doctrine utterly transcend man's intelligence, and in some instances actively violate human intelligence. Thus the belief in a triune God or the belief in a God-man are paradoxes whose very nature is to be incomprehensible to man's reason. But this need not be embarrassing to orthodox Christianity since it is a system of belief which acknowledges readily the inadequacy of man's reason. Faith is necessary at the very point at which understanding has reached its limits. *"Credo quia absurdum est",* is neither a failure of nerve nor an abdication of reason. It does not make every absurdity worthy of belief, for while it sees the divine as absurd, it never sees the absurd as divine. It is merely a humble acknowledgement that there are severe limits to human understanding, and that the mysterious aspects of the universe are those with which man's inner being needs most to come to terms.

While Judaism admits the limitations of man's intellect and the presence of certain cosmic mysteries it does not lay its primary stress on this side of things. Instead one finds in the rabbinic sources a rather steady inclination to make sense out of the apparently senseless. As one surveys the rabbinic literature dealing with the *akedah* it becomes clear that the tendency of the rabbis was to reject the view that Abraham's ready compliance with God's commandment was an act of blind faith. Certainly no one would deny that Abraham acted out of faith and love. But his faith, according to the rabbinic view was not blind. The absurdity is apparent so long as we rely only on the scriptural text. Jewish tradition, however, was unwilling to admit that the scriptural story was the whole story, precisely because as it stands the story is absurd. If God, who is the foundation of all morality, requires Abraham to perform a wicked and immoral act, if God, whose word is eternal requires the performance of an act whose result will be the violation of His own promises concerning the future of Abraham's children, and if Abraham goes forth quietly and unquestioningly to do as he is bidden -could anything be more senseless?

It is the very absurdity of the story as it stands that forced the rabbis to expand.it and to give it a different meaning. Kierkegaard, in presenting Abraham as a prototype of the "knight of faith", tends either to forget or to misread other episodes in Abraham's career. The same Abraham on other occasions openly doubts God's promises and questions His justice. Though God has repeatedly assured him that he will have a legitimate son who will be his heir, Abraham laughs at the idea. In fact, so profound is his skepticism that his only response to the divine promise is the request that at least Ishmael be permitted to live. That Sarah should bear him a son is something that Abraham refuses to believe will ever happen. This Abraham is so skeptical that he questions God's justice when he learns of the impending destruction of Sodom and Gomorrah.[7] Yet, in Kierkegaard's interpretation, this same man is ready to offer up his own son without a single murmur of protest at God's behest, though the command is absurd, or better yet, because the command is absurd.

This is a view which is wholly unacceptable to the teachings of the rabbis. Instead as they fill out the story of the *akedah* they give us a doctrine that is insistent on turning an apparent absurdity into a perfectly understandable and reasonable event. Just as Abraham was not required to accept the apparently absurd in other instances so was he not required to do so here. In the cases of the promised birth of Isaac and of the threatened destruction of Sodom and Gomorrah Abraham openly expresses his doubts and his objections. And God does not grow angry with him, because there is very good reason to doubt. Judaism does not require a man to believe what intelligence clearly cannot accept. Maimonides laid down the principle that even "a miracle cannot prove that which is impossible; it is useful only as a confirmation of that which is possible."[8]

In this framework, the rabbis taught that in actuality God's demand for the sacrifice of Isaac was not a moral absurdity at all. On the contrary, God, Abraham, the angels, and even Isaac, all knew and understood that there were very good reasons for God's demand, and these reasons were far more earnest than a mere protest against child-sacrifice. The midrashim pivot around a central theme. The scriptural text relates that when Isaac grew and was weaned Abraham made a great celebration. It was then that God tested him. The rabbis describe what happened in this way:

> Satan said to the Almighty: 'Sovereign of the Universe! To this old man Thou didst graciously vouchsafe the fruit of the womb at the age of a hundred, yet of all the banquet which he prepared, he did not have one turtle-dove or pigeon to sacrifice before Thee Hath he done aught but in honor of his son". Replied He, 'Yet were I to say to him, "Sacrifice thy son before Me", he would do so without hesitation. Straightway, "God did tempt Abraham..."[9]

In another version Abraham is represented as realizing himself that in his joy over his son he had neglected to give thanks to God. Thus he says, "I have rejoiced and caused all to rejoice, but I did not set aside even a ram or a bullock for God."[10] Still another interpretation as the ministering angels present the same complaint before God.

In any case it is clear that the rabbinic teachings did not conceive of God's demand as arbitrary or incomprehensible. Nor is Abraham's act of faith based on a moral absurdity. On the contrary, there is a perfectly understandable reason why God asks and Abraham is ready to offer up such a sacrifice. Nor does the comprehensibility of the act lessen its significance as an act of faith. Even when a man knows why the sacrifice is required of him he still must be distinguished by his love of God and his faith in God to be able to do as God commands. In Kierkegaard's version Abraham did not argue or protest because he was faced with a demand which made argument or questioning inappropriate, and even impossible. The Jewish version remembers that this is still the Abraham who argued and protested, questioning God's justice, even in behalf of the wicked Sodomites. How then could he do less in behalf of his own son? The answer is that what struck him dumb was not the utter paradox and absurdity of God's demand, but rather the recognition of the truth of the charges brought against him. Words would have been meaningless at this point. As a man of faith, understanding what was required of him, he could only go forth at once to justify himself.

The rabbis took pains even to give the episode a special meaning for Isaac. In the rabbinic view Isaac was not an innocent child being led to the slaughter. According to the usual count Isaac was thirty-seven years old, and for him, too, this was a meaningful and comprehensible event. He is represented as he compares his own merits with those of Ishmael. Ishmael argues that he is superior in God's sight because he was already thirteen years old when he was circumcised yet he made no effort to run away from the painful operation, while Isaac was only eight days old at his circumcision and thus had made no real sacrifice for God. To this Isaac replies that unlike Ishmael who served God with only one limb he would be prepared to offer up his very life if God should require it of him. As with Abraham we have here great faith and great love, but not an act whose foundations are absurdity. Like Abraham, Isaac too understands why he is being bound to the altar.[11]

Moreover the *akedah* is an event which is meaningful for all mankind, in the interpretation of the rabbis. Its purpose was to demonstrate to all men that God does not act arbitrarily. Lest any man might think that God chose Abraham arbitrarily or that He gave him a preeminent position for no special reason, he was commanded to sacrifice his son so that all the world would know how great was Abraham's love of God. The *Midrash Tanchuma* expresses this idea in a magnificent passage. It pictures Abraham standing before God and arguing in the following manner:

> Master of the Universe! A man ordinarily tests his friend because he does not know what is in another's heart. But You, who examine the hearts and reins of men, should you have found it necessary to test me in this way? Surely it must have been evident to you that if you commanded me to offer up my son I would hasten to do so with a perfect heart. The Holy One, Blessed be He, answered him: I did it only to let the peoples of the world know that I did not choose you arbitrarily.[12]

What more striking instance could there be of the Jewish conception of the reasonableness and comprehensibility of the *akedah!* One could not imagine Kierkegaard's Abraham addressing God in this way, nor Kierkegaard's God replying in this way.

IV

The heart of the issue lies in the fact that for Kierkegaard the paradox of faith "is rooted in an antithesis ... between God and man, between God's understanding of what human life ought to be, and man's."[13] Judaism is rather inclined to emphasize the close tie between God and man, and the common elements of understanding that bind God and man together. Man's highest life is one in which his understanding of his ideal ends coincides with God's understanding. One of the ultimate purposes of the revelation at Sinai is to give man a clear picture of what human life ought to be in God's sight. The very center of this conception of religion is the belief that God is not far removed from man, but is instead closely bound to him. Kierkegaard's God transcends the world absolutely. He is completely separated from man, perhaps even opposed to man, and, therefore, there is, according to his doctrine, almost inevitably an antithesis between God's view of things and man's view of things. The Jewish God is "nigh unto all them that 'call upon Him, to all that call upon Him in truth." Jewish teaching frequently goes so far as to suggest that God is, in some degree, dependent on man, and even that he is bound by the laws of men.

These ideas are developed in a striking way in some of the rabbinic commentary on the *akedah*. In much of the commentary one finds the feeling that the *akedah* is not only Abraham's trial, but also God's trial. God must prove himself to humanity, just as Abraham must prove himself. It would be a mistake to think of this view as blasphemy, since what underlies it is a very deep and sensitive piety joined together with a profound love of humanity. So long as men are imperfect God is necessarily on trial. It may be that an Abraham can achieve perfect faith even when God hides his purposes from him, though, as we have shown, the rabbis did not think so. The Torah teaches, in the story of the water issuing forth from the rock, that Moses lost faith momentarily. If Abraham, who is the father of faith, sometimes questions God, if Moses, who alone spoke with God directly, could lose faith, then what can be expected of ordinary men? God is always on trial. In times of trouble men are forced to doubt, and God must prove Himself if humanity is to be redeemed.

How else will men come to a knowledge of God? Judaism, in its classic form, does not teach that God arbitrarily bestows His grace on some men, while in His detachment from humanity he leaves others to remain ignorant of His glory, He is rather the ever loving Father who seeks to redeem and elevate every one of His children. He is ready to stand trial in man's court of justice. Through His prophets He pleads His own cause. "Thus saith the Lord! What unrighteousness have your fathers found in Me, that they are gone far away from Me?" And as God pleads, his witness is man. More than signs and wonders, more than every miracle, the testimony of the man of true faith justifies God and brings him close to men.

We see this feeling expressed in a well-known comment on the *akedah* in which the rabbis picture God as coming to Abraham with the following words:

> I have tried you with many trials and you have passed them all successfully. Now, I beg of you, for my sake, withstand also this trial, so that men will not say that all the earlier ones were without true worth.[14]

God acknowledges his dependence on Abraham, for if men are to find their way to Him then they must be led by Abraham. If Abraham fails, then God, too, has failed. As Schechter has expressed it, "it is this witnessing... to revelation by which God is God: without it He could not be God."[15] Indeed, we find Abraham saying, according to the Midrash, "Before I made Him known to His creatures He was only the God of the heavens; but once I made Him known to his creatures he is also the God of the earth."[16]

The angels, too, are aware of God's need for man. Interpreting the verse in which the angel calls to Abraham to stop him from killing Isaac, the tradition tells the story in this way. As Abraham lifted the knife, the angels began to cry bitterly before God, reminding Him of His promise that Isaac would carry on Abraham's line. But if Abraham slaughters Isaac, they demanded, "to whom will you say at Sinai: I am the Lord your God; and who will sing before you at the sea; This is my God and I will glorify Him"?[17] Just as man needs God, for without Him he becomes a beast, so does God need man, else he remains unknown to the world. For His own sake, say the angels, God must not permit his faithful to be destroyed.

Of course, this is only one side of the picture. Judaism also recognizes God's majesty, and knows that there are times when man can do little more than prostrate himself before God. There are many familiar instances in the traditional liturgy where man humbly and tearfully acknowledges his own unworthiness. Judaism never ceases to impress man with his own creatureliness, and with the consequent fact that he is limited and imperfect. So far Judaism has no quarrel with Kierkegaard. The quarrel arises when Kierkegaard makes this the whole of man's relationship to God, while Judaism teaches that prostrating oneself is only one way of approaching God.

The difference can be even more sharply delineated if we reflect on the fact that the rabbis did not only teach that God sometimes needs man, but even that he is sometimes bound and judged by the laws of men. The classic instance in which Rabbi Levi Yitzchok of Berditchev called God to judgement before a court of men is by no means an isolated occurrence. It is just one in a series of episodes of this general character. The epitomization of this idea is contained in the midrashic explanation of the meaning of "Moriah". Depending on the relationship of "Moriah" to the root which means "teaching", the rabbis explain that the name refers to "the place at which the righteous issue forth their teaching before the Holy One, Blessed be He, and He carries out their instruction."[18] Or in an even stronger version they speak of Moriah as "the land from which the righteous give forth their teaching, issuing decrees to God which He fulfils." This same conception of God as bound by the laws of men is evident in a number of other rabbinic comments on the *akedah*. The Jewish God is not opposed to man. His own fulfillment depends on man, even as man's fulfillment depends on God. It would be blasphemous to suggest that God and man are on the same level. But it is equally wrong to forget that man is the culmination of God's creative work, that he is made in the divine image, that he is "but little lower than the angels". Such a man must recognize his limits and, in deep humility, pay homage to his Creator. But such a man is also duty bound to recognize his highest possibilities, to know where he stands in the cosmic scheme, and to insist on his rights, even before God, as well as to do his duty with unquestioning obedience.

V

The essential opposition between Kierkegaard and the Jewish tradition is also apparent in another aspect of the interpretation of the *akedah*. For Kierkegaard Abraham is "the knight of faith who in the solitude of the universe never hears any human voice but walks alone with his dreadful responsibility."[19] In the moment of trial when a man faces God he stands completely alone, according to Kierkegaard. He is neither understood by others, nor does he seek to guide others. His detachment from the world is complete, and Kierkegaard applauds this as a very high achievement, "The true knight of faith," says he, "is a witness, never a teacher, and therein lies his deep humanity, which is worth a good deal more than this silly participation in others' weal and woe which is honored by the name of sympathy, whereas in fact it is nothing but vanity".[20]

This is a doctrine which violates one of the most deeply rooted convictions of Judaism. When a Jew stands before God, even in the moment of trial, he is not completely alone. He is a member of *k'lal Yisrael,* of the community of Israel. He bears with him responsibility for his people, and his own merit is increased through *z'chuth avoth,* the merits of the fathers. When he stands before God, even on Yom Kippur, he does not pray only for himself, but for the group. The very confession of sins is expressed in a plural form—"for the sin which *we* have sinned before Thee". Kierkegaard is filled with contempt for "silly participation in others' weal and woe". Judaism has always considered such participation one of man's highest duties.

It is for this reason that Kierkegaard imagines Abraham as standing before God in complete solitude, totally detached from the rest of mankind. But the Jewish tradition was certain that at the very moment of his trial Abraham did not stand alone, but that, at the very least, he must have asked God's mercy for the future of Israel. One of the most typical expressions of this view is found in a comment on the words, "By myself have I sworn, saith the Lord". One rabbinic tradition describes the scene this way:

> The Holy One, Blessed be He, opened the firmament and the darkness [as witnesses] and said: By myself have I sworn. Abraham said to Him: You have sworn Your oath ' but I too have sworn an oath that 1 shall not leave this altar until I have said all that needs to be said. God told him to speak. Said Abraham: Did You not once promise me that my children would be numerous as the sands on the shore of the sea and as the stars in the heavens? Yet when You commanded me to offer up Isaac 1 did not answer by reminding You of Your promise [but I went directly to do Your will]. Therefore, I ask that in the future when Isaac's children will sin and will suffer that You shall remember in their behalf the binding of Isaac.[21]

One of the measures of Abraham's greatness is that he did not stand alone before God. It is to his eternal credit that in the midst of the severest trial which any man can suffer he remembered to ask God's mercy for his future generations. Because the rabbinic tradition could not imagine a great spirit doing otherwise it was only natural for it to picture Abraham in this way. Abraham's act would be far less impressive if he did not, in the midst of his own suffering, participate in others' weal and woe".

To Kierkegaard this appears to be a kind of vanity. To the Jewish tradition such participation in the lives of others is one of man's highest duties. A truly pious man never approaches God in the solitude which isolates him from his fellow men. Even when the high priest stands all alone in the holy of holies he prays not only for himself, but for his household and for all Israel. Abraham could do no less.

One can hardly resist at this point a brief mention of an earlier episode in Abraham's career. We are told that "the Lord appeared unto him by the terebinths of Mamre, as he sat in the tent door in the heat of the day; and he lifted up his eyes and looked, and, lo, three men stood over against him." The Torah goes on to tell how Abraham ran toward the men and pleaded with them to accept his hospitality. From this the rabbis drew a lesson concerning the importance of hospitality. Abraham, though he was ill, and though it was hot, ran to the strangers in order to offer them what comforts he could. But most important of all, the rabbis conclude, is that Abraham left the divine presence in order to extend a hand of welcome to strangers who were hungry and weary. For this reason the rabbis rule that hospitality to a needy traveler is an even greater act than receiving the Presence of God. For Abraham left God in order to receive the wanderers. To Kierkegaard this would be utterly incomprehensible. In his view, when a man stands before God he is completely detached from men. In the Jewish view, a man's worthiness to stand before God is directly related to his love and concern for his fellow men.

VI

This leads us to one final comment which in its own way illuminates the fundamental difference between Kierkegaard's Abraham and the Jewish Abraham. The only emotion that Kierkegaard attributes to Abraham during the *ake*dah episodes is "fear and trembling". He stresses the dread which Abraham suffers when he has to make the terrible choice between his love for his son and his desire to fulfill God's commandment. Kierkegaard describes with artistic mastery the father's anguish during those three long days of the journey to Moriah, as well as the horror which must have been Abraham's as he lifted the knife to slaughter his beloved son. How else could it be?

But the rabbinic tradition is able to imagine the events in another way. It would be foolish to think that Abraham was so lacking in ordinary human sentiment that he could prepare to slaughter his son without feeling any pain. But even in the midst of his tears, the rabbis tell us, he also felt joy.

> And Abraham stretched forth his hand and took the knife to slay his son." He stretched forth his hand to take the knife, and tears fell from his eyes into the eyes of Isaac, because he felt the mercy of a father. But *in spite of this he went joyfully to do the will of his Creator.*[22]

This same idea is expressed in a number of other places. Abraham hastens to do God's will, and even when it requires of him the greatest sacrifice which anv man can make he is still able to do i; with joy, because he knows that he is fulfilling a divine commandment. He feels the joy because he is not performing an act which is absurd, but one which is meaningful. He feels the joy because he does not stand before God alone, but as a representative of the children of Israel. He rejoices because he knows that his personal suffering may be the source of Israel's future redemption. Above all else the Jewish Abraham can rejoice even in such trying circumstances because he knows that he is doing God's will. The Psalmist teaches, "Happy is the man that feareth the Lord, that delighteth greatly in his commandments."

It is clear that what distinguishes Jewish doctrine from Kierkegaard's doctrine is the Jewish conception of the religious life as involving a kind of dialectical movement. Kierkegaard is aware of only one dimension of religious reality, namely the dimension in which man is so overpowered by the sense of his own unworthiness that he can do nothing but prostrate himself before God. Judaism sees this as only one aspect of the religious life, and conceives of man as moving between a humble acknowledgement of God's majesty and a forthright assertion before God Himself of human claims and human rights. Kierkegaard sees only the somber and solitary side of the religious life. Judaism sees instead a movement between the somber and the joyous, between solitude and sociality.

I am very much aware that in this essay I have, at best, pointed to many fundamental questions while dealing with them at the surface. To pursue all of these questions to their proper depth would require far more space than is available to any article. My main purpose has been only to illuminate some of the most fundamental differences between Kierkegaard's akedah and the Jewish *akedah,* and to show how far the differences between the Kierkegaardian Abraham and the Jewish Abraham are symptomatic of the differences between Kierkegaardian religion and Jewish religion.

NOTES

[1] *Cf.*, Joseph H. Gumbiner, "Existentialism and Father Abraham", Commentary, February, 1948, and David Baumgardt, "Man's Morals and God's Will", Ibid., March, 1950.

[2] Gumbiner, *op. cit.,* pp. 144 and 148.

[3] *Ibid.,* p. 148.

[4] Baumgardt, *op. cit.,* p. 247.

[5] S. Kierkegaard, *Fear and Trembling,* (Princeton, 1945), p. 100.

[6] *Ibid.*, p. xxiii, quoted in Editor's Preface.

[7] Kierkegaard holds that "When the righteous punishment was decreed upon Sodom and Gomora... Abraham came forward with his prayers." But it is quite clear from the Biblical text that things were quite different. Abraham does not acknowledge the righteousness of the punishment, but questions it. He does not pray for Sodom and Gomora; but demands that justice be done. Moreover, he is clear and unequivocal in his suggestion that God is not doing justice. But when Kierkegaard reads even such an open text he sees it through the transforming powers of his own conception of Abraham.

Kierkegaard stresses the fact that Abraham pleaded the cause of Sodom and Gomora, but that when God demanded the sacrifice of Isaac "he did not pray for himself." What Kierkegaard overlooks completely is that Abraham might have prayed for Isaac; he might have seen this as Isaac's cause, as well as his own. Kierkegaard does not see at all that the son has to be spared, not only the father.

[8] Maimonides, *Guide for the Perplexed,* Part III, Ch. XXIV.

[9] *B. Talmud,* Sanhedrin, 89b, Soncino translation.

[10] *Bereshith Rabbah,* XLV.

[11] *Cf. B. Talmud Sanhedrin,* 89b; also *Tanchuma* Vayera, 42.

[12] *Tanchuma,* Vayera, 46.

[13] From a review by David Swenson, quoted in the Editor's Preface to *Fear and Trembling,* p. xxiv.

[14] *B. Talmud, Sanhedrin,* 89b.

[15] Solomon Schechter, *Some Aspects of Rabbinic Theology,* (New York, 1910), p. 24.

[16] *Bereshith Rabbah,* XLIX.

[17] Cited in *Torah Shelemah,* Vol. 3, Tome 4, p. 897, item 131.

[18] Cited in *ibid.,* p. 775, item 37, and footnote.

[19] *Fear and Trembling,* p. 122.

[20] *Ibid.,* pp. 122-123.

[21] Cited in *Torah Shelemah,* op. *cit,* p. 909, item 184 note.

[22] *Bereshith Rabbah,* XLVI.

13

REVIEW: ABRAHAM JOSHUA HESCHEL
God in Search of Man. A Philosophy of Judaism

God in Search of Man: A Philosophy of Judaism, by Abraham Heschel, Jewish Publication of Society of America, Philadelphia, 1956, pp. 437.*

The true philosopher is a man who "demands for himself a verdict, a Yea or a Nay, not concerning science, but concerning life and the worth of life. He learns unwillingly to believe that it is his right and even his duty to obtain this verdict, and he has to seek his way to the right and the belief only through the most extensive (perhaps disturbing and destroying) experiences, often hesitating, doubting and dumbfounded." In these instructive words Nietzsche has reminded us of something that most of our contemporaries prefer to forget. Philosophy is not an intellectual chess game which uses concepts in place of rooks and pawns. Nor is it merely another one of the sciences. Only when human thought reaches the level of deepest earnestness does it become philosophical. Only when a thinker addresses himself to the deepest human questions can he become a philosopher. By these standards, Professor Heschel is one of the few genuine philosophers in this country, a rarity among intellectual mechanics and clever technicians who amuse themselves by treating man's ultimate questions as linguistic mistakes.

In his most recent book, Dr. Heschel offers us more than dogmatic philosophical conclusions. He takes us into his study and allows us to participate in the processes of his thinking as he moves toward the goal that Nietzsche set,—"a verdict... concerning life and the worth of life." The path he follows will scandalize some and amuse others, but this is a risk that every profound spirit takes when it stands before the world without a protective mask. In writing this remarkably open and forthright book, Dr.

Heschel has exposed himself to the slings and arrows of those readers and commentators, who, failing to understand him are determined to have their petty revenge by substituting insult for analysis. Whatever view one may hold regarding Heschel's position every responsible reader will recognize that this book is the product of a remarkable combination of wide erudition, incisive intellect, and spiritual sensitivity.

We would do well to take careful note of Professor Heschel's initial word of caution. He is anxious to protect his readers from the danger of confusing philosophy with religion. Metaphysics does not create the world of nature on which it frequently reflects; neither does philosophy of religion create the religion which is its subject-matter. In both cases the phenomena are given and the task of philosophy is to provide us with "a method of clarification, examination, and validation," a method, that is, of evaluating our insights. An adequate philosophy of religion will, therefore, be concerned first to understand the special nature of the insights of religion and then to deal with these insights in a way which is uniquely appropriate to them.

Because of the dominance of the natural sciences in our day there is a widespread tendency to suppose that the methods of the sciences are the only reliable methods of inquiry. If this were the case, then there would be no possibility of any serious examination of tne contents and claims of religion, since these are admittedly not open to testing in the laboratory. Many students of religion have substituted for empirical verification a more modest test, namely, that religion is intellectually acceptable to the degree that it accords with canons of discursive reason. Judaism, in particular, is often presented as the strictest rationalism, a religion, presumably, whose truth every intelligent man ought to affirm with the same ease and conviction with which he acknowledges that the sum of two and two is four.

Dr. Heschel does religion, in general, and Judaism in particular, an invaluable service by his forthright attack on this superficial view. "The widely preached equation of Judaism and rationalism is an intellectual evasion of the profound difficulties and paradoxes of Jewish faith, belief, and observance." Judaism is more than a set of superficially popularized rational affirmations. It depends on an explicit recognition of the insufficiency of man's intellect, on the awareness that our very insistence on intellectual responsibility forces us to take a stand on issues which cannot be settled by way of intellect alone. "Religion is not within but beyond the limits of mere reason. Its task is not to compete with reason but to aid us where reason gives only partial aid. Its meaning must be understood in terms *compatible with the sense of the ineffable.*"

When man responds to the world around him in his most sensitive moments he is aware that there is a higher dimension of reality than that which is ordinarily known. In such moments he penetrates beyond the limits of reason, beyond rules and prescriptions, beyond simple order and system to the very foundations of all being, to God. Ordinarily these moments of exaltation are infrequent, but their overwhelming truth transforms our lives. The occasions on which a man discovers the highest and noblest demand and merit his continuing loyalty. Our faith in God depends, not on rational arguments or demonstrations, but on the absolute claim of those insights which, having once been experienced can never again be denied. Our faith may waver, but it must not be destroyed.

The immediate certainty that we attain in moments of insight does not retain its intensity after the moments are gone. Moreover, such experiences or inspirations are rare events. To some people they are like shooting stars, passing and unremembered. In others they kindle a light that is never quenched. The remembrance of that experience and the loyalty to the response of that moment are the forces that sustain our faith. In this sense, *faith is faithfulness,* loyalty to our response.

When a man betrays this faith and loyalty he betrays himself. Even when illumination and discernment leave him, even when the light turns to darkness, he has no choice but to remain faithful. Having once discovered the source and the meaning of his own existence, an honest man must strive with relentless effort to return to that source, to recapture that meaning. We cannot always live at the highest level of exaltation, but a life which knowingly abandons that ideal is an unforgivable blasphemy. It is a deliberate rejection of the possibility of divine perfection. "He who has ever gone through a moment of radical insight cannot be a witness to God's non-existence without laying perjury on his soul."

The foundation of religious commitment depends on more than rational analysis. However, this does not mean that we reject reason or look for easy certainties. "The sense of wonder and transcendence must not become a 'cushion for the lazy intellect.' it must not be a substitute for analysis where analysis is possible; it must not stifle doubt where doubt is legitimate." We are obligated to press reason to its outer limits, but having done so we cannot stop at those limits. All knowledge begins in direct experience, but it is not exhausted by a rational analysis of that experience. The experiences in which God reveals Himself to us generate a supra-rational certainty which neither offends nor violates our reason. But may not our intuitions be mistaken or illusory? "Indeed," says Dr. Heschel, "there is no perception which may not be suspected of being a delusion. But there are perceptions which are so staggering as to render meaningless the raising of such a suspicion." Against these perceptions the conventional doubts seem curiously irrelevant. The man of faith wonders that such doubt is possible.

The orientation required of us in religion differs essentially from that which is appropriate to scientific inquiry. "In the realm of science, a question may be asked and an answer may be given by one man for all men. In the realm of religion, the question must be faced and the answer given by every individual soul." The scientist is searching for general truths. Once he has answered his questions the answers become the common property of all men. We need not repeat all of the scientist's procedures in order to possess his answers. We need only understand them. In religious matters each man must ask and each man must answer for himself. It is true, as we shall see shortly, that Judaism requires us to ask and answer as members of the community of Israel. But it is equally true that no one can ask and no one can answer in behalf of another. If we lack the tradition we are lost. If we have only the tradition we have failed to take the most essential step, the step of personal commitment. Though rabbinic opinion differs considerably over the question of the necessity of appropriate intention in fulfilling divine commandments it is practically unanimous in its insistence that the *Shema* must be recited with the appropriate intention, i.e., with an explicitly conscious affirmation of the divine rulership over all creation. Here, we cannot rely on tradition alone. In relationship to God every man must take his own stand and must speak for himself.

But how can the individual find God? For Dr. Heschel this is the wrong question. It is not man who pursues God, but God who is pursuing man. The Bible is the most striking record of God's search for man, from the "Where art thou?" with which He sought out Adam to the abiding love with which He continues to search for all Israel. "Yea, I have loved thee with an everlasting love; therefore, with affection have I drawn thee." God's love for us has caused Him to reveal Himself in the Torah and the works of the prophets. By way of our study of that revelation we can develop the spiritual sensitivity which will lead us one day to proclaim with Job, "I had heard of Thee by the hearing of the ear; but now mine eye seeth Thee." It is through our mastery of God's revelation that we come to see that even the ordinary is extraordinary, that even the commonplace is uncommon, that all existence is a source for us of "radical amazement."

Can we be certain of revelation? Is it not too much to ask of man that he believe that the Infinite Being addresses Himself to finite man, that the Eternal enters into the stream of temporal events, that God concerns himself with history? There is only one way for man to be convinced of the truth of revelation, and that cannot be the way of rational demonstration. "Revelation is a mystery for which reason has no concepts."

There are no proofs for demonstrating the beauty of music to a man who is both deaf and insensitive, and there are no proofs for the veracity of the prophet's claim to a man who is spiritually deaf and without faith and wisdom. Proofs may aid in protecting but not in initiating certainty; essentially they are explications of what is already intuitively clear to us.

One of the main obstacles in our understanding both the fact and the content of revelation is our stubborn literal-mindedness. Language, even at its poetic best, is not adequate to describe revelation. All it can do is evoke responses which lead to insight. If we read literally, then the words become barriers to our understanding and belief. We must read the report of revelation with the aim of participating in the event, not of conceptualizing it. Because revelation is unique we cannot compare it with other experiences of knowing. At best we can only hope to penetrate the outer edges of the mystery, to gain some dim impressions. But even these dim impressions are enough to rouse us from our spiritual lethargy. They make us receptive to the divine call; they make it possible for each man to answer God's search for him, to present himself before the divine glory and majesty.

Fortunately, the individual Jew is not dependent exclusively on his own insights which are vague and insecure. They are organized and integrated for him through Torah, the great document of God's public revelation. "If other religions can be characterized as a relation between man and God, Judaism must be described as a relation between man *with Torah* and God. The Jew is never alone in the face of God; the Torah is always with him. A Jew without the Torah is obsolete." The Torah serves as a check against individual insight. It serves to guide, direct, and deepen that insight. Having been given to all Israel for all its generations it is the one absolute touchstone against which every moral and theological claim must be measured. Without Torah we are completely dependent on the relative inadequacy of our own vision and understanding. With Torah that vision is deepened and is anchored in the one ultimately reliable expression of divinity in history. Moreover, it is not our private, individualized view of Torah that we regard as normative, but rather the Torah as it has been understood by the sages of Israel, the Torah of Jewish tradition. "Our attitude to the Bible is more than a problem of isolated individual faith. It is as members of the community of Israel that our ultimate decision must be made. Estranged from the community of Israel and its continuous response, who could understand the voice?"

Our approach to the Bible through our membership in the community of Israel does not free us of our own share of the task. The tradition may illuminate the obscure, it may call to our attention marvels which we would otherwise pass without notice. But the community and the tradition of Israel cannot think and cannot feel for the individual. The purpose of revelation is to widen our horizons, to extend our understanding. Revelation which is used to suppress thinking and inhibit understanding is distorted and perverted. With the aid of revelation we must grow in spiritual stature so that we are capable of recognizing the divine when it confronts us. It would be a tragedy for man to have been so dulled by mechanical external contact with the text of revelation that his spiritual sensitivity is impaired rather than heightened.

The Jewish technique for bringing man to spiritual grandeur is not by way, initially, of theological speculation. The Bible is not merely a theological textbook. "If God were a theory, the study of theology would be the way to understand Him." However, God is not a theory but the highest reality, and the way to knowledge of Him begins in action. Judaism is a "science of deeds"; the *Mitsvah* is our key to faith, and thus to the Almighty Himself. "Religion is not the same as spiritualism; what man does in his concrete, physical existence is directly relevant to the divine." The commandments of the Torah are our way to the spirituality and holiness which is our ultimate goal. "By living as Jews we may attain our faith as Jews. We do not have faith because of deeds; we may attain faith through sacred deeds."

Mitsvot are not to be thought of as devices which serve man's needs. They are not divinely ordained palliatives whose purpose is to bring us health and comfort. The *Mitsvah* is frequently itself a mystery, its meaning obscure and its purpose hidden. Only by committing ourselves to observance of the precepts of the Torah can we discover their inner significance. To the man who stands on the outside no explanation can be satisfactory. To the observant Jew who follows the established way of Jewish piety, no explanation is necessary. The law can never be understood if it is treated as a series of disjointed particular rules. The parts and the whole must be seen together in their mutual interrelatedness. For the Jew who not only studies, but lives Torah in this way the *Mitsvot* are an art which refine his nature, elevate his spirit, and make him progressively more receptive to the divine call. By way of the *Mitsvah,* the Jew serves God, not himself, and in the act of divine service he draws closer to the divine being.

"The purpose of religion is not to satisfy the needs we feel but to create in us the need of serving ends, of which we otherwise remain oblivious." It hardly requires divine commandments to make us feel the need for food and drink, for rest and security. Such needs are the common heritage of mankind. The religious life aims at making us feel with equal urgency the need for moral and intellectual perfection, the need to rise above our natural state and to realize the divine potential that lies within each of us. Regular observance of the *Mitsvot,* which are a divine discipline, makes us feel these latter goals as pressing needs. Judaism asks that we commit ourselves to God's commandments, knowing that when we have made this commitment we have taken the first step toward the true service of God. When we reach higher levels of development we begin to penetrate the inner spirit of the law. At this point we come to know the end which *Halakhah* serves. We understand that, '*Halakhah* must not be observed for its own sake but for the sake of God. The law must not be idolized. It is a part, not all, of the Torah. We live and die for the sake of God rather than for the sake of the law."

In this summary explication of Professor Heschel's philosophy of Judaism, we have been able to touch on only a few of the main topics which he treats. His position is worked out with extreme care and in much detail. It is consistently supported by a wealth of citations from and references to the whole of our sacred literature, beginning with the Bible and ending with some of the writings of the most recent rabbinic and chasidic sages. His book, however, is far more than just another work of scholarship.

It is, rather, the exposition of the self-understanding of a deep religious spirit whose roots and whose goals are in Judaism. As such it both teaches and challenges every Jew. It teaches us to understand our faith more profoundly, and challenges us to move out of the drabness of ordinary living to the spiritual exaltation which is the heritage of all Israel. That heritage is beautifully depicted in Dr. Heschel's answer to the philosopher's question, his "verdict concerning life... He who seeks an answer to the most pressing question, what is living?, will find an answer in the Bible: man's destiny is to be a partner rather than a master. There is a task, a law, and a way: the task is redemption, the law to do justice, to love mercy, and the way is the secret of being human and holy."

MARVIN FOX
Ohio State University,
Columbus, Ohio

NOTES

*A reprint from *Judaism: A Quarterly Journal of Jewish Life and Thought* Vol. 6, No. I Winter 1957

14

HESCHEL, INTUITION, AND THE HALAKHAH

The growing popularity of the works of Professor Abraham Joshua Heschel attests to the fact that his approach has struck a responsive chord in the hearts of thinking contemporary Jews. Heschel draws heavily upon Jewish mysticism and Hasidism, and his mastery of English prose lends his work great charm. Professor Marvin Fox, a member of *Tradition*'s Editorial Committee, here presents an analysis of two problems in Heschel's writings, one of a general theological nature and the other specifically Jewish. Dr. Fox is professor of philosophy at Ohio State University and is active in a number of national Jewish organizations. He received his Jewish education at the Hebrew Theological College of Chicago. His articles have appeared in both academic philosophic journals and various Anglo-Jewish periodicals. He is currently working on a comprehensive study of the philosophy of Maimonides.

In the drabness of the landscape of Jewish thought in America the writings of Professor Abraham Joshua Heschel stand out brilliantly. His works are fresh and vital, casting light where it is sorely needed, and helping us to achieve a renewed understanding of what it means to be a Jew. While we can learn much from Heschel, there are some points in his philosophy of religion and of Judaism which require revision or, at least, a different emphasis. This brief essay proposes to examine several of these points in order to see whether Heschel's position is sound and whether it is in accord with the main body of Jewish teaching.[1]

I

Philosophy of religion, according to Heschel, is concerned, among other things, with clarifying and validating the claims of particular religions. If we want to validate religious insights we must have a method, and, the only method which Dr. Heschel offers us is intuition. He explicitly rejects the claim that religious truth can be established by some kind of empirical technique or by discursive reason. The existence of God, revelation, God's working in history, the uniqueness of human nature—none of these can be established either by observation or demonstration. Our certainties about these matters are ultimately dependent on direct intuition.

The most common objection to any theory based on intuition is that we have no reliable way to distinguish between those experiences which are genuine perceptions of a higher reality and experiences which are mere delusions or hallucinations. How can we be certain whether a given intuition is a prophetic vision or the aberration of a madman? Dr. Heschel has taken note of this difficulty and has tried to deal with it. His answer consists of the assertion that the man who has had a true experience of the divine is so completely in the power of that vision that he is absolutely incapable of doubt or uncertainty. Obviously this is not a solution of the problem, but merely an avoidance of it, since we are given no criterion by which we can distinguish between genuine and delusory experiences.

There are some other aspects of this same problem which Professor Heschel has not dealt with in his book, but which require some comment. Must we not admit the equal validity of every religious doctrine which bases itself on intuition? Can we reject all but our own? Surely we, as Jews, are bound to insist on the truth of our own position and to reject any religious view that contradicts our teachings. Presumably, devout Christians will find themselves in precisely the same position with regard to the articles of their faith. But on what ground do we make such a selection? Is there any element in the intuitive experience that should lead us to believe that our intuitions alone are correct and that all others are false? Can any persuasive arguments be formulated in favor of one given set of intuitions as *the true set?* In the market-place of competing and often contradictory religious ideas the appeal to intuition seems to be a self-defeating weapon. If it is used to justify one doctrine it can be used with equal success to justify every other doctrine. The net result, it would appear, is an intolerable theological chaos, which offers a fertile field for the saccharine inanities of the "good-will" movement.

Furthermore, a religion which depends on intuition as its primary method restricts itself to a very small segment of mankind. Great spiritual sensitivity is not very widespread. What are we to do about the largest proportion of mankind, those who are neither prophets nor the sons of prophets? According to Rabbinic tradition, during the revelation at Sinai even the untutored hand-maidens had greater prophetic visions than Ezekiel was to experience at a later time. But we, the Jews of this age, do not have this rare prophetic gift. Flashes of insight, moments of spiritual exaltation, soul-shattering visions are available to very few of us. A conception of religion which is rooted in such experiences automatically restricts the realm of faith to a small group of the spiritually elite.

Professor Heschel believes that "the supreme problem in any philosophy of Judaism [and, presumably, in the other major religions as well] is: what are the grounds for believing in the realness of the living God?" and he asks whether man is capable of discovering such grounds. According to his analysis there are three ways that lead man to God, three ways of reliable intuition. Man can come to a knowledge of God by sensing His presence in the world, in things... sensing His presence in the Bible... sensing His presence in sacred deeds. "But each of these three ways, it can be argued, is open only to the man who is already responsive to the reality of God; they will be of little help to others.

If one looks at the world with the eyes of the spirit closed, he is likely to see nothing at all of religious significance. It is true that a man who already conceives of the world as a divine creation can see evidence of divinity throughout the realms of nature and history. However, the mind that finds in nature nothing but matter and motion and that sees man as only one more animal in the natural order is not likely to achieve religious insight through this route. To see the sublime, and the more than sublime, in the world one must look with the eyes of faith. There is no evidence that men can achieve that faith by inspecting the world.

The proposal that men can find God in the Bible involves us in a similar difficulty. The reader who approaches the Bible in the conviction that it is a divine book will have his religious awareness deepened and intensified by study of the sacred text. What reason have we to hope that the reader who denies the divinity of the Bible will also be able to find his way to God through the instrumentality of that great work? All that Professor Heschel has to say about the divine character of the Bible will be convincing only to those who already agree with him. There is perhaps a tacit recognition of this fact in his almost too vigorous defense of the Bible. Each of his arguments begs the question, since it presupposes what is to be proved. A typical example may be seen in his basic argument which states that failure to respond to the Bible is testimony of the limitations of the reader and not the book. "No sadder proof can be given by a man of his own spiritual opacity than his insensitiveness to the Bible." "We accept it because in approaching, it our own splendid ideas turn pale, because even indisputable proofs appear vulgar at the sound of prophetic words... Ultimately, then, we do not accept the Bible because of reasons, but because if the Bible is a lie all reasons are a fake."

True as we believe these claims to be, they are not an argument. Men who stand outside the world of the Bible will only be perplexed or enraged by such strong demands. Having examined the very same pages, they often discover nothing more than a collection of superstitions and errors, which seem to be the work of relatively undeveloped primitive minds. To these men belief in the Bible is evidence of a shallow intelligence and a weak character. Exchanging epithets will not solve the problem, nor will vociferous reassertions of our counter-claims. We, who have found light and inspiration in the Bible, must acknowledge that we are dependent on intuition. By way of this intuition we sense the presence of God in even the most ordinary words of sacred Scripture. But how can the Bible serve as a pathway to God for those who approach it without religious faith and without any sense of the spiritual impoverishment of their humdrum lives?

The third of Professor Heschel's ways to God seems also to suffer from essentially the same difficulty. At first glance it appears that even men who stand outside the world of faith may be able to discover God through the performance of sacred deeds. Presumably this is a way which is open to men whose intellectual orientation has closed their eyes to the presence of God in nature, in history, in the Bible. For no matter what they think or believe, they can act as if they believed: שלא לשמה בא לשמה מתוך. As Professor Heschel himself puts it, "A Jew is asked to take a *leap of action* rather than a *leap of thought*. He is asked to surpass his needs, to do more than he understands in order to understand more than he does... Through the ecstasy of deeds he learns to be certain of the hereness of God. Right living is a way to right thinking."

This, too, is a road which can lead to religious conviction only if it presupposes some measure of such conviction. If a man performs deeds without any sense of their spiritual significance whatsoever how can they be effective in leading him to God? In his later exposition of the *mitzvot,* Dr. Heschel himself argues impressively against mere mechanical observances which reduce the religious life to a kind of "sacred physics." A "leap of action" must be religiously motivated if it is to lead a man to awareness of the reality of God. As Dr. Heschel puts it, "At the beginning is the *commitment, the supreme acquiescence."* Without the commitment of faith a man is most unlikely to undertake the performance of "sacred deeds," and if he should they will be mere posturings without any spiritual effect.

This very point, I believe, is the one that should be stressed most of all. We cannot depend on direct intuition. Perhaps this is what Rabbi Yochanan meant when he taught that since the destruction of the Holy Temple prophecy was taken away from the prophets and given to madmen and children. Sober men know how utterly unreliable intuitions can be. Those who envision themselves as having direct insight into ultimate truth too often turn out to be either mad or infantile. Professor Heschel's position would be far sounder if he consistently put the main emphasis on the initial act of faith, on "the supreme acquiescence."

Contemporary Jews can come to live a life of Torah-loyalty in one of two ways. Some simply accept the entire tradition as valid because they received it from parents and teachers. For them there are no very serious personal or intellectual obstacles to a Torah-true life, and it is not to them that Professor Heschel has addressed his writings. Their faith is firm.

The Jew who is perplexed and searching is our special concern. He will never be persuaded to live as a Jew by an appeal to religious intuitions which he does not have and cannot understand. Instead of being asked to look for evidences of God in nature or in the Bible, he must be confronted with the greatest of all challenges—the challenge to find meaning in his own life. He must be forced to see that without God and His Torah men are reduced to being animals and automata. Our faith does not derive from personal prophetic visions or from moments of personal revelation. It is forced upon us as the only alternative to forfeiting our very humanity. Only when we recognize the depth of our own need are we ready, in faith, to pass beyond the limits of our discursive knowledge. We then affirm that "In the beginning God created," because we recognize that to deny God means to destroy ourselves. With this faith we are endowed with heightened awareness so that the evidence of God's presence in nature and history are apparent to us. With this faith we are able to discover something of the divine truth hidden in each letter of sacred scripture. Not in vain did Maimonides set down as the first principle in his Code the obligation to know that God exists and that He is the source of all being. Without this conviction there can be no religious thought, no religious intuition, and no religious action.

In summary, our difference with Professor Heschel on this point is one of direction. He seems to suggest in many places that intuition is the way to faith. We are arguing that faith must precede intuition. This view seems more consistent with post-exilic Jewish tradition which saw the age of prophecy as ended, and a more realistic approach to the religious dilemma of the contemporary Jew.

II

Dr. Heschel's philosophy of Judaism reflects his general philosophy of religion. The Judaism which he sets forth is a religion of deep spiritual craving, of an insatiable thirst for God. While he acknowledges and even stresses the absolute importance of Halakhah it is quite clear that he demands something beyond Halakhah. "The meaningfulness of the mitzvot," he says, "consists in their being vehicles by which we advance on the road to spiritual ends." The implication is that the *mitzvot* themselves are insufficient for the elevation of man's spirit, that they are a means to a higher end. In fact, very early in his book Dr. Heschel affirms that "Religion is, indeed, little more than a desiccated remnant of a once living reality when reduced to terms and definitions, to codes and catechisms."

There can be little quarrel with the ideal representation of Judaism which Professor Heschel has formulated. Any fair examination of the authentic Jewish tradition will recognize, with Dr. Heschel, that it seeks a disciplined life whose pattern is set by Halakhah with the aim of bringing man as close as possible to God. But even among faithful and pious Jews the exalted spiritual moments are infrequent. One has the feeling that Professor Heschel has over-emphasized this dimension of the religious life, that he places too little value on the ordinary routine of piety and demands far too much spiritual fire of the ordinary Jew.

Is it necessary to go as far as Dr. Heschel does in his absolute requirement of spontaneity, burning religious feeling, and inner devotion? Must we, in effect, scorn the piety of the vast numbers of meticulously observant Jews because it is often routine and mechanical? Does not such a view of Judaism grant (without intending to do so) the old (and probably malicious) charge that the letter kills while the spirit gives life? With all of Dr. Heschel's repeated affirmations of the fundamental need for Halakhah in the religious life, his qualifications and restrictions of the place of Halakhah undermine the effectiveness of his stand. Jewish tradition devoted its major efforts to the development of Halakhah without qualifications or apology. Judaism recognized (in Heschel's own words) that "man may be commanded to act in a certain way, but not to feel in a certain way; that the actions of man may be regulated, but not his thoughts or emotions." A Jew who lives in accordance with Halakhah has done all that can be asked of him. Whenever he acts in response to the *mitzvah*, he draws close to God, even if he never has a mystical experience, even if he never knows the anguish of craving for the divine presence and the transcendent joy of breaking through the barriers. Professor Heschel seems to underestimate the worth of the most prosaic fulfillment of the divine commandments.

While we applaud the skill with which he has explicated and defended the often neglected Aggadah we must note that this enthusiasm seems to have blinded him somewhat to the special place of Halakhah in Judaism. For, according to Dr. Heschel, "Halakhah does not deal with the ultimate level of existence." He believes that "The law does not create in us the motivation to love and to fear God, nor is it capable of endowing us with the power to overcome evil and to resist its temptations, nor with the loyalty to fulfill its precepts. It supplies the weapons; it points the way; the fighting is left to the soul of man."

The greatest Jewish sages were, of course, cognizant of the importance of Aggadah and many of them made brilliant contributions to aggadic literature. Nevertheless, they consistently centered the bulk of their study and concern on Halakhah. Their preference for Halakhah indicates that they found in it far more than Professor Heschel does. They were convinced that Halakhah *does* deal with the ultimate level of existence. They understood that Halakhah is more than a dry legal code and that halakhic study is more than intricate mental gymnastics. By way of Halakhah Judaism grasped in a clear and communicable form the profoundest religious insights. Dr. Heschel fails to see this when he attacks "pan-halakhic theology" as "a view which exalts the Torah only because it discloses the law, not because it discloses a way of finding God in life." Jewish tradition has always taught that Halakhah is the only reliable way of finding God in life. In Halakhah Judaism bridges the gap between the man of rare spiritual genius and the rest of the people. The great religious insights, which are ordinarily restricted to men of prophetic sensitivity, are made available and real through Halakhah to every Jew in all the ordinary circumstances of his every-day life.

"Insights are not a secure possession; they are vague and sporadic; they are like divine sparks, flashing up before us and becoming obscure again, and we fall back into a darkness 'almost as black as that in which we were before."' Because he sees very clearly that we cannot rest with such insights, Professor Heschel goes on to ask the most earnest questions. "The problem," he says, "is: How to communicate those rare moments of insight to all the hours of our life? How to commit intuition to concepts, the ineffable to words, insight to rational understanding? How to convey our insights to others and to unite in a fellowship of faith?" Surely Dr. Heschel must admit that the historic Jewish answer to his questions has always been a reliance on Halakhah. Given the vagueness and insecurity of our moments of insight they must be translated into terms that are related to man's life in order to be effective. This is precisely what Halakhah does. It is an objectification of Israel's collective religious experience, a concrete expression, in human terms, of those elusive truths granted us through divine revelation and grasped in especially sensitive moments by our choicest spirits. The entire structure of Halakhah is the Jewish way of committing "intuition to concepts, the ineffable to words, insight to rational understanding." This is neither a rejection of religious thinking, nor a derogation of theology. It is not a condemnation of the restless craving of men for spiritual exaltation and overpowering insight. What we are insisting upon is that all of these are present in Halakhah.

In spite of his strictures Dr. Heschel will surely grant that the talmudic discourse concerning "the ox which gored the cow" is not merely an and discussion of certain technical problems in the law of damages. It is the Jewish way of concretizing the presence of God in the most mundane aspects of daily life. Rabbi Elazar ben Chisma made this point eminently clear when he laid down the principle קנין ופתחי נדה הן הן גופי הלכות. This is the view of the world of Halakhah as an ideal world in which we meet God face to face. What seems impractical and irrelevant is shown in that world to be especially meaningful. What seems ugly and indelicate is transformed in that world to the highest level of beauty and refinement. In his life and in his study, the halakhic Jew renews continually the essence of his own being. Though he may have no great moments of mystical insight he is, nevertheless, always very close to God, for it is the objectification of divine reality in Halakhah that stands at the center of the halakhic life. It is only in Halakhah that moments of genuine religious awareness are given a stable, intelligible, and communicable form.

This explains the consistent priority which rabbinic tradition gave to halakhic literature as a subject of study. How revealing is the rabbinic observation that the study of sacred Scripture is only a partially satisfactory activity, while the most desirable of all study is the study of *Gemara:* "They who occupy themselves with the Bible (alone) are but of indifferent merit; with Mishnah, are indeed meritorious... with Gemara—there can be nothing more meritorious" (*B. M.*, 33a). This teaches us that the apparently dry legalisms of halakhic debate encompass all of the divine beauty and wisdom of the Bible. Even more than this—divine revelation receives its most specifically concrete and crystallized form in halakhic discourse and halakhic decision. However lovely and moving the flights of aggadic imagination may be, they lack the stability and clarity of Halakhah. Aggadah may inspire us, but only Halakhah can give direction to our actions. The need for aggadic inspiration is granted without question, but Aggadah is effective only with halakhic discipline and direction. God and man can find each other only by way of the bridge of halakhic study and action, for we have been taught that "Since the day that the Temple was destroyed the Holy One blessed be He has nothing in this world but the four cubits of Halakhah alone" (*Berakhot*, 8a). The world of Halakhah is the distillation of all our authentic efforts to encounter the divine. It is in that world that man elevates himself so that he can be with God.

Repeatedly, in his writings, Professor Heschel affirms this very same point, only then to back away from it because of a fear of "pan-halakhism." It is this hesitation about the full power of Halakhah that is inconsistent with the normative Jewish tradition. At his best, Dr. Heschel offers us a superb exposition of the ultimate significance and the ultimate claim of Halakhah. His philosophy of Judaism would be immeasurably strengthened if he held to his own insights with complete consistency.

NOTES

[1] This essay is based on Heschel's book, God *in Search of Man* (Philadelphia: Jewish Publication Society, 1956). All quotations, unless otherwise noted, are from this volume.

15

HESCHEL'S THEOLOGY OF MAN

The writings of Professor Heschel have had a growing impact upon modern religious thought. In this essay Professor Fox, who wrote on "Heschel, Intuition, and Halakhah" in our Fall 1960 issue, discusses some recent works by Professor Heschel. Dr. Fox is Professor of Philosophy at Ohio State University and a member of *Tradition*'s Editorial Board.

"Who is man?" In the very phrasing of the question Professor Heschel directs our attention to a number of crucial issues.[1] In asking "who," and not "what," he presupposes a certain kind of answer. Man must be a person and not a thing. He must belong to a special order of being, for there is nothing else on earth that we can think of or refer to as "who." And clearly, since we place the highest value on personality, this man whose nature we seek to know belongs not only to a unique but to a most dignified realm. His humanity is something specially precious, something to be cared for and cherished.

All this might seem to be a set of commonplaces, and in less skillful hands it might have become just that. But Heschel is not frightened by this danger, for his roots are in the Jewish tradition, and as he views it, *"The teaching of Judaism is the theology of the common deed. The Bible insists that God is concerned with everydayness, with the trivialities of life.*

The great challenge does not lie in organizing demonstrations, but in how we manage the commonplace." It is the merit of Heschel's writing that he can transform the commonplace with such skill that we see all of its marvels. He helps his readers share his own sensitivity and teaches them to respond to ordinary events and ordinary people with wonder, with reverence, and with a profound sense of personal renewal. He has often commented on the traditional Jewish practice of reciting a benediction before partaking of food or drink. In the benediction on drinking water we express thanks to God "by Whose word everything was created." To see all the marvels of creation in a simple glass of water is a high achievement indeed. When we not only see but also respond with awe and gratitude for the water itself and for all that it mirrors, that is an even higher achievement. A major goal of Heschel's literary effort over the past twenty years has been just this—to teach us to see and to respond, to discover and be grateful for the marvels that surround us at every moment.

While he wants us to respond even to the glass of water, his greatest aim is to teach us to understand and appreciate man, to value human personality as we find it in our own selves and as we discover it in every other man. Heschel sees in the devaluation of man, the greatest danger to contemporary society. Where man is reduced to a thing, a tool, or a number, nothing of genuinely human value can be preserved.

In The Insecurity of Freedom[2] he has collected twenty essays published (with one exception) during the last ten years. Though these are occasional pieces with such diverse titles as, "Religion in a Free Society," "Israel and the Diaspora," and "The Vocation of the Cantor," they are all, as the subtitle of the volume suggests, "essays on human existence." In *Who is Man?* Heschel has developed his theme in a more sustained way. However, even here his method is not that of the analytic philosopher. He rarely constructs a formal argument, and even more rarely does he engage in what contemporary philosophy would call "analysis." His aim is kerygmatic, i.e., to proclaim his own insight with such force that it is convincing, and in language fashioned with such skill and care that his readers share his vision. His method assumes that one who has not caught the vision will never be persuaded by argument alone. There are some who find Heschel's rhetoric inflated, and others who are suspicious of his tendency to express a profound insight in a pithy epigram. Such critics miss the point of Heschel's approach to the problems about which he writes. His strategy is to appeal simultaneously to mind and heart, to engage the intellect and the emotions; for he seeks more than the assent of the understanding; he aims at the transformation of feeling, the awakening of sensitivities, the heightening of imagination. Heschel is a poet, as well as a philosophical theologian—a poet with a mission, the saving of man from self-destruction. His unusual style is ideally suited to the purposes for which it has been fashioned and to the audience to which it is addressed. His own words make the point most successfully:

Life must be earned spiritually, not only materially. A good conscience is the invention of the devil. Man knows more than he understands. He senses more than he is able to say. Reducing knowledge to the limits of understanding is to stultify our intelligence. To maintain that everything we know we are able to understand, that everything we sense we are able to say, is an invention of idiots. *Intellectual embarrassment*, awareness of our inability to say what we sense, is a prerequisite of intelligence.

And what cannot be said discursively must be evoked with sympathetic imagination. For,

Sensitivity to the mystery of living is the essence of human dignity. It is the soil in which our consciousness has its root, and out of which a sense of meaning is derived. Man does not live by explanations alone, but by the sense of wonder and with mystery. Without it there is neither religion nor morality, neither sacrifice nor creativity.

In his numerous epigrams Heschel often succeeds in penetrating the heart of an issue in very few, but memorable, words. Concerning the moral base of human relations he says, "No man has a place in this world who tries to keep another man in his place." Of the relationship of institutional Christianity to Judaism he observes that, "The children did not arise and call the mother blessed; instead, they called the mother blind. Some theologians continue to act as if they did not know the meaning of 'honor your father and your mother'; others, anxious to prove the superiority of the church, speak as if they suffer from a spiritual Oedipus complex." The pathetic state of contemporary Jewish education is painfully expressed in the statement that, "We say that we have given the Bible to the world. Have we not given it away?" It is by the power of this kind of writing more than by any formal arguments that Heschel consistently makes his strongest and most persuasive appeal to his readers.

In these two books Heschel is concerned with developing a philosophical anthropology, or more accurately, a theology of man. This has been a central theme in his work for many years, as even a quick glance at the titles of his various books will indicate. Taking his stand against the reductionism of some contemporary theories of human nature, Heschel opposes vigorously every effort to understand man as merely an animal, or merely a biochemical organism. Our greatest need is "to think of man in human terms," for anything less misrepresents and falsifies. When we confront man in his own terms we come to see that he cannot be legitimately understood on the model of animals. For even the smallest effort at self reflection shows us that unlike other living creatures that simply are what they are, man "is a problem intrinsically and under all circumstances." He is a problem because he is capable of measuring the actual against the ideal, what he is against what he ought to be.

The glory and the burden of man is that he is never free of responsibility for the development of his own humanity. And every man knows this, however vaguely. In his self-confrontation, man becomes aware of his possibilities and these, in turn, imply his responsibilities. He cannot merely rest easily, being what he is, for he is driven to reflect on what is demanded of him, to aspire toward the realization of the human ideal. "To claim to be what I am not is a pretension. To insist that I must be only what I am now is a restriction which human nature must abhor. The being of a person is never completed, final. The status of a person is a *status nascendi*. The choice is made moment by moment. There is no standing still."

The central characteristic of man, as Heschel understands him, is that he lives in consciousness of obligation, that he is laden with responsibility. "I am commanded therefore I am." This is the key to human nature. Without duty, obligation, commandment, there is no true humanity. Because man is fully aware that he is not his own creator, he recognizes a debt to the source of his being. This insight is as old as the normative tradition, as old as the Biblical story of the first man. In that story the first words spoken to man are commandments, divine commandments. First, "God blessed them and God said to them, 'Be fertile and increase, fill the earth and master it...'" (Gen., 1:28). When he spoke to man again, "The Lord God commanded the man, saying 'Of every tree of the garden you are free to eat; but as for the tree of knowledge of good and bad, you must not eat of it...'" (Gen., 2:17). It is only in being commanded that man discovers who he is, only in the recognition of debt and duty that his humanity is defined.

The rabbinic tradition saw this point clearly when it commented on the verse which follows the sin of Adam and Eve. "Then the eyes of both of them were opened and they perceived that they were naked." In explaining this verse the Midrash teaches that the reference is not to their physical nakedness. "They had been given a single commandment and they were stripped bare of it." In rejecting the commandment they rejected the very idea of being commanded, and at that moment they were stripped of their humanity. Heschel's representation of man is directly in line with this old rabbinic tradition.

But what is it that is asked of us, what are we commanded? Though Heschel is known to be an observant Jew, he does not, in these books, resort to the classical answer. Instead of simply saying that the 613 divine commandments are a summary of our duties and obligations, Heschel tries to penetrate into the inner meaning of this version of human responsibility. Of course, the ideals of kindness, 'generosity, love, and the whole collection of Biblical virtues provide the norm. However, he is concerned with the inner state of man that underlies that norm and makes it vital and meaningful. Abandoning pat formulas, Heschel invokes certain categories which have become familiar to us from his earlier works. To begin with we must have a sense of indebtedness just for the fact of our existence. This leads to an awareness of dependence, to the knowledge that "man is not alone," to the recognition that without God man is incomplete. Freed of our illusions of self-sufficiency, we can see our world with new insight.

In spite of our pride, in spite of our acquisitiveness, we are driven by an awareness that something is asked of us; that we are asked to wonder, to revere, to think and to live in a way compatible with the grandeur and mystery of living.... All that is left to us is a choice - to answer or to refuse to answer.

Concretely, Heschel calls for a human life which fulfills its own potentialities by being always on the side of the angels. Our reverence for the marvel which is man should lead to active battle against poverty, racial discrimination, ignorance, greed, and the whole set of familiar social ills. We enter on these battles aware of our own limitations, and yet fully convinced that we are called and that we must answer. This is, literally, our vocation, a vocation which daily awaits our response. "I am afraid of people who are never embarrassed at their own pettiness, prejudices, envy, and conceit, never embarrassed at the profanation of life. A world full of grandeur has been converted into a carnival... Social dynamics is no substitute for moral responsibility."

What exalts man above all other creatures is that he is needed, needed by God. This is not a blasphemous limitation on God's perfection, but rather an indication that He has given a special role to man. Says the Psalmist, "The heavens are the heavens of the Lord; but the earth hath He given to the children of men." Man alone is witness on earth to divine truth. Man alone can bring into being the kind of society which is worthy of being called the kingdom of God on earth. Heschel follows rabbinic teaching in viewing man as cosmically creative, as God's partner in the daily renewal of the world. The Torah sets down the path and sets forth the teaching, but only man can breathe life into the fixed patterns of practice. In the exalted moments of awe and reverence for all creation, in the discovery of the marvels that surround us, man first comes to know himself. Only then can he truly devote himself to that service of humanity which is the highest and most vital service of God. This is the true meaning of faith. Religion is not a set of dogmas, though these have their proper place. "Jewish faith... is not a formula. It is an attitude, the joy of living a life in which God has a stake... Faith comes with the discovery of being needed, of having a vocation, of being commanded."

Given this conception of man, it follows that he is supremely valuable. This is expressed by Heschel in two ways, either by speaking of man as divine, or as sacred. And these are, of course, two sides of one coin. Our humanity is a revelation of divinity, for at his best man is truly a mirror in which we can see reflected the image of God. Where else in the world do we find the delicacy and sensitivity which characterize man at his best? Where else do such qualities as love and generosity manifest themselves? At this highest level of his possibilities man is not continuous with animal nature, but his "human being is a disclosure of the divine. The grandeur of human being is revealed in the power of being human." Every man is sacred because this divine potential is present in him, and by "sacred" Heschel means "ultimate preciousness."

It is important, finally, to note that the personal categories which Heschel sets forth are not mere passing episodes of human self exaltation. Heschel sees these qualities of personality as basic structural features of reality, to be taken as seriously as traditional metaphysical categories. He holds that we cannot hope to understand the world by way of classical ontologies alone, nor will reflection on substance and cause unlock the door to the inner mysteries of existence. In his view, the dignity of man and the preciousness of human life are the elements of a metaphysic that is more profound, more perceptive, and more revealing than classical first-philosophy. Heschel is an existentialist in the best sense of the term, namely, in affirming that the deepest dimensions of human existence reveal the most fundamental aspects of ultimate reality.

It might be said, with justice, that in these books Heschel has created nothing new; he has simply restated the classical Biblical-rabbinic doctrine concerning man. Yet, his contribution is of enormous worth, for he has found a way to recast these old teachings so as to give them renewed relevance and contemporary power. The confirmed, doctrinaire skeptic is unlikely to be affected by these books; but those to whom the religious view of man is a live option will be as deeply moved by Dr. Heschel's rhetoric as they are instructed by the scope of his learning and the luminosity of his mind.

NOTES

[1] *Who Is* Man?, by Abraham J. Heschel, Stanford University Press, 1966.
[2] Abraham J. Heschel, *The Insecurity of Freedom: Essays On Human Existence,* Farrar, Straus and Giroux, 1966.

16

SOME PROBLEMS IN BUBER'S MORAL PHILOSOPHY

Maurice Friedman begins his excellent study of Martin M. Buber with a characterization of Buber's thought as proceeding along a "narrow ridge," a ridge which Buber himself tells us is located "between the gulfs where there is no sureness of expressible knowledge." Many philosophers have had as their aim the building of a complete system which would provide certain and unambiguous answers to the fundamental questions which concern men. Buber thinks of Aristotle, Aquinas and Hegel as the three classic instances of philosophers who aimed at security. In these philosophies "all insecurity, all unrest about meaning, all terror at decision, all abysmal problematic is eliminated."[1] But such security is not possible today when "the question about man's being faces us as never before in all its grandeur and terror-no longer in philosophical attire, but in the nakedness of existence."[2]

In his treatment of the problems of ethics, in his analysis of the phenomenology of moral decision, Buber avoids rigorously any easy security. Walking along the "narrow ridge" he tries to account both for the absolute moral demands which are made on every man and the flexible open way in which we must meet those demands. Every moral decision is a moral risk, because there are no final answers available to us. Yet we have no choice but to take the chance, else we reduce ourselves to mechanical automata and destroy our humanity.

And if one still asks if one may be certain of finding what is right on this steep path, once again the answer is No; there is no certainty. There is only a chance; but there is no other. The risk does not ensure the truth for us; but it, and it alone, leads us to where the breath of truth is to be felt.[3]

Buber believes that moral values must be absolute and must be related to an absolute else they cannot be binding at all. When a man is concerned to know what it is that he really ought to do there is no possible answer except in terms of an absolute demand. Like Glaucon in Plato's Republic Buber denies that anything less than an absolute can be binding. Social conformity, personal interest and fear of punishment are only considerations of expediency, not of morality. Man has to make his decisions as if he were in possession of the ring of Gyges, as if he could do whatever he likes without fear of being found out.

> We find the ethical in its purity only there where the human person confronts himself with his own potentiality and distinguishes and decides in this confrontation without asking anything other than what is right and what is wrong in this his own situation.[4]

Ethics is concerned with the "radical distinction" between human actions which makes choice depend not on "their usefulness or harmfulness for individuals and society," but on "their intrinsic value and disvalue."[5] If man wants to know what is right and what is wrong, if he seeks to discover what is intrinsically valuable, then, Buber believes, he must appeal to the Absolute.

In this commitment to absolute values we see one side of Buber's moral philosophy, namely the conviction that the Absolute (i.e., God) exists, that He is the source of values and of moral obligation, and that all men are accountable to Him. "Over and above all the countless and varied peoples there is an authority... to which communities as well as individuals must inwardly render an account of themselves."[6] Without such an authority man could not possibly make basic value distinctions, for "only an absolute can give the quality of absoluteness to an obligation."[7] And every genuine obligation is absolute. When a man affirms that he is duty-bound to act in a certain way he is affirming that he is bound absolutely. Duty is not an arbitrary matter, nor is it merely a name for a psychological state. Kant was right in seeing the awareness of duty as the key to morality because each man does experience as real the fact of obligation. Every moral decision (as distinct from prudential choice) presumes the absoluteness of the claim which is made on us, the absoluteness of our duty. This absoluteness does not derive from ourselves. It is not a feeling within us. It is an ontological reality which we discover when we allow ourselves to face our duty and to hear that which is addressed to us. "I am constitutionally incapable," says Buber,

> of conceiving of myself as the ultimate source of moral
> approval or disapproval of myself, as surety for the absoluteness that I,
> to be sure, do not possess, but nevertheless imply with respect to this
> yes or no. The encounter with the original voice, the original source of
> yes or no, cannot be replaced by any self-encounter.[8]

Only in relationship to the Absolute can man discover true values. One must stress Buber's view that values are discovered and not freely chosen. No man would feel bound by any value-claim if he were convinced that it was only his own invention. Neither would a man feel bound if he had made a free choice from among a range of possibilities. What is demanded of me here and now in this particular situation is not chosen arbitrarily. If it were it would not bind me absolutely. Buber distinguishes himself from Sartre, who declares that "someone is needed to invent values," else life will be meaningless. Sartre, therefore, understands by value "nothing else than this meaning which you choose." To this Buber replies,

> One can believe in and accept a meaning or a value, one can
> set it as a guiding light over one's life if one has discovered it, not if one
> has invented it ... not if I have freely chosen it for myself from among
> the existing possibilities and perhaps have in addition decided with
> some fellow-creatures: This shall be valid from now on.[9]

For Buber our moral decisions and our relationship to God derive from revelation. A detailed examination of Buber's views concerning revelation would take us beyond the subject of this essay. Moreover, the problem will undoubtedly be treated in other essays in this volume. For our purposes it is sufficient to draw attention to Buber's passionate assurance that revelation means real meeting between man and God. It cannot be adequately understood from without but must be known directly and from within. There are some who try to reduce revelation to symbolic meanings and others who seek to dilute its breath-taking immediacy by speaking of it as a vague cosmic process. Either such men have not truly encountered the divine or else they have failed to reflect on the inner character and the profound effects of that meeting.

> What is the eternal, primal phenomenon, present here and
> now, of that which we term revelation? It is the phenomenon that a man
> does not pass, from the moment of the supreme meeting, the same being
> as he entered into it ... rather, in that moment something happens to the
> man. At times it is like a light breath, at times like a wrestling-bout, but
> always it *happens*. The man who emerges from the act of pure relation

that so involves his being has now in his being something more that has grown in him, of which he did not know before and whose origin he is not rightly able to indicate. However the source of this new thing is classified in scientific orientation of the world, with its authorised efforts to establish an unbroken causality, we whose concern is real consideration of the real, cannot have our purpose served with subconsciousness or any other apparatus of the soul. The reality is that we receive what we did not hitherto have, and receive it in such a way that we know it has been given to us.[10]

Revelation transforms man by introducing into his being new dimensions of insight and awareness. It is in the meeting with the eternal Thou that man becomes what he is; here alone does man become truly human.

Revelation is not restricted to a few isolated and spectacular moments in history. "The mighty revelations which stand at the beginning of great communities and at the turning point of an age are nothing but the eternal revelation."[11] Man encounters God not only in the events of the Bible or in the ecstatic moments of mystical union. Each moment of human existence, the quiet as well as the dramatic, is a possible moment of revelation. We have only to open ourselves to the voice which addresses us. Thunder and lightning and the cloud of darkness overhanging Sinai are no guarantee of revelation. It becomes revelation only when he who is addressed "listens to that which the voice, sounding forth from this event, wishes to communicate to him, its witness, to his constitution, to his life, to his sense of duty."[12]

It is in revelation that we are confronted with the Absolute; it is through revelation that we discover absolute values and that we know what is asked of us.

However, the matter is not quite so simple. There are two problems which each moment of revelation poses for us, problems to which Buber is deeply sensitive. The first is the question which plagues every man who wonders whether he has truly heard the voice of the Absolute. Surely, we always risk being mistaken. Buber, himself, cautions that whenever we feel ourselves directed to act in a way which is radically different from the established ethical norms we must be very cautious. When we believe ourselves to be commanded by the Absolute to a "suspension of the ethical" then "the question of questions which takes precedence over every other is: Are you really addressed by the Absolute or by one of his apes?" Buber admits, moreover, that "in our age especially, it appears to be extremely difficult to distinguish the one from the other."[13]

Professor Buber seems to feel that the problem is especially acute in our own time, because now more than ever, "False absolutes rule over the soul, which is no longer able to put them to flight through the image of the true."[14] In other ages of human history men were also subject to the danger of confusing the one true voice with crude imitations. Yet they had, according to Buber, some more-or-less valid image of the Absolute to which they could appeal and which could serve as a control. In our day we have lost this capacity to form even crudely valid images of the Absolute; "the image-making power of the human heart has been in decline so that the spiritual pupil can no longer catch a glimpse of the appearance of the Absolute."[15]

Out of this view of Buber's arise a number of specific questions which I would like to pose. If we admit that individuals can be mistaken when they believe that they have been addressed by God, must we not have some reliable criterion for distinguishing between the false and the true address? But what criterion can there be? So long as man judges revelation by his inner light, is not every claim to revelation equally valid? Nor does it help to distinguish on the basis of the spiritual sensitivity which varies during the various ages of human history, since exactly the same problems which we find as we try to evaluate individual claims are present when we try to evaluate the claims of nations or religious groups who appeal to the superior validity of great moments in their past. Admittedly, the man who is completely convinced that the Absolute has addressed him directly needs no further evidence even if what he hears violates ethical convention. But such men, at least in our society, are a small minority. What of the vast numbers who experience claims and counter-claims, who hear many conflicting voices, how are they to distinguish the true from the false, the voice of God from the voices of those who mimic the Divine? Can any genuine guidance be given to such men? Can a way be opened to them?

The problem grows more aggravated when we consider a second aspect of Buber's view of revelation. The man who encounters God is not a *tabula rasa*. He is not a blank neutral tablet on which the divine finger writes its message. What he is conditions what he receives, for revelation is a "mixture of the divine and the human."

> The revelation does not pour itself into the world through him who receives it as through a funnel; it comes to him and seizes his whole elemental being in all its particular nature, and fuses with it. The man, too, who is the 'mouth' of the revelation, is indeed this, not a

speaking-tube or any kind of instrument, but an organ, which sounds
according to its own laws; and to sound means to modify.[16]

No revelation is pure and wholly divine, according to Buber. What
a man hears reflects, in part, what he brings to his meeting with God.

This raises some further questions. Why is a man's own
modification of revelation binding on him? We said earlier that man requires
the absoluteness of absolute values in order to give ground to his moral
decisions, that values cannot bind us if they are our own inventions. But to
the extent that we modify revelation is not the result our own invention?
We cannot hope to disentangle the divine from the human elements because
they are forged together in the meeting between man and God. How then
can we rely on the results of that meeting? It is not sufficient to answer that
a man who has been seized with the divine fire *does* feel bound, that each
revelation is a "summons and a sending." For one can easily adduce instances
of equally deep commitment without any claim to revelation, and Buber,
himself, cautions us against the allurements of false Gods who so readily
command our loyalty and win our devotion.

The "narrow ridge" which Buber walks with respect to problems
of moral decision is a result of his denial that the meeting with the Absolute
yields a clear and certain moral program. On the contrary he believes that,
"As no prescription can lead us to the meeting, so none leads from it."[17] A
set of moral rules which is proclaimed to be absolute and permanently
binding on all men is most probably a falsification of revelation. "God has
truth, but he does not have a system. He expresses his truth through his
will, but his will is not a program."[18] So certain is Buber of this that he
believes that any other way trivializes both the meeting with God and man's
moral struggle. His comments on a verse in the book of Psalms are most
revealing. Speaking of the verse, "Thou dost guide me with good counsel,"
Buber insists that it cannot mean that the speaker expects to receive from
God direct and explicit moral instruction. The Psalmist does not believe
that God is an oracle who will guide his every action. Buber tells us, "Just
because I take this man so seriously I cannot understand the matter in this
way."[19]

In Buber's analysis of the phenomenology of the moral decision
he has become convinced that to know the right way is almost never an
easy or simple matter. Each genuine moral decision is the result of great
struggle and searching. There are no cheaply won answers to our perplexities
about right and wrong. Men,

who are seriously laboring over the questions of good and
evil, rebel when one dictates to them, as though it were some long
established truth, what is good and what is bad; and they rebel just
because they have experienced over and over again how hard it is to
find the right way.[20]

If one takes the moral struggle seriously then he must recognize
that it is a struggle. Revelation does not alleviate the struggle by providing
us with a set guide to moral practice.

Even the great historic revelations which are set down in such books
as the Bible cannot be properly understood as presenting us with finished
and set programs of action. The laws which are recorded in the sacred
writings of the great religions are interpreted by Buber as human rather
than divine. They are the record of what men have done with and to
revelation, but they are not the literal text of revelation. In his
correspondence with Franz Rosenzweig Buber expresses this view with
great clarity, "I do not believe," writes Buber, "that *revelation* is ever a
formulation of a law. It is only through man in his self-contradiction that
revelation becomes legislation. This is the fact of man."[21] Whatever it is
that we derive from revelation it is not a set code of practice.

The reason for this view lies, in part at least, in Buber's
understanding of man's moral situation. He sees every instance of moral
trial as unique. It has to be decided in terms of the particular circumstances
and the particular demands. To decide for the right and the good is an act
which can never be performed mechanically, nor can it be accomplished by
implementing long-established rules of behavior. There can be no rules to
cover the unique and the particular, since rules always are generalizations
which must ignore specificity and particularity. A man must know what is
asked of him here and now. No set course of action which has been chosen
in advance can serve as a guide when the moment of decision is upon us.

Every case, if it is taken seriously in its unique character and
situation, proves itself to be something that cannot be anticipated,
something withdrawn from planning and precautionary measures. No
traditional formulae and rhythms of any kind, no inherited methods of
exercising power, nothing which can be known, nothing which can be
learnt, are of any use to the man of sacramental existence; he has ever to
endure through the moment which is not and cannot be foreseen...[22]

Though these words are spoken of the "man of sacramental
existence" they find their echo in many places in Buber's writings and can

be fairly taken as an expression of the moral situation of every man.[23] Buber's attitude toward supposedly revealed legislation is clear in the light of his insistence on the uniqueness of each case of moral decision. If the only question I may properly ask is, "What is demanded of me?" then no law as such binds me. Only when the "Thou shalt" or the "Thou shalt not" speaks personally to me does it command my loyalty and submission. As a general formula it does not touch me at all. With this attitude Buber, the Jew, rejects much of the legislation of the Hebrew Bible. About this Buber is completely unambiguous when he writes to Rosenzweig, "for me, though man is a law-receiver, God is not a law-giver, and therefore the Law has no universal validity for me, but only a personal one. I accept, therefore, only what I think is being spoken to me...[24] And Buber believes that when the law is addressed to me it binds me, not because it was set down in ancient days, but because in the uniqueness of the present moment the one true voice speaks through it. For the most part, however, we must find our way without the law which has been set down. We must, rather, keep ourselves open to whatever way may be opened to us as we meet in true relationship with God.

What then does revelation achieve, according to Buber? In man's meeting with God something happens which Buber believes to be far more significant than the receipt of specific instructions about how to act. In this meeting a man becomes bound to God and this fact transforms the man in a radical way. For, though he has not been told explicitly what to do, he has discovered that man is responsible for what he does, that he is held accountable and that he must give an account of himself. When man and God meet

> the human substance is melted by the spiritual fire which visits it, and there now breaks forth from it a word, a statement, which is human in its meaning and form, human conception and human speech, and yet witnesses to Him who stimulated it and to His Will.[25]

No act can be right, Buber teaches us, unless it arises from our bond with God. No act can be morally significant unless it is linked to God. Whatever we do must be done in and through the burning reality of our relationship to the Absolute. "To do the right thing in the right way, the deed must spring from the bond with Him who commands us. Our link with Him is the beginning, and the function of the teachings is to make us aware of our bond and make it fruitful."[26] This is what comes out of revelation-not codes and not rules, but the reformation of the human spirit. Through revelation man knows that he is commanded, that demands are made of him.

But only the man himself can decide what specifically is asked of him; he alone knows how to respond.

It is no wonder, then, that Buber repeats so often his caution against supposing that we can ever be certain that we have done what is right. Men usually find moral assurance by depending on established moral codes to which they try to conform, or by developing independent but convincing theories about the nature of moral duty which they then live by, or by appealing directly to a conscience which they are certain does not mislead them. As we have seen, Buber denies that any of these ways is absolutely reliable. Nor does revelation itself give me any clear course or program of action. This is why Buber is forced to conclude that "there is not the slightest assurance that our decision is right in any way but a personal way."[27] All we can do is to decide in the light of what we feel is being asked of us, in the light of what the particular circumstances demand. We do so with the consciousness that we are running a risk, but that this is the most and the best that is open to us. A morally sensitive man "knows that he cannot objectively and reliably know whether that which he intends to do is the correct answer to the problem presented to him." This is why he "lives through these moments daringly, in fear and trembling."[28]

In summary, we can say that Buber sees man as obligated by revelation to make a decision in a set of circumstances so unique that only he alone can decide what it is that he ought to do. This seems to place Buber almost at the opposite extreme from his position that values must be absolute. Does he not violate his own doctrine of the absoluteness of the moral demand by making each individual man the sole, but uncertain, judge of what he ought to do? Does he not substitute the privacy of the individual decision for the absolute value? Revelation which does not communicate with man directly seems to make God's word dependent on man's response. But is this not a reduction of the divine to the human? Even if a man believes that a recorded revelation, such as the Pentateuch, is to be understood literally, he still does not have final certainty in every act. There are always conflicts of equally pressing duties and equally just claims. No man can be certain that he has always given priority to the right duty or that he judged correctly in deciding in favor of a given claim. However, if he believes that he is bound by God's word and that that word is known with much explicitness he can feel secure in many (if not in all) of his decisions. For he does not substitute his opinion for God's commandment. Is this not what Buber would have us do? Does Buber's kind of revelation reveal anything more than the views of individual men?

There is still another difficulty that arises out of this aspect of Buber's moral philosophy. If I understand him correctly he takes the position that there can be no general moral rules or codes which are binding, that each moral situation is unique and requires its own unique solution, that this solution is made responsibly only when the individual man responds to the divine voice with his own act of decision, and that, therefore, there is in the last analysis a kind of complete privacy to each moral decision. Moreover, it would follow from this that we can make no moral judgments of men or societies, and, perhaps, not even of ourselves. But does this not in effect make any kind of human society impossible? We are forced in the ordinary circumstances of our lives to judge men and societies, to throw in our lot with those whom we believe to be good and to oppose those whom we believe to be evil. Can we ever make such judgments without some general principles by which we are guided? Even individual action and decision would become almost impossible. Is each man really expected to be a prophet speaking with the assurances of the divine word, or a creative moral genius who carves his own way out of the dark forest of moral doubt and uncertainty? Most men (perhaps even all men) do need guidance and direction, and without such guidance they would be completely paralyzed. Is it not enough that a man decides for the good? Must he also create out of himself an understanding of what constitutes the good?

Buber partially admits the justice of these objections when he says,

> I do not in the least mean that a man must fetch the answer alone and unadvised out of his breast. Nothing of the sort is meant; how should the direction of those at the head of any group not enter essentially into the substance out of which the decision is smelted?

However, he adds immediately that "direction must not be substituted for decision."[29] Yet if there is to be direction at all what role does it play, and what am I to decide? Is each man to decide only whether to accept that direction which he already acknowledges leads to the good, or must he decide also whether the direction does as a matter of fact lead to the good? In the latter case what principles or criteria shall he invoke? Does he not, in spite of Buber's disapproval, have to "fetch the answers alone and unadvised out of his breast"?

Apparently Buber wants to meet this problem by admitting that the existence of society does require norms of behavior, but that adherence to these norms is not to be confused with genuine moral decision.

> Provided society does not insist that the moral and legal forms into which it has transformed the Ten Commandments, that that product which is an I-and-Thou deprived of the I and the Thou, is still the Ten Commandments its activities are unobjectionable; it is as a matter of fact impossible to imagine how society could exist without them.[30]

Though these rules of behavior are necessary conditions of social existence Buber hastens to add that there could be no greater calamity than that which would befall us "if society were to have the temerity to pretend that its voiceless morals and its faceless law are really the Word," if we were to substitute, that is, conformity with social rules for the sense of being personally commanded. And what is to be done with the man who knows only the rules of his society, or the man who accepts on faith the Ten Commandments without feeling any immediate personal address? Or, what is even more troubling, what shall we do with the man who chooses a way in opposition to the norms of society or to the Ten Commandments? Shall we condemn him as evil? But we cannot for he may be acting in accordance with what he is convinced is the voice of God. Neither is Buber prepared to accept such men and to approve of them. For we discover that Buber himself, in spite of his theories, makes many moral judgments, establishes general rules of approved conduct, and appeals to those rules frequently. He, too, seems to acknowledge that without such rules there would be moral chaos. It would be illuminating, indeed, if Professor Buber would help us to see how he reconciles his setting down of such moral norms with his insistence on the uniqueness of each moral situation and the exclusive prerogative of the individual who is called upon to choose a way of acting.

Let us first cite the evidence in order to make certain that we have not misunderstood or misrepresented Buber's intentions. We must first take note of the fact that there are passages in which Buber speaks of revelation as having specific content. In explicating the view of Hasidism, for example, he states that "the Torah [i.e. established Jewish law] marks the circumference of revelation as it is up to the present."[31] This seems to imply that this is a valid revelation and that those who accept it are bound by the norms of behavior which are contained therein. Buber adds that "it depends on man whether and to what extent this expands," how far the act of hallowing the world is to go. But one thing is eminently clear, namely that men have no authority to contract the sphere which is under the revealed commandments-not even the man who does not feel that they are spoken directly to him. (It cannot be argued that this is not Buber's own view, but only his explanation of Hasidism. For in his foreword to the book from which these sentences are taken Buber tells us that he considers "Hasidic truth vitally important for Jews, Christians, and other," and that "because of its truth" he is carrying Hasidism "into the world against its will.") It appears, then, that Buber also admits that revelation involves specific commandments and commandments which are set down as general rules.

He even seems to believe that there are times when we can and should give concrete moral instruction, when it is a moral failure to shirk a request for moral guidance. One such situation is that of the teacher in relationship to his pupils.

> The teacher who is for the first time approached by a boy with a somewhat defiant bearing, but with trembling hands, visibly opened-up and fired by a daring hope, who asks him what is the right thing in a certain situation-for instance, whether in learning that a friend has betrayed a secret entrusted to him one should call him to account or be content with entrusting no more secrets to him-the teacher to whom this happens realizes that this is the moment to make the first conscious step towards the education of character he has to answer, to answer under a responsibility, to give an answer which will probably lead beyond the alternatives of the question by showing a third possibility *which is the right one*. To dictate what is good and evil in general is not his business. His business is to answer a concrete question, to answer what is right and wrong in a given situation.[32]

But how on Buber's own ground can or ought any man answer such a question for another? And how can he know "what is right and wrong in a given situation" without having some general principles to which he can appeal?

Let us note further that Buber makes specific judgments of men and of peoples. He speaks disapprovingly of Hitler as "the sinister leading personality" of his time and is convinced that we can distinguish qualitatively "between the charisma of Moses and that of Hitler."[33] In a moving and courageous statement made in Germany in 1953 Buber condemns with the deepest bitterness those of the Germans "who killed millions of my people in a systematically prepared and executed procedure whose organized cruelty cannot be compared with any previous historical event." Of these

Germans Buber says, "They have so radically removed themselves from the human sphere, so transposed themselves into a sphere of monstrous inhumanity inaccessible to my conception, that not even hatred, much less an overcoming of hatred, was able to arise in me."[34] It is hardly necessary to say that we share Buber's sentiments. What we are moved to ask, however, is how even such men can be condemned as evil unless there are general moral rules which bind all men. If there are no such rules, then what is the ground for our judgment? May not even such men also be acting in response to their own understanding of the divine voice? Surely Buber meant his statement to be a true and correct moral judgment and not merely an expression of arbitrary personal feelings.

Buber also makes a considerable number of moral pronouncements which take the form of general rules. He rules that lying is evil. "The lie is the specific evil which man has introduced into nature... In a lie the spirit practices treason against itself."[35] From the standpoint of biblical faith, which is Buber's own standpoint,

> deceit is under all circumstances regarded as disgraceful... even if it is prompted by a desire to promote the cause of justice; in fact, in the latter case, it is the more pernicious, since it poisons and disintegrates the good which it is supposed to serve.[36]

In fact, in revelation, Buber believes, God "distinguishes between truth and lies, righteousness and unrighteousness," and "He challenges us to make such distinctions within the sphere of our life."[37] Not only is lying evil, violence is also evil.

> What is accomplished through lies can assume the work of truth; what is accomplished through violence, can go in the guise of justice, and for a while the hoax may be successful. But soon people will realize that lies are lies at bottom, that in the final analysis, violence is violence, and both lies and violence suffer the destiny history has in store for all that is false.[38]

If violence is evil then murder must surely be judged evil. And Buber does make precisely this judgment. "In the realm of Moloch," he says, "honest men lie and compassionate men torture. And they really and truly believe that brother-murder will prepare the way for brotherhood There appears to be no escape from the most evil of all idolatry."[39] Not only such outright violence, but the drive for power itself is condemned by Buber. "A will-to-power, less concerned with being powerful than with being 'more powerful than,' becomes destructive. Not power but power hysteria is evil."[40] In another passage Buber adds the seduction of women to those acts which decent men must reject. It is an evidence of their diseased moral condition that "Don Juan finds absolute and subjective value in seducing the greatest possible number of women, and the dictator sees it in the greatest possible accumulation of power."[41] No man with correct moral perception, Buber believes, would judge these as absolute values.

Just as he makes strong general pronouncements about which things are morally evil Buber also takes a stand with respect to what is good. So, for example, he asserts that the social legislation in the Pentateuch, which seeks to bring about a basic equality of persons and possessions, is good, and, what is even more important, that these laws were explicitly revealed by God.

> Communal ownership of the land, regularly recurrent leveling of social distinctions, guarantee of the independence of each individual, mutual aid, a general Sabbath embracing serf and beast as beings with an equal claim to rest, a sabbatical year in which the soil is allowed to rest and everybody is admitted to the free enjoyment of its fruits-these are not practical laws thought out by wise men; they are measures which the leaders of the nation, apparently themselves taken by surprise and overpowered, have found to be the set task and condition for taking possession of the land.[42]

That Buber should feel such enthusiasm for the social legislation of the Bible is understandable in the light of the conviction which he shares with Hasidism that all men are equal and that discrimination between men, especially discrimination in favor of myself is evil. "Nothing disturbs the unity of God's work, the foretaste of Eternity, as much as... overbearing discrimination between myself and my neighbour, as if indeed I excelled in one way or another above someone else."[43] From this rejection of discrimination between men follows the positive need to extend our love to every man. We must love the world if we are to love God; this must be the aim of every good man.[44]

If we open ourselves to this commandment we will discover, Buber assures us, still another duty. We will know that we must seek peace. This is one demand which God makes of all men without exception. For we are told by Buber that "if we consult our deep inner knowledge about God's command to mankind, we shall not hesitate an instant to say that it is peace."[45] "There is a purpose to creation; there is a purpose to the human race, one we have not made up ourselves... No, the purpose itself revealed its face to us and we have gazed upon it... Our purpose is the great upbuilding of peace... The world of humanity is meant to become a single body."[46]

I have quoted so extensively from Buber in the last several pages because I wanted to allow him to speak for himself without the possibly distorting mediation of paraphrases and explanations. From these quotations it seems to me to be clear, beyond any doubt, that Buber does make numerous positive and negative moral judgments which he intends to be universally and permanently binding. My question has been stated before and can now be restated. How does Professor Buber reconcile such universal moral judgments with his view that even in revelation there are no set moral principles, and that men can only come to moral decisions in the light of the uniqueness of their particular circumstances? Does this not make impossible judgments and the proclamation of principles of the kind that Buber has so frequently offered us in his writings and in his speeches?

Buber's readiness to take so firm a stand in favor of certain kinds of actions as good and against certain others as evil is even more puzzling when we consider his analysis of the nature of the good and the evil. He repeatedly defines the good as "direction" and the evil as "lack of direction."[47] This direction may either be understood as the movement toward becoming that which I am uniquely intended to be, or else it is understood as the direction toward God.[48] In the former meaning Buber's intention is most beautifully expressed in the Hasidic tale which he has recorded and which has been very widely quoted. "Before his death, Rabbi Zusya said 'In the coming world, they will not ask me: Why were you not Moses? They will ask me: Why were you not Zusya?'"[49] Man's only duty is to become what he uniquely is. All that is asked of a man is that he realize his own particular nature.

In substance, moving in the direction of self-fulfillment is thought by Buber to be the same as moving in the direction of God.

> In decision, taking the direction thus means: taking the direction toward the point of being at which, executing for my part the design which I am, I encounter the divine mystery of my created uniqueness, the mystery waiting for me... Every revelation is revelation of human service to the goal of creation, in which service man authenticates himself.[50]

What is demanded of man, above all else, is that he recognize his responsibility, that he make a decision. When the decision is made with the whole strength of a man's being and in the full awareness of the depth of his responsibility then the decision is upright; it is in the right direction. The only real evil is to fail to come to any decision. "If there were a devil it would not be one who decided against God, but one who, in eternity came to no decision."[51] For a man cannot truly make a decision with less than his whole being and when he has so unified himself that his entire being moves in a single direction he has done all that can be asked of him. Buber, in one place, defines sin as "what a man cannot by its very nature do with his whole being."[52] On the other hand, when a man has made a genuine decision, i.e., a decision with his whole being, he is assured of doing good. For "man can decide only for the direction of God."[53] Consistently with the rest of his doctrine Buber adds no more content to his definitions of good and evil than that which we have set forth. A man must decide. He must direct his entire being toward an end. That end is the realization of his own uniqueness. And this is simultaneously a movement in the direction of God. There is, as there must be, a studious avoidance in all of this of any more specific identification of the good. But this raises again the very same questions which troubled us before. First, how does Buber explain, in the light of these definitions, the many specific statements he makes about good and evil? Secondly, are we not forced to do exactly what Buber has done, namely to add content, rules, prescriptions and prohibitions? Otherwise would not every kind of act possibly be one which was in the direction of some person's true self-realization? Can men not murder or lie with their whole being?

There is still one more dimension of Buber's moral philosophy that we must examine. We have defined the good as direction and have understood this as a dedication of man's being to his own fulfillment. However, Buber is deeply committed to the view that true humanity, and hence true morality, is only possible when men are related to each other in a living community. Every true culture is such a community, and the same man who, we were told, must make his own decision and find his own way must also act as a member of his culture. At least this is the case so long as the culture is live, integrated, and effective. Cultures express morally valid ways of living and morally valid ideals. These ideals are not arbitrary, nor are they the inventions of men or the results of some sort of general agreement. "The patterns familiar to us from the history of culture are never personal or arbitrary... from the *polites* pattern of classical Greek antiquity to the 'gentleman' of the great era in English history."[54] Such patterns arise from the deepest levels of the life of a people and embody a valid ideal within the history and civilization of that people. Even if we grant Buber's contention that when a culture breaks down man has no choice but to seek his own direction, we should still be disturbed by his claims about the status of men in vital and integrated cultures. Surely Buber would not have us believe that the ideal of every culture is morally acceptable Must we not distinguish between the moral worth of cultures? What principles, what general criteria shall we employ if we follow Buber's guidance? Buber may well be correct when he teaches us that "though something of righteousness may become evident in the life of the individual, righteousness itself can only become wholly visible in the structures of the life of a people."[55] This does not mean that the institutionalized life of every people is righteous. How, then, can we judge?

Buber is aware of the problem, but his answer leaves us somewhat unsatisfied. He stresses the fact that each man belongs to his community. Yet at the same time we must note "that true membership of a community includes the experience... of the boundary of this membership." However, this boundary "can never be definitively formulated."[56] We must be critical of our community, recognizing its limits and knowing its evils. Yet, Buber says, there are no external criteria that we can call on. Only one way is open to the man of moral concern, and that is to stand before God in a completely open and receptive way. In so doing he will discover, in pain and agony, where the boundary lies. Again we are turned back to the inner life of man and to the problems which this generates.

In this essay 1 have not attempted to set forth in all of its detail and richness the whole of Buber's moral philosophy. Some topics have been dealt with sketchily. Some topics, e.g., freedom, the dialogical relationship, the moral implications of I-Thou and I-It, have not been dealt with at all. It is my belief that the basic problems which have been raised here would not be materially affected by Buber's treatment of these topics. For we have seen in Buber's moral philosophy an attempt to defend moral anarchy while pleading for moral order. It is my hope that Professor Buber will favor us with a clarification of his position.

MARVIN FOX
Ohio State University

NOTES

[1] *Between Man and Man*, p. 139.
[2] *Ibid*, p. 145.
[3] *Ibid.*, p. 71.
[4] *Eclipse of God* (Harper Torchbook edition), p. 95.
[5] Ibid.
[6] Israel and the World, p. 220.
[7] *Eclipse of God*, p. 18.
[8] *Ibid.*, cf. also P. 98.
[9] *Ibid*, P. 70; cf. also, *Between Man and Man*, P. 108.
[10] *I and Thou*, p. 109.
[11] *Ibid.*, p. 117.
[12] *Israel and the World*, p. 98.
[13] *Eclipse of God*, pp. 11 8-119.
[14] *Ibid.*
[15] *Ibid.*
[16] *I and Thou*, p. 117.
[17] *Ibid., p.* I 10.
[18] *Israel and the World*, p. 114.
[19] *Good and Evil: Two Interpretations*, p. 43.
[20] *Between Man and Man*, p. 105.
[21] Letter to Franz Rosenzweig, June 24, 1924. Contained in Franz Rosenzweig, On *Jewish Learning* (New York, 1955), p. III.
[22] *Hasidism*, p. 135.
[23] Cf., e.g., *Between Man and Man*, p. 68; *Israel and the World*, pp. 163, 216.
[24] In Rosenzweig, *op. cit.*, p. 115.
[25] *Eclipse of God*, P. 135.
[26] *Israel and the World*, P. 145.
[27] *Between Man and Man*, p. 69.
[28] *Hasidism*, p. 162.
[29] *Between Man and Man*, p. 69.
[30] *Israel and the World*, p. 87.
[31] *Hasidism*, p. 27.
[32] *Between Man and Man*, p. 107. Italics mine.
[33] Eclipse of God, pp. 77-78.
[34] *Pointing the Way*, p. 232.
[35] *Good and Evil*, P. 7.
[36] *At the Turning*, p. 53.
[37] *Israel and the World*, p. 209.
[38] *Ibid.*, P. 238.
[39] *Eclipse of God*, p. 120.
[40] *Israel and the World*, p. 216.
[41] *Between Man and Man*, p. 108.
[42] *Israel and the World*, p. 229; cf. *Pointing the Way*, p. 143.

43 *Hasidism,* pp. 181-182.

[44] *Ibid.,* pp. 157-8, 165; *I and Thou,* pp. 107-109.

[45] *Israel and the World,* pp. 236-237.

[46] *Ibid.,* p. 186.

[47] Cf. *Between Man and* Man, pp. 74-75, 78-79, 114; *Hasidism,* p. 105; *Good and Evil,* pp. 125-128.

[48] Cf. *Good and Evil,* P. 140.

[49] *Tales of the Hasidism,* 1, 251.

[50] *Good and Evil,* p. 142.

[51] *I and Thou,* p. 52.

[52] *Hasidism,* p. 59.

[53] *Israel and the World,* p. 18.

[54] *Ibid,* p. 150; cf. *Between Man* and Man, pp. 102-103.

[55] *Israel and the World,* p. 210.

[56] *Between Man and Man.,* p. 66.

17

REVIEW ESSAY
BERKOVITS' TREATMENT OF THE
PROBLEM OF EVIL

Although the title of Professor Berkovits' book suggests a limited concern with the problem of religious faith only in the light of the horrible events of recent Jewish history, he is, in fact, working on a larger canvas. His purpose in *Faith After the Holocaust** is to present a viable mode of understanding and dealing with the classic problem posed by the presence of evil in the world. While his primary example is the holocaust and the challenge which it has posed for faith in our own time, he fully understands that it is only an example, and not a case that presents unique problems. He shares the anguish of all decent men over the destruction of European Jewry, but he does not make the common mistake of supposing that the holocaust has introduced a new dimension into the classical problem of evil. Even if it is true that the actions of Hitler's hordes were unparalleled in all of human history for their cruelty, it does not follow that we are now facing the problem of God's apparent injustice in a unique way. With sound philosophic understanding, Berkovits argues that the dimensions of evil in the world and the depth of human suffering in no way affect the basic issue. If God is both perfectly beneficent and absolutely powerful, then the presence of any unjustified suffering poses a problem. The pain suffered by the Jews of our time is surely greater than that of other periods of Jewish sorrow, and the emotions run higher, but for the sober thinker this in no way affects the basic problem. A just and compassionate God, who has the power to control the destiny of all men, should not permit any evil in the world, unless it is merited. The pain of a single innocent child is no less a challenge to faith, in principle, than the pain of the millions whose agonies form the melancholy history of our age.

In his approach to this classical theological-philosophical problem, Berkovits rejects the familiar and overly easy solutions which have been offered over the centuries in the vast literature on the subject. He sees, with keen perception, that they are, on the whole, solutions which do not solve anything, that they buy faith at the expense of integrity, or at the expense of ordinary notions of justice and compassion. The view that all suffering must be punishment for sin is dismissed by him contemptuously as a kind of obscenity. To decide that the millions who were tortured and put to death during the Hitler years were all wicked, that the men, women and even the children were all guilty of crimes so great that they merited their gruesome fate, is to be guilty of unspeakable moral perversion. This is no way to defend God. In an expression of admirable force, Berkovits writes, "Not for a moment shall we entertain the idea that what happened to European Jewry was divine punishment for any sins committed by them. It was injustice absolute. It was injustice countenanced by God." That same God condemned Job's friends for their easy answer to the very difficult question of Divine justice and mercy. We owe him no less than the seriousness of thought and the moral sensitivity that He demanded of them.

Neither is Berkovits prepared to accept the medieval philosophic teaching that evil is privation. The standard argument goes that if evil is only something negative, then God cannot be accused of having made it. Berkovits sees in this, at best, a kind of philosophical ingenuity, but not a serious answer to the anguished question. Men who suffer for no apparent reason will not be satisfied with the philosophic assurance that their suffering is mere negation and is, therefore, without ontological status. This does nothing to lessen the reality of pain, nor does it in any way justify God in the eyes of the ordinary believer. The wild bestiality of the German oppressors was "no mere absence of good. It was real, potent, absolute."

Professor Berkovits is equally vigorous in his rejection of the opposite solution. The deniers of faith affirm that God is detached from the world, if He exists at all. This is a God who doesn't care, for whom human affairs are a matter of indifference, under whose governance there is neither justice nor a judge. This is not a solution to the problem of evil. It is the final rejection of religious conceptions of God, and the substitution for them of a world-picture in which all events are due either to blind chance or rigorous natural causation. No God can be blamed for human suffering, for injustice or the absence of compassion in the world, for there is no ultimate power which is either just or compassionate. Berkovits is fully aware of the force of such an argument when it is based on a reading of the facts of human experience. One of the characters in Hume's *Dialogues Concerning Natural Religion* gives strong expression to this view of the world. "The whole earth... is cursed and polluted. A perpetual war is kindled amongst all living creatures. Necessity, hunger, want stimulate the strong and courageous; fear, anxiety, terror agitate the weak and infirm. The first entrance into life gives anguish to the new-born infant and to its wretched parent; weakness, impotence, distress attend each stage of that life, and it is, at last, finished in agony and horror." It is not difficult to see why anyone who experiences the world in this dark and dismal way might conclude that it is anything but the product of a just and compassionate power. Without trying in any way to cover over the force of this perception of the world, Dr. Berkovits still argues effectively against it.

He takes great pains to show that this pessimistic view of reality is self-defeating. It has the effect of making all life and all human striving absurd, and, in the process, it results in the denial of all objective status to values. In a world without God there will be no right and no wrong, no good and no evil. There can only be whatever it is that individual men happen to find pleasing. Kindness and cruelty are of equal status in such a world, since all depends on individual preference and tastes. "It is the most uncomfortable aspect of such a position," Berkovits soundly argues, "that-if carried to its logical conclusion-it leads to a justification of Nazism itself. If there is no possibility of a transcendental value reference, if existence as such is fundamentally meaningless and man alone is the creator of values, who is to determine what values are going to be or what the man-made meaning is to be? In a universe in which all values are based on human choice and decision anything may become such a value." This is a consequence which we men are prepared to confront honestly and seriously. Even those moral philosophers who deny all objectivity to moral values are still determined to preserve the moral distinction between Hitler and his victims. They are unwilling, morally unwilling, to accept the claim that all that separates the oppressor and the oppressed is a difference in personal values. It is monstrous to suggest that, in the last analysis, we have no possibility of sound moral judgment, and that we can only say that each man has the right to create his own values. Yet, it seems to be the case, if we study modern moral philosophy carefully, that, despite their dislike for the position of total moral relativism, it is exactly to that position that naturalistic moral philosophers are inevitably led. Happily, they are better than their theories, and they continue to affirm the classical distinctions between good and evil even though they cannot provide any ultimate sanction for the values which they cherish.

Having disposed of the unacceptable approaches to the problem of evil, Professor Berkovits turns to his own constructive treatment of the problem. From the outset he lays down the rule that a proper response to the holocaust (and presumably to any other instances of evil in the world) can only come from those who were present and suffered personally. We must view all other responses as less than perfectly authentic. Both faith and rebellion, he rightly argues, are primarily the prerogative of those who were there. None of us who knew of the events from a distance has the moral or intellectual right to take a final position, to stand in judgment about matters of such gravity. Affirmations of faith are cheap and unconvincing when they come from those who did not themselves endure and witness that ultimate degradation of humanity which occurred in the Nazi death camps. With what justice can we proclaim the supremacy of faith to men who lived through physical, moral, psychological agonies which transcend even the most debased imagination? We, who lived in the comfort and safety of civilization, have not earned the right to preach faith to our brothers whose world was destroyed before their eyes. Those among them who could only rebel against God merit our sympathetic understanding, our reverent regard for their integrity, for their rebellion may be far greater praise of God than a faith which is won at little cost. Neither may we feel free to imitate their rebellion. There is a kind of self-pride, an almost vulgar self-assertion about the public declarations of rebellion that come from men who have not themselves suffered. As Dr. Berkovits puts it, "The disbelief [of those who were there] was not intellectual but faith crushed, shattered, pulverized; and faith murdered a millionfold is holy disbelief. Those who were not there and, yet, readily accept the holocaust as the will of God that must not be questioned, desecrate the holy disbelief of those whose faith was murdered. And those who were not there, and yet join with self-assurance the rank of the disbelievers, desecrate the holy faith of the believers."

Initially we may question the soundness of this position. If the problem of evil is a philosophical or theological problem, then it must be addressed with sober analytic thinking. Why, then, is it necessary to have experienced the force of evil directly in order to have the moral and intellectual right to formulate a response to it? As we study carefully the approach which Professor Berkovits has worked out to the problem, it becomes clear that he is not willing to grant that it is a purely intellectual puzzle which can be resolved (if at all) by purely intellectual devices. On the contrary, what makes ordinary philosophical approaches to the problem of evil unsound and unconvincing is that they are no more than intellectual. Either they find an answer which is intellectually satisfying, but do so by closing their eyes to ordinary human experience, or they take human experience seriously and in so doing are driven to deny that there is any satisfactory solution to the problem of evil. It is the merit of Berkovits' approach that he carefully avoids falling into either trap. He tries, instead, to show that all reflection on our problem ends in a paradox. We are genuinely confronted with irreconcilable opposites, with contradictories which necessarily exclude each other. Our position is at that point one in which we are finally called upon to make an affirmation, to take a stand that goes beyond the limits of what can be established by any argument. Whether we affirm the just and compassionate God of traditional religious faith, or whether we deny such a God because of the apparent injustice and sorrow in the world, we must, in both cases, go beyond what philosophic argument can sustain. This is precisely why we are cautioned by Berkovits not to stand in judgment on those who reacted to the holocaust out of the depth of their own experience. They were reacting authentically to a reality which they could only interpret in their own way. Some saw it with the eyes of a faith more powerful than all the forces of evil. Others could only deny God in the light of the horrors which they witnessed. Both were beyond intellect alone. Both were responding to the challenge and the obscurity of the world which they knew. In both cases they were taking their stand in the face of, or beyond, paradox. This, according to Berkovits, is the inescapable situation of all who confront the mystery of God's place in history. "We adorn God with a great many attributes which mean to describe his actions in history even though they are contradicted by the facts of history. Fully aware of the facts, with open eyes, we contradict our experience with our affirmations."

As the ground for his position, Berkovits introduces several basic elements. To begin with, he argues that good and evil are so related that there cannot be one without the other. Only a being capable of both has the capacity for either. It is for this reason that he allows himself to make the surprising (and, for some, the troubling) assertion that God is beyond good and evil, that He cannot be either. This is because, by definition, God cannot be evil, from which it follows that, in any strict sense, He cannot be good either. "God, being incapable of the unethical, is not an ethical being.

Goodness for him is neither an ideal, nor a value; it is existence; it is absolutely realized being. Justice, love, peace, mercy, are ideals for man only... God is perfection... He is all light; on just that account, he is lacking the light that comes out of the darkness."

For man, who is not perfect, whose very nature is finite, and whose whole life can only be striving but never complete realization, there is the possibility of good, only so long as there is also the possibility of evil. God, as the creator of all, is not the creator of good and evil. He is, rather, the creator of the possibilities of both, possibilities which are open to man to realize in his own way. This is a fruitful way to formulate the principle that man is free, that he must be free in order to be man. God is the ground of all being, but man alone is responsible for the manner in which he actualizes that which God created as potential. It follows from this that if God is guilty of anything, it is that He created man. Whether this was a desirable thing to do is hardly a matter which we can settle. Man is here, after the fact of his creation, and all that is open to him is to reflect on his own condition and to strive for the realization of his noblest and most elevated potentialities.

As to God, His situation can only be seen, at least from a human perspective, as paradoxical. If He prevents man from doing evil, then, by virtue of that intervention in human affairs He also prevents man from doing good. Berkovits sets the paradox forth in its full force when he says that God must necessarily withdraw from history. "If man is to be, God must be long-suffering with him; He must suffer man. This is the inescapable paradox of Divine providence. While God tolerates the sinner, He must abandon the victim; while He shows forbearance with the wicked, He must turn a deaf ear to the anguished cries of the violated. This is the ultimate tragedy of existence: God's very mercy and forbearance, His very love for man, necessitates the abandonment of some men to a fate that they may well experience as Divine indifference to justice and human suffering. It is the tragic paradox of faith that God's direct concern for the wrongdoer should be so directly responsible for so much pain and sorrow on earth."

Given the paradox, we can easily enough understand the skepticism of those who turn away from God because they feel themselves alone and abandoned in a world that gives no evidence whatsoever that justice and mercy are built into the cosmic value structure. However, how shall we understand the faith of those who continue to believe in God, who in the midst of suffering and pain continue to proclaim that God exists and that He is the only and ultimate ground for all true human and humane values?

Answering from a Jewish perspective, Berkovits sees God's might precisely in the fact that He does not use His limitless power to deny man's freedom. Despite His compassionate concern with man, God does not prevent men from the exercise of truly free choice. It may pain and grieve Him to see the innocent victimized, but to intervene would mean to turn man into an automaton. "God is mighty, for He shackles His omnipotence and becomes 'powerless' so that history may be possible." In this view, God, like man, shows His strength primarily in self-restraint.

Yet, this by itself is insufficient as a way of justifying faith. Berkovits sees another aspect of Divine power in the mysterious existence and the persistent survival of the Jewish people. Jewish history, he holds, is not explicable in natural categories. By every rule of nature, by all the canons of the history of man, the Jews should long ago have disappeared. Their continued existence, despite their utter powerlessness in a world where power counts, is testimony to a dimension of being which is beyond all that is ordinarily known to men. A people that exists not by virtue of its power, but only by virtue of its commitment to witness to God, provides by its very survival the best of all testimonies to God's presence. This is the central point in the philosophy of Jewish history which Berkovits sets forth. It is also the strongest ground he is able to offer in favor of religious faith in a world where so much evil is evident. Jews, from the perspective of their experience, may understandably rebel against God as they contemplate their own melancholy history. For the very same reason they can retain their faith in God, for without God in the world the history of the Jews surpasses all explanation.

If we expect a demonstrative proof that God is good and just, Berkovits does not have it to offer. In fact, he holds that it is, in principle, impossible. What he has tried to do instead is to show that the stance of faith, like the stance of skepticism, has its deepest roots in immediate human experience and in a certain mode of reflection on that experience. We confront an insoluble paradox effectively, not by ingenious attempts to resolve the irresolvable, but rather by trying to discover what it means and what direction it can offer for our lives. That discovery can only come from a confrontation with our own reality, with the world which we know, be it beautiful or ugly. The Jew who confronts his world will be aware of the depth of sorrow and injustice in it. He will also be aware of the remarkable survival of the Jewish people. If the former predominates, he is likely to deny God. If he truly reflects on the latter, he should find it possible to affirm God, no matter how inexplicable the massive evil that he knows.

What Professor Berkovits has offered us is a searching and perceptive variation on a familiar theme.

Evil is explained, though never justified, as a consequence of human freedom. God is understood, though not justified, as permitting evil, because it is a necessary condition for the possibility of good. In this book this familiar theme is presented anew with freshness and insight which helps us to see the power of the argument in a new light. When the special fact of the uniqueness of Jewish existence is added to the old argument, what emerges is a stimulating and helpful treatment of one of the oldest and most painful of all the problems that confront men who are genuinely seeking God.

Having said this, we cannot overlook the fact that even this treatment of the problem of evil, like almost every other, leaves as much unanswered as it has answered. We shall consider only a few of these unanswered questions very briefly. However successful his treatment of the problem which is generated by the evils which free men do to each other, Berkovits has given us no way at all of coping with the more difficult problem of human suffering due to natural causes. Perhaps the holocaust can be fully attributed to the wickedness of men, but what shall we say of the suffering caused by earthquakes, typhoons, disease, and similar non-human agencies. No identifiable human act is responsible for the suffering of the child dying of a malignancy, nor can we charge any man with guilt for having brought about climatic conditions that result in widespread famine. it is evident from the whole tone of his book that Berkovits would not resort to the simple explanation that these sorrows are the direct consequence of human sin. He knows perfectly well the biblical and rabbinic texts which make just such an explanation, but he cannot accept them as literally true. Given the seeming arbitrariness of the suffering which such natural disasters cause, it is, indeed, difficult to maintain the simple cause and effect picture. Yet, once we find ourselves forced to give that up we have nowhere to go. Berkovits does not discuss the question at all, perhaps because he has chosen to use the holocaust as his model. It is, however, clear that no treatment of the problem of evil is complete which does not try to come to terms with this dimension of human suffering. It is by far the most difficult aspect of the problem to deal with, the most intractable, the least open to solution. The suffering caused by natural disasters, even more than the evils caused by men, subjects faith to its most severe test. We need thinkers of the stature of Professor Berkovits to help us find our way through the darkness which natural disaster casts over our picture of a just and compassionate God.

Berkovits' representation of God as beyond good and evil also poses some difficult problems. It may be that he would interpret texts that speak of God as having positive moral attributes with the method of Maimonides or other philosophers who deny any positive attributes to God. In that case, we need to know what it can possibly mean for man to imitate God. How can man, whose life consists of striving for the realization of his values, imitate a God who is the ground of value, but is Himself beyond all value? Berkovits' treatment of the problem of evil is distinguished by his consistent refusal to allow philosophical ingenuity to replace the rich texture of human experience. Yet, when it comes to the canons for the ordering of man's life, He requires us to engage in that very philosophic subtlety which he has previously rejected. Either there is some specific sense in which man can imitate God, or else the ideal of *imitatio dei* is nothing more than a kind of philosophic sleight of hand.

To take a final case, we are forced to conclude that the theory which Berkovits sets forth deals much too casually with the problem of miracles. In the Bible the miracle is the classic case of God's visible control of human affairs. It is the public evidence of the presence of God in history. The oppressed slaves are freed from Egypt only by direct Divine intervention. The Israelites are saved at the sea, again by Divine intervention. And so it goes through a series of such events over many centuries. This seems to contradict the assertion that God is present, but withdrawn. It seems to refute the claim that God's strength is manifest above all in His restraint. Once we see that God can and sometimes does enter into battle on the side of the meritorious, we are forced to ask, with respect to every case of human suffering, why God does not intervene here. It is not sufficient to assert, as Berkovits does, that "All God's miracles occur outside of history. When God acts with manifest power, history is at a standstill. The only exception to the rule is the historic reality of Israel." Just what does it mean to speak of miracles as outside history, when they involve events that are part of human history. If the exodus is not history, then what is it? More important, whether historical or trans-historical, it is a saving event at a time of great human need. God heard the outcry of the oppressed masses and chose to come to their aid. This, in itself, gives us a model which forces the question on us throughout subsequent history. Why were they saved, but not our contemporaries? Why should God, by His own testimony, have denied freedom to Pharaoh, yet felt constrained to allow freedom to Hitler? We are very close, after all, to the old Epicurean paradox. If God is both all-powerful and perfectly benevolent, how can we account for evil in the world?

These critical questions are raised, not for the purpose of discrediting the work of Professor Berkovits, but rather to point up again the melancholy fact that, after all our best efforts at solutions, we still have no final and fully satisfying understanding of the ways of God in the world. The defect is surely not that of Berkovits, nor of any other serious thinker. It is simply our inability to comprehend ultimate things with our finite understanding. This seems to be, in certain respects, the most significant result of Berkovits' study. He is exactly right when he insists that we are dealing with a problem that does not yield to intellectual resolution. After using our intellect to the fullest measure in order to clarify the issues as fully as we can, we are still left with the need to take our stand on grounds that transcend the limits of human understanding. The greatest testimony to the victory of faith is not only the continued existence of the Jewish people, but, as Berkovits so clearly shows us, their continuing witness to the presence of God and to the objectivity of divinely ordained values. We may never resolve fully the philosophical and theological puzzles which evil poses for us. We may never find ourselves in circumstances in which we can be men of pure faith, without any edge of doubt, without any element of rebellion. Yet, our very existence as Jews, our very persistence as a people committed to the search for the holy in a world which is profane, is itself the most powerful answer to our own skepticism. It is an equally powerful response to the skepticism of others.

NOTES

* New York, Ktav Publishing Co., 1973.

18

THE MORAL PHILOSOPHY OF MaHaRaL

Rabbi Judah Loew ben Betzalel, the MaHaRaL of Prague, was one of the most important Jewish thinkers of the sixteenth century. As Jacob Katz points out, during this period MaHaRaL was "the only Jewish author... to expound Judaism as a comprehensive conception."[1] His work includes contributions to most of the main branches of Jewish thought, and among them his expositions of Jewish ethics occupy a central place. While there are comments on matters of ethical interest in every one of his works, the most concentrated treatment is contained in *Neviot Olam* and in his commentary on Mishna *Avot* under the title *Derekh Hayyim*. In these works he deals with almost every aspect of ethics, but he does so in an unstructured and unsystematic way. No single subject is fully developed in one place, nor is there an explicit set of connections between the subjects which forms them into a coherent and comprehensive theory. The MaHaRaL did not produce a great systematic treatise on ethics on the order of the major works of Greek antiquity or of modern philosophy. Neither are his Studies of the genre of the Jewish works of philosophical piety such as *Hovot ha-Levavot*, or of the intensive explorations of the later *musar* literature. Yet, careful study shows him to be a Jewish ethical thinker of great interest and illuminating insight.

Our task is to construct the system which is lacking in the writings of MaHaRaL and to do so without imposing upon him thought-forms and structures which are alien and which distort or misrepresent his intentions. We begin with a methodological premise, namely, that there is a latent system underlying the seemingly disconnected thoughts in the works of MaHaRaL and that this system was clearly present in his mind, although not in his form of writing. Having chosen the genre of commentary, he was largely tied to the occasions provided by his particular texts. Yet, through it all, whether he is beginning from a biblical verse, a Mishnah, an Aggadah or a halakhic passage, there are consistent lines of thought which bear witness to a clear formulation in his mind of an approach to the basic questions of ethics. The text on which he is commenting is often the occasion for an excursus which is only loosely and in the most general sense a "commentary." The attentive reader cannot help but conclude that MaHaRaL had important ideas to share with his readers and that he frequently used whatever text was before him as an opportunity to express himself on a subject of general importance. As we assemble these seemingly isolated notes and comments we can see that they constitute a comprehensive and important treatment of our subject. We shall engage in an exercise of the intellectual imagination as we try to formulate the main themes in MaHaRaL's moral philosophy as he might have done himself had he chosen to write a single systematic treatise on this subject.

Let us first consider briefly the place of MaHaRaL in the history of Jewish ethical thought and in the wider context of general religious and philosophic thought. While some writers have tried to make much of the deep roots that MaHaRaL presumably had in the culture of sixteenth-century Europe, there is no evidence that his thinking about ethics was affected by his particular time and place. His sources are in the classical Jewish works and, in considerable measure, in some of the main trends of medieval Jewish philosophy. There are also important points where he is clearly affected by Kabbalah, but for the most part this is more a matter of atmosphere than of particular doctrines. Scholem correctly includes MaHaRaL among those who attempted in some degree "to explain kabbalistic ideas without using technical language."[2] However, as we shall see, some of his doctrines which appear to be kabbalistic may well have their origins in standard rabbinic sources. Finally, with respect to ethics, there is no reason to think of MaHaRaL as a bridge between the Middle Ages and the modern world. He is primarily a Jewish thinker standing fully inside the classical Jewish tradition, one who at the same time reflects in his ideas and terminology the effects of his studies in both philosophy and Kabbalah.

The most fundamental principle that MaHaRaL sets forth with respect to human behavior is that there is an unbreakable connection between the moral and the metaphysical realms. The order of reality includes rules for human action, and human action, in turn, has significance for the entire cosmic order. The ultimate source of virtuous human behavior is more than just a code of laws. True human virtue embodies the structure and pattern of all reality. MaHaRaL begins his *Netivot Olam* with this theme. "The Torah is the order of man which directs him to the actions that he should perform, the way in which he should perform them, and how he should be ordered with respect to his actions. This is the concern of the Torah. And just as the Torah is the order of man, so is it the order of the world and ultimately the order of all that exists."[3] The manifest content of the Torah is its Commandments, which are essential for the proper ordering of human life, while the deep content of the Torah includes the structural principles of all reality. So direct is the connection between human behavior and the cosmos according to MaHaRaL, that the destiny of the world rests on man. When the righteous observe the commandments they are a force helping to sustain the entire world, and when sinners violate the commandments they are a counter-force which tends to destroy the world .[4]

MaHaRaL describes the Torah in its essential nature as supernal divine wisdom which exists apart from, and independently of, the created world. Following the well-known midrash,[5] he conceives of the Torah as the pre-existent pattern which God consults as He creates the world. The Torah is pure reason unsullied by any corporeal elements. As such it would seem to be far removed from the world of man and of human concerns. Yet, in a characteristically dialectical turn, MaHaRaL simultaneously roots the essence of the Torah in its relationship to man. He affirms, on the one hand, that nothing that is created is worthy of existence in and of itself. Only insofar as its existence is connected with the Torah does anything become endowed with true value and gain conjunction with true being. Even the human intellect, sometimes spoken of by MaHaRaL as man's glory, is in this connection seen as of relatively low-grade and inconsequential status. "Although man has intellect, this is only human intellect which is tied to matter. The world is not worthy of sustained existence because of this good which is of low and inferior standing."[6] Only when the human intellect is connected to the wisdom of Torah does it become truly worthy and thus help to sustain the world. Yet, at the same time, the value of the Torah itself arises from its connection with man. All the world was created for man and he has the highest rank among all existents. The order of reality is thus a reflection of the order of man, since "God created the world in accordance with what would be appropriate for the human order."[7] This is the true meaning of the statement that God consulted the Torah when He created the world, since the Torah is *seder haadam,* the ordering principles for human existence and fulfillment. From one perspective the Torah is pure being, a transcendent reality whose manifest content reveals to our limited intelligence only glimmers of its perfection. At the very same time its perfection, which man never fully grasps, results from its connection with the human order to which it gives ideal form.

We have here the metaphysical basis of the moral dimension of reality. Ideal human behavior is determined by the Torah. It derives from the supernal world and helps to determine the very order of that world. What is true of the formal ideal is also the case with respect to individual human actions. Man's behavior is seen as having cosmic effects. We see in this theory, which provides the philosophical-theological foundations for morality in the thought of MaHaRaL, a cluster of influences. MaHaRaL bases himself on standard scriptural and aggadic texts. The understanding of these texts is filtered through both philosophic and kabbalistic modes emerging finally in the form which MaHaRaL makes available to us.

A second layer in the theoretical structure of MaHaRaL's moral philosophy is his understanding of the metaphysical source of evil in the world. The Torah is conceived as the intermediary power created by God to give being to the world. Good is identified with being and evil with non-being. It follows that only the good can truly exist, and since the Torah is the model of all good, it alone among created things can be said to have absolute fullness of being. The reason for this is that reason can only be directed toward the good, and a world which derives from the divine creator must be ordered in accordance with reason. One is reminded here of the passage in Plato's *Phaedo* in which Socrates argues that if *nous* is the ordering force of the world, then all things must be disposed toward the good.[8] Reason is the antithesis of non-being, and the Torah which is regularly conceived by MaHaRaL as perfect reason in its pure essence is the created ground of being, just as God himself is the uncreated and eternal ground of being. When the world is oriented toward the Torah, it achieves the force of being standing against non-being.[9]

What then is the source of evil in the world? Evil is identified with privation or non-being, and this, in turn, is identified with matter or the corporeal. When the created world is oriented toward the Torah it overcomes its inherent non-being, which is its evil. "Because of the fact that this world is material and is far removed from the realm of reason, the Torah which is itself reason has no place in the world. But the moment the desire of the nether world for the rational Torah is aroused, the Torah answers, 'Here I am,' since all things that are rationally ordered have positive ontological status."[10] We should note in passing that familiar Zoharic ideas and terminology are used here.

This doctrine translates into a very clear picture with respect to specifically human experience and concerns. Sin is explicitly and repeatedly identified by MaHaRaL with privation or nonbeing.[11] The source of sin in man is his matter which is essentially privation. Human virtue is conceived as the victory of form over matter, intellect over the body, being non-being.[12] *Tshuva* is the removal of sin. The cause of sin is matter, and if man were totally without matter, he would be like an angel and would be totally without sin."[13]

This sharp break between body and spirit is characteristic neither of biblical nor of much rabbinic thinking on this subject. The philosophic tradition, absorbing Platonic and Neoplatonic influences, introduced this theme into the center of Jewish religious thought.[14] One hears in MaHaRaL echoes of familiar passages in Maimonides and other medieval Jewish philosophers. "All man's acts of disobedience and sins," says Maimonides in an oft-quoted passage, "are consequent upon his matter and not upon his form, whereas all his virtues are consequent upon his form... His eating and drinking and copulation and his passionate desire for these things, as well as his anger and all bad habits found in him, are all of them consequent upon his matter."[15] What separates even Moses from the perfection of virtue which would come with a complete apprehension of God is the fact that "his human intellect is still resident in matter."[16] For MaHaRaL this principle is fundamental to an understanding of all human evil. It is a theme which pervades all of his works.

Yet, unlike Plato and those who follow him, MaHaRaL does not reject the body completely. The Platonic ideal is that of the philosopher who is always pursuing death. To the fullest extent possible he seeks to achieve the separation of soul from body even in this life.[17] Despite Maimonides' explicit concern with *tikun haguf*, he exhibits strong attachment to the Platonic ideal.[18] MaHaRaL works out an important compromise with the inescapable fact that human beings are corporeal and thus inevitably subject to sin. The matter out of which man is constituted can be progressively refined. Since we are not angels, but men, our task is not to reject matter or cast it off completely, but rather to transform it so that it can serve to advance rather than inhibit our achievement of the highest virtue. Some men are born with refined matter and this enhances from the first their moral-spiritual development.[19] Even those who are less fortunate are still able to concentrate their powers in such a way as to overcome the threat of non-being inherent in their material substratum and to live a life of virtue and ultimate fulfillment.

In fact, the ideal model is Abraham, who is represented by MaHaRaL as having achieved perfection of the material element and was thus fully able to rise to the highest level of spirituality. If the spirit alone is cultivated while the body is ignored, we have a perilous situation in which the "branches are stronger than the roots." What distinguished Abraham from earlier generations is that his roots, i.e., his body, were perfected, and this provided the basis for his spiritual ascent. "For when man achieves the true perfection of the body which is his foundation and root, he is then fit to receive the full perfection of form... the glory of the divine *tzelem* at the highest level which is appropriate, and finally the intellect controls matter fully."[20] In this respect MaHaRaL understands each man to be unrealized potentiality seeking actualization. The soul is a pure unblemished entity housed in the human body. Man must first realize the highest potentialities of the body itself so that, in turn, the soul may be completely actualized.[21]

As a corporeal being seeking full moral-spiritual-intellectual actualization, man lives in the world of action, not only in the realm of thought and contemplation. The Torah, which is the model for ideal reality, is both supernal wisdom and a concrete guide to human behavior. MaHaRaL considers it to be a major and irredeemable error for man to concentrate on knowing to the exclusion of doing. "Wisdom without action is not proper for man, since man is not pure intelligence. What is required rather is that man's actions should follow after his intellect."[22] Similarly, actions alone that are blindly performed without relation to man's higher intellectual-spiritual nature are unworthy of human beings. To paraphrase a well-known Kantian aphorism, actions without thoughts are blind, and thoughts without actions are empty. The Torah as pure perfected wisdom is inaccessible to man. Only by way of *mitzvot* which are simultaneously directed to body and soul does man establish his connection with the true Torah. It is a mark of man's superior nature that he must concentrate deliberate effort in order to actualize his potentiality. Creatures which exist only in the order of nature achieve whatever measure of actualization is open to them in the normal course of events. Aristotle's notion of *orexis*, the striving of all things for their own proper fulfillment, does not necessarily entail struggle and labor. Only for man is there the possibility and demand for intense and conscious effort to become what he might properly be. MaHaRaL sees this uniquely human situation as evidence of man's special worth. Unlike a plant or an animal he will not automatically fulfill himself. At the end of the road, however, his active effort is rewarded when he rises to an ontological status which is shared by no other earthly beings.[23]

This leads us directly to those practical questions regarding human behavior and its values which concern every moral philosophy. Given the general metaphysical framework which we have set forth, we must now consider the criteria of good and evil according to MaHaRaL. We must determine what kinds of human action meet those criteria and also what the grounds are upon which MaHaRaL bases his judgments. The foundation of the entire system is God. All being is good, as over against privation which is evil. As necessary being, God is fully and necessarily good.[24] However, His fullness of pure being does not, in and of itself, provide us with imitable models of virtuous behavior. We require some source of moral guidance which translates the divine perfection into human terms. This is the function of the Torah, considered now as a body of commandments, not just as the model of supernal wisdom. As the concretized expression of the perfection of divine being, the Torah alone provides man with full and proper criteria for virtue and with explicit rules for good actions. It is by way of the commandments, which are wholly good, that finite man is transformed into a being who has commerce with God.[25]

This general statement now requires careful analysis and explication, Once we begin to set forth rules of behavior within an ethical system we confront all the problems of specification which are inherent in this task. Like every other moral theorist, MaHaRaL distinguishes between types of rules, grounds of obligation, orders of priority within the rules and similar matters.

With respect to the grounds of obligation within the Jewish religious ethic, his most general principle is that all the commandments are *gzerot*, divine decrees which are imposed upon man from above. At this level of the discourse he gives no consideration to the reasons for the commandments or to what might recommend them to us as desirable from a purely human perspective. The basic stance which MaHaRaL requires in his structuring of the Jewish system of obligation is pious submission to the absolute authority of the divine decree. At this stage man sees himself as unworthy of independent judgment or decision. The word of God has been transmitted to man and that is sufficient for the determination of human duties. MaHaRaL associates this with a psychological stance which he calls *busha*. In his usage this term cannot mean "shame" in any ordinary sense of that term. What it refers to is rather a state of retiring modesty arising from acute awareness of our human limitations. This is in sharp contrast to *azut*, an attitude of confident, even arrogant, self-assertion.

> One who is opposite in character from the arrogantly self-assertive (*az panim*) is not likely to sin. For all the divine commandments are gzerot which God imposes on man. When a man is retiring in nature (*ba'al busha*) he is prepared to accept and submit to the edicts and commandments which are ordained by God, since the definition of *busha* is a state in which one is fully open to being affected by others without asserting oneself. It follows that one who is able to submit to the divine decree will not transgress it.[26]

The virtuous life, defined by God's commandments is rooted in man's ready and unquestioning acceptance of the "yoke of the commandments."

It does not follow, however, that these commandments are arbitrary or capricious expressions of the divine power. We accept them as binding because they come from God, but a proper understanding teaches us that these divinely ordained modes of virtuous behavior are intrinsically good. When he considers the virtues in this light MaHaRaL rejects categorically any claim that they are good because of their instrumental or utilitarian value, although he is fully aware of the extent to which the commandments have social utility. However, when he considers them from a purely axiological perspective, it is not their usefulness which he sees as the ground of their binding value. Neither are they binding on us because they reflect a *consensus gentium*. "Vices are intrinsically bad and virtues are intrinsically good."[27] No direct philosophical argument or analysis is offered in defense or explication of this claim. It is clear, however, that MaHaRaL derives it from the general principle that the Torah is perfect wisdom and that, as such, there can be nothing arbitrary in it. As MaHaRaL explains, everything in the Torah is pure rational necessity which derives directly from the absolute truth of God. It follows that "there cannot be a single thing, not even a single dot, in the Torah which might be other than as it is"[28] We can conclude from this that whatever is divinely commanded through the Torah is intrinsically good. The social utility or wide-spread general acceptance of particular commandments may add to their attractiveness from our limited human perspective. Their ultimate ground, however, is their intrinsic value. Since we are incapable of grasping this fully through our own resources, we submit in modest awareness of our creaturely finitude to the divine wisdom.

MaHaRaL takes it to be added evidence of the intrinsic value of some of the virtues that they are also practiced by certain animals.[29] The fact that they seem to have been built into the order of nature gives added support, in his opinion, to the claim that they are divinely ordained values.[30] We have here two poles of a dialectical exposition. On the one hand, virtues are conceived as divine decrees to which man can only submit in faithful self-suppression. On the other hand, virtues are conceived as intrinsically valuable and thus commanding the freely given assent of any intelligent person. Thesis and antithesis are synthesized in the actual situation of man. The very process of submission grants him the illumination which in turn leaves no doubt about the intrinsic worth of the commandments. Thus, the man of true piety will observe the commandments with a combination of loyalty to God's word and intelligent apprehension of the supreme wisdom implicit in that word.

A similar dialectical pattern is present in the way in which MaHaRaL structures the specific modes of human behavior. He identifies three types of good. At one extreme is the absolutely obligatory, that which is fully and unequivocally mandated in the law. At the opposite extreme is good action which is purely voluntary and gracious, action which lies beyond the line of the law. Midway between them is a less clear category which consists of actions which are neither fully mandated nor fully acts of grace, but are a combination of the two.[31] The extreme categories are *mishpat* over against *hesed, din* over against *lifnim mi-shurat ha-din.*

The extreme of *mishpat* consists of the strict rule of justice as commanded in the Torah. This is represented by MaHaRaL as a particularly prized moral ideal. Considered by itself strict justice is a model of moral perfection. For in justice there is nothing arbitrary, nothing unclear or uncertain. Its terms can be defined precisely, and in principle it is possible to apply justice strictly and to perfection. Justice is thought in this respect to be a paradigm of the action of God in the world. Like God Himself, Justice is rationally necessary. For Israel to have received from God a rule of justice is a mark of His special favor, since it provides a rational connection between human society and the divine realm. "Justice, more than anything else, is directly associated with God, and therefore God is present whenever true justice is rendered."[32] Moreover, while the basic principles of justice are set forth in the Torah, human intelligence is sufficient for understanding and applying them properly. Unlike the ritual prescriptions whose rules and applications can only be known to us when they are divine commands, justice can be rendered in society completely through human insight and understanding.[33] Other commandments demand of us acceptance in faith since we do not fully understand them, but the rule of justice recommends itself directly to human intelligence. Not only do we recognize it as God's command, but we also see its intrinsic worth. Justice evokes our acceptance at all levels.

Having set forth this one extreme of the ethical, MaHaRaL is driven both by psychological reality and an inner logic to reject it, even while he affirms it. An unremitting commitment to strict justice carries its own seeds of destruction within itself. Such an unyielding commitment tends to harden the human character to the point of harshness, and drives man almost inexorably to a perversion of justice itself. In the words of MaHaRaL, "How great is the sin of one who rests everything on strict justice alone!" He becomes so determined to yield nothing, so insistent on receiving his due, that before long justice turns into the worst of injustice, ending up as robbery and self-serving.[34] The divine ideal of justice is readily corrupted when it is in imperfect human hands. Righteousness turns into self-righteousness and then into self-seeking tinder the guise of justice. Human society demands something beyond justice, as is evident in the aggadic statements which teach that God had to abandon his original intention to create the world in accordance with Justice alone.[35] Without the addition of grace and compassion the world could not have survived. Inescapably, human imperfection and limitation will always tend to corrupt perfect justice.

It is this that forces the dialectical movement to the opposite extreme. Within the ethical system there must be a counterbalance to strict justice. As MaHaRaL sets forth Jewish moral teaching, justice is tempered by *hesed*. The most general definition of *hesed* is that it is action in behalf of another which goes beyond the requirements of the law.[36] It is not justice which is the primary criterion here, but love and compassion. To go beyond justice in the direction of injustice is sinful corruption. To go beyond justice in the opposite direction of loving concern is the highest virtue. *Hesed* is now construed as the essence of the Torah, the most virtuous human behavior and the true human good. "The Torah is the absolute good, and for this reason it is know as *torat hesed* since that is what constitutes the absolute good.[37] The introduction of a rule of justice into the world is seen by MaHaRaL as a concession to human imperfection. If men were not inclined to sin, if they were not subject to those corporeal drives which are the ground of human corruption, there would have been no need for the imposition of rules of Justice. In a perfect state of affairs *hesed* would prevail naturally. In our imperfect condition we live by the minimum decencies which justice requires, but our full humanity is expressed only through *hesed*. This is the meaning of the rabbinic statement that the Torah begins and ends with *hesed*.[38]

For that is the essence of Torah, and it is only when we live with *hesed* as our guide that we become what we ought properly to be, beings who are fully formed by, and exemplify, the values of Torah. MaHaRaL notes that symbolic support for this contention is found in the fact that the numerical value of Torah and of *gemilut hasadim* is identical. *Hesed* is thus man's true virtue.[39]

Above all *hesed* is considered by MaHaRaL to be the one true way of *imitatio dei*. We walk in God's ways only if, like God, we behave in total freedom and with absolute independence of choice. Since justice is both commanded by God and imposed upon us as a rule of- reason, we observe its demands as duty rather than as free choice. We behave justly, or at least recognize the demands of justice, because we must. In this case our reason necessitates our will. We may, in our corruption, violate principles of behavior, but even then our reason forces us to acknowledge that there is a rule of justice. In contrast, every act of *hesed* is completely free. We behave lovingly and graciously because we choose to do so, not because we are required to do so. In this way we truly imitate God, who acts only of His own volition and is never subject to external powers. For "only when one performs *hesed* which is beyond the demands of the law do we behave fully in accordance with our own personal decision and choice. It is such behavior that can properly be termed walking in the ways of God."[40]

Mishpat and hesed live in man in dialectical tension. MaHaRaL speaks in enthusiastic support of each of these virtues when he is expounding them. He also recognizes the limitations of each. A world of pure *hesed* is not possible in the context of human history. We cannot rely exclusively on man's generosity and love to establish a good society. For, as we noted earlier, men are not angels. Lacking the rigorous controls of justice, human society would be exposed to the unrestrained self-seeking assertiveness which is present in some measure in every man and in intolerable measure in those who are coarse and tend toward the beastly. A rule of justice functions to restrain such impulses. Justice alone, however, is also unsatisfactory, for it contains the seeds of its own corruption. *Hesed* is its necessary counterbalance. In the Jewish moral system, as set forth by

MaHaRaL, these opposed modes of human behavior live in a continuous and mutually corrective relationship.

The objective virtues come into human practice as a result of basic attitudes and orientations. Most fundamental are the motivating forces which are classified tinder the headings of love of God and fear of God. Here again MaHaRaL sets out a dialectical relationship between two opposed tendencies, each of which has a significant role in the affirmation of the life of virtue and piety. Taken separately, love and fear are polar opposites which have distinct functions and serve distinct ends. Love of God is held by MaHaRaL to be positive and constructive, while fear is negative and destructive. The former is judged to be particularly good and pleasing to God, while the latter "sows ruin because of the terror which it brings into the world."[41] Love moves us to the fulfillment of the positive commandments, while fear causes us to avoid transgressing the negative commandments. The one concentrates on the pursuit of the good and the right, the other on avoidance of the evil and the wrong.[42] Fear stems from our painful awareness of our own finitude and our creaturely limitations. We are acutely conscious of the fact that we are nothing but effects of the divine causation, and that, as such, we are utterly dependent beings. We stand in awe of the divine Majesty and of His transcendent power.[43] Our fear rests on our recognition that God is the wholly other whom we can never approach in intimate relationship. Rather, like the Israelites at Sinai, we must keep our distance lest we be destroyed when drawing excessively near to God.[44] We should not underestimate the significance of this approach to God and to His commandments, since it is not mere emotion, but the result of sound intellectual apprehension. Only one who understands the role of God in the order of reality will draw the contrast between God's greatness and man's unworthiness. Only one who recognizes God as the commanding presence will be filled with anxiety at the thought of transgressing His commandments. Fear of God is valuable and necessary for the virtuous life. Yet it has its destructive elements, as we noted, and these can be balanced only by love.

Identical facts are seen in radically different colors when they are refracted through the prism of the love of God. MaHaRaL uses almost the same expressions when he speaks of the ground of our love of God that he used in expounding our fear of God. He points out that love of God is generated in man when he recognizes that "he is nothing in his own right, but that all he is comes from God and that all will return to Him. Furthermore man knows that nothing exists apart from God."[45] Given a shift in attitude and perspective, what initially generated fear now evokes love. We love God because He is the ground of our being, because what we are and what we can become in the process of self-perfection all derives from Him. The very knowledge which caused us to feel awesome distance now fills us with a sense of intimate connection. We now think of ourselves not as the impersonal effects of a remote and overpowering cause, but rather as the children of God, attached in love and intimacy to their father.

The extremes introduce differing moments into the same set of-perceptions, responses which color in distinctive ways all of our striving for lives which are virtuous. But as MaHaRaL's thought develops on this subject the extremes come together in a synthesis which interpenetrates their seemingly separate domains. In the final analysis, fear of God is not only tempered by love, but derives directly from love. Love fills us with an intense desire to do whatever is pleasing to our beloved, and this, in turn, causes us to be anxious, even fearful, concerning any act which might violate the desires of our beloved. One who loves God truly also fears any transgression of His commandments.[46] This is no longer the destructive fear which we discussed earlier, but a fear informed by love and therefore a fear which is sound and constructive both as emotion and as a guide to action.

Having set forth the foundations and structure of the main elements in MaHaRaL's moral philosophy, we must give some consideration to one further type of virtuous behavior which is often misunderstood. I refer to that extensive constellation of recommended actions which goes under the name of *derekh eretz*. Some writers claim to find in rabbinic rules concerning *derekh eretz* an independent natural morality. It is their view that the rabbis were teaching us about a realm of moral principle which is based on unaided human reason and is not derived from divine commandment. They go on to construe this as a natural moral law which has full status with the divine commandments within the Jewish moral system. At least so far as MaHaRaL is concerned this view has no foundation. *Derekh eretz* is a kind of natural virtue within MaHaRaL's system, and it is known independently. It is not, however, part of morality as such, nor does it in any way exist as an independent body of obligation parallel to the commandments of the Torah.

Of the various elements that are included by MaHaRaL under the heading of *derekh eretz*, the least interesting for our purposes is that which is purely etiquette or propriety. MaHaRaL follows the rabbinic sources in recognizing the worth of such behavior, but he certainly does not confuse it with morality. In its key meaning *derekh eretz* refers to that whole body of practice which is required for human life to be sustained and for man to be able to function within society. It is *derekh eretz* in this sense which preceded the Torah, as we are repeatedly told, and which made life possible on earth before the Torah was revealed. This *derekh* eretz is nothing more than behavior which is based on good sense, on what we learn from human experience, and on a healthy concern for our own welfare and that of our society. "*Derekh eretz* is the practical ordering of human life in this world (*hanhagat ha-olam ha-ze*). A person who does not behave with *derekh eretz* has no place in this world and is not considered part of our reality."[47] Under the rubric of *derekh eretz* MaHaRaL includes "the work that a man does in order to support himself and everything else that is required for maintaining one self in this world."[48] We are not dealing here with commandments of the Torah, nor with some sort of law of reason, but simply with the fact that every human being must do certain things in order to survive. Specific prescriptions and rules of behavior, in accordance with *derekh eretz,* derive from the general principle that one should use one's intelligence for appropriate practical ends. MaHaRaL sometimes includes under *derekh eretz* basic rules of morality, but he explicitly labels these as commandments which are binding on us and whose violation is a sin.[49] This is an extended usage which neither affects the root meaning of *derekh eretz* nor adds to the basic concept.

Having set forth the structure of the moral system in MaHaRaL's thought, we must now turn to the place of man within that system. We cannot here attempt a full account of MaHaRaL's theory of human nature, but shall concentrate our attention only on those aspects which are immediately related to man as a being who is commanded to do the good. In his analysis of this aspect of human nature, MaHaRaL again follows a dialectical pattern. Viewed from one perspective, man is conceived of as thoroughly good in his essential nature. God created man perfectly so that man has no natural tendency toward evil. Uncorrupted, man's whole being is directed exclusively to the good. "Man was originally created without sin."[50] This is both a moral assessment and a metaphysical judgment. Having been created directly by God, man shares the divine purity and perfection. Given his divine source, man is not only created without sin, but by his very nature loves and pursues the good and the wise.[51] Righteousness is natural to man, so much so that he becomes wicked only when he violates his own natural way by a deliberate decision.[52] It should follow from this that if man would only allow his natural tendencies to prevail he would be perfectly virtuous.

There is, however, an opposed picture of man set forth by MaHaRaL. In this version man is beset by strong natural tendencies to evil. The most extreme portrait of this aspect of man's nature represents man as desiring evil for its own sake. There is a force in man which attracts him to evil not because of the pleasure that evil may offer or any other benefit that it may confer, but simply because it finds evil attractive in itself.[53] In fact, "if man were to follow his natural inclinations, he would perform no good deeds whatsoever."[54] Considered from this perspective man is a creature from whom no good or virtuous action should ever be expected.

The polar tensions are reflections of contradictory aspects of human nature. Man is constituted out of fundamentally opposed elements which cause him to live in a constant state of tension between forces which pull in contrary directions. He is created in the image of God and, as such, shares in the divine perfection. This is man's ultimate ground of value, that which confers upon him his unique status in the world of created things.[55] However, this quasi-divine being is housed in a physical body, and, as we saw earlier, that body is conceived by MaHaRaL as the source of evil. When he describes man as having strong natural tendencies toward evil, MaHaRaL is always speaking in the context of man's material corporeality. "So long as man is encased in his body he cannot follow the path of righteousness... because the body in its very nature tends toward that which is a privation of righteousness."[56]

From this it follows that virtue is not automatic for man but must be acquired with much effort and struggle. All other creatures are whatever they are in the fullness of their nature from the time that they come into existence. Man alone is created with the open possibility of becoming more or less than he initially is. Should he allow the material element to dominate him, he will be less than a man, even less than the beasts, for he will have corrupted his higher nature. If the intellectual-spiritual element prevails then man becomes more than he initially is. He actualizes his highest potentiality and belongs to the realm of the divine.[57] The mediating power between the two extremes is the Torah. This is the force which alone addresses itself successfully to the material dimension and gives man the capacity to overcome it. It is at the same time the force which embodies the supernal wisdom that transforms man into a higher being.[58]

This brings us back to our starting point. We have seen how the various elements in MaHaRaL's thought are articulated into a systematic moral philosophy. It is essential to restate at this point our initial premise.

Although there is in the works of MaHaRaL no single extended systematic discussion of these themes, it seems clear that he has offered us far more than isolated and unconnected thoughts. Careful reading makes it possible to discover the system which is implicit in the works of MaHaRaL and to construct a faithful account of his moral philosophy. What we have attempted here is an initial sketch of the main features of that system. Each of these themes needs to be further elaborated and the moral philosophy of MaHaRaL must then be considered within the larger context of his thought.

Nothing in the ethical theory that has been presented here would serve to identify MaHaRaL unmistakably as a sixteenth century figure. His sources are traditional and fits style of thought fits far better with the rabbinic tradition, with medieval Jewish philosophy, and with Kabbalah than with any emerging modernism. One has only to contrast MaHaRaL's moral theory with that of Moses Mendelssohn in the eighteenth century or with Jewish Kantians of the nineteenth century to see how traditional he was. However, modernism is not by itself an absolute value, and we can find in the traditional thinking of MaHaRaL an illuminating and permanently valuable Jewish understanding of the moral life.

NOTES

All references to the works of MaHaRaL are to the Jerusalem, 1971 reprint of the London edition by Honig. The following abbreviations have been adopted:

            D. H.   = *Derekh Hayyim*
            N. O. I   = *Netivot Olam*, Vol. I
            N. O. II= *Netivot Olam,* Vol. II

[1]   Jacob Katz, *Exclusiveness and Tolerance* (New York, 1962), p. 138.
[2]   Gershom Scholem, *Kabbalah* (Jerusalem, 1974), p. 77.
[3]   *N. O.* I, p. 4a; cf. ibid., pp. 4b, 6b.
[4]   *N. O.* I, p. 4a.
[5]   *Gen. Rabbah* I, 1.
[6]   *D. H.,* p. 25b.
[7]   *D. H.,* p. 275a.
[8]   *Phaedo,* 97B.
[9]   *D. H.,* p. 172b.
[10] Ibid.
[11] *N. O.* I, p. 43a.
[12] *D. H.,* p. 197a.
[13] *D. H.,* p. 192b.
[14] Cf. E. E. Urbach, *Hazal: Pirkei Emunot ve-De'ot* (Jerusalem, 1969), pp. 190ff.
[15] Maimonides, *Guide of the Perplexed,* tr. S. Pines, III, 8, p. 431.
[16] Maimonides, *Eight Chapters,* ed. Gorfinkle, VII, pp. 82-83.
[17] *Phaedo,* 64c-67a.
[18] Cf. for example, *Guide,* 1III, 51.
[19] *D. H.,* p. 91a-b
[20] *D. H.,* p. 220b.
[21] *N. O.* I, p. 63ab.
[22] *N. O.* II, p. 185b.
[23] *N. O.* I, p. 72b.
[24] *N. O.* II, p. 123b.
[25] *D. H.,* p. 123b.
[25] *D. H.,* p. 182a.
[26] *N. O.* II, p. 199b.
[27] *N. O.* II, p. 104a-b.
[28] *D. H.,* p. 117a-b.
[29] *N. O.* II, p. 104a-b.
[30] Ibid.
[31] *N. O.* I, p. 153b.
[32] *N. O.* I, p. 156a.
[33] *D. H.,* p. 21a.
[34] *N. O.,* I, pp. 164bff.
[35] *Gen. Rabbah* XII, 15.
[36] *N. O.* I, p. 146a.
[37] *N. O.* I, p. 16a.

[38] *N. O.* I, p. 150a.
[39] *N. O.* I, p. 152a.
[40] *N. O.* I, p. 148b.
[41] *N. O.* II, p. 44b.
[42] *N. O.* II, p. 45a.
[43] *N. O.* II, p. 23ab.
[44] *N. O.* I, p. 120a.
[45] *N. O.* II, p. 39a.
[46] *N. O.* I, p. 22b.
[47] *N. O.* II, p. 250b.
[48] *D. H.*, p. 153b.
[49] *N. O.* II, p. 249a.
[50] *N. O.* II, 152a.
[51] *N. O.* I, pp. 31b, 33a.
[52] *N. O.* II, pp. 138ab, 141a.
[53] *N. O.* II, p. 40a.
[54] *D. H.* p. 141a.
[55] *N. O.* II, p. 52b.
[56] *N.O.* II, p. 7a.
[57] *D. H.*, p. 138ab.
[58] *D. H.*, p. 25ab.

19

RAV KOOK: NEITHER PHILOSOPHER NOR KABBALIST

My purpose in the seemingly provocative title of this essay is not to cast any doubt on the eminence of Rabbi Abraham Isaac Kook. He was, by the most rigorous standards, one of the most interesting and creative Jewish thinkers of this century. Unlike certain other modern Jewish thinkers whose knowledge of the primary sources of Judaism was limited, Kook was a great rabbinic figure who had superb mastery of the entire classical literature. There was no area of classical Jewish learning that he did not control. Bible, Talmud and its associated literature, philosophy, kabbalah, hasidism— he was equally at home in all of them. He spoke always with an authentic voice that reflected his deep roots in Jewish learning and in Jewish faith. There was a dimension of originality, even a touch of genius, about everything that he wrote, whether it was a halakhic treatise, an essay on a contemporary issue, reflections on basic questions of Jewish thought, or his mystical soul giving expression to its loftiest visions. This makes him a figure worth our most careful attention, one who should be studied, despite the difficulties of his style, far more seriously than has been the case until now.

It is therefore no derogation of his stature or eminence to say that he was neither a systematic philosopher nor a systematic kabbalist. It is not a service to his thought to try to force it into artificially constructed systematic forms since this is certain to distort its inner meaning and to rob it of its force.[1] Kook was fully conscious of the unsystematic character of his thought, a point evident in his open struggle with the problem of expressing his vision in language that can communicate adequately. In his private diary he recorded the following statement: "My thoughts are broader than the very sea; I cannot express them in prose. Although it is not what I most prefer, I am forced to be a poet, but a poet who composes in free verse. I cannot be chained by consideration of meter and rhyme."[2] In a poem that is frequently quoted, Kook gives vent to the frustration and anguish he suffers because he cannot give full and adequate expression to his unique vision.

> Expanses, expanses,
> Expanses divine my soul craves.
> Confine me not in cages,
> Of substance or of spirit.
> My soul soars the expanses of the heavens,
>
> Who will voice my bitterness,
> The pain of seeking utterance?
> I thirst for truth, not for a conception of truth,
> For I ride on its heights,
> I am wholly absorbed by the truth,
> I am wholly pained by the anguish of expression.
> How can I utter the great truth
> That fills my whole heart?
>
> Whatever I say
> Only covers my vision.
> Dulls my light.[3]

This incapacity to give satisfactory expression to a mystical vision is typical of the greatest mystics of all religious traditions. It is one of the ironies of this phenomenon that the very mystics who complain most bitterly about the ineffability of their vision produce some of the most magnificent literary expressions of that vision. In this respect, Kook is no exception. What lies behind their bitter complaint is not their lack of language, but their intense awareness that no language, however sensitive and beautiful, can ever be a satisfactory vehicle for their subject.

Philosophers may sometimes have difficulty in conveying their insights to their readers. Yet in the very nature of their work, philosophers, who are explicators of the *logos*, are comfortable the language that is the product of their very existence as rational (i.e., *logos*—bearing) beings. Since their entire enterprise is systematic form to a rational apprehension of ultimate things, it is natural that they should consider it possible to achieve that goal. The same can be said, *mutatis mutandis,* of the systematic kabbalists, those who attempt to give expression, in however esoteric a form, to a structured account of the world of the divine. In the case of the Zohar, to take the most familiar example, the system of the *sefirot* is not evident on the surface and the terminology is anything but fixed. Nevertheless, the system is there, and a diligent student can uncover it and even recast it in a less obscure form.

For Kook, unlike the philosophers and kabbalists of the type we have been discussing, the lack of system is inherent in his subject matter and in his method. The episodic aphoristic style is not just a matter of taste or of a preference for a particular rhetorical form. It is certainly not due to any inability on his part to write extended systematic essays. The corpus of his writings gives the lie to any such claim, since there are numerous extended essays that are clear and systematic in structure. This is the case not only with his halakhic works, but also with his publicistic works and with much of his extended correspondence. However, when he comes to give expression to his vision of the ultimate, he can only adopt a poetic or quasi-poetic mode of expression. Perhaps this is because the infinite, by its very nature, cannot be confined by definitions or captured in any linguistic formulation. Plato is explicit in saying this about his own vision of ultimate being, namely, the Form of the Good. Socrates refuses to talk about it directly just because it cannot be captured adequately by human reason, nor can it be expressed in the discursive language which the philosopher ordinarily uses. He must therefore satisfy himself with giving a systematic philosophical account of the nature and structure of reality up to the point where reason breaks down. It appears, however, that this is precisely the point at which Kook wants to begin his thinking. He feels deeply the frustration of not being able to express his vision in language which is adequate to it, but he is wise enough to know that to reduce the indefinable to definitions is a gross distortion of truth.

This is what is meant by the statement that Kook was not a 'philosopher. In his work we find hardly any argument or marshaling of evidence in a way that is characteristic of the work of the philosopher. He shares his insights, but we can exercise no control over the truth claims of those insights. If he succeeds in helping us to experience his vision, argument and evidence become irrelevant. What one experiences directly is verified by the experience itself and does not require arguments to establish its reality. In fact, arguments alone cannot convince one that he experiences what he does not, nor are arguments needed to convince him that he experiences what he actually does. Thus, if he fails to help us share his vision, then nothing he can add will be of any use. This amounts to saying that Kook does not do philosophy in any normal sense of the term because his subject matter and his goals are not those of the philosopher.

In his essay in this volume, Lawrence Kaplan points out correctly that Kook had a deep and reverent regard for Maimonides. Kaplan goes on to note that Kook put great emphasis on the Jewish legitimacy of the thought of Maimonides, and he wisely distinguished between legitimacy and truth. As Kaplan puts it, "Rav Kook's... reply to Yawetz is not so much a defense of the truth of Maimonides' views but rather of their legitimacy as authentically Jewish views." Again Kaplan makes the point that Rav Kook takes the position that "if Maimonides . . . could be inspired by his own views to attain almost unparalleled heights of holiness, faith, and divine service, that in itself is proof of the legitimacy of those views-their legitimacy, not their truth. Indeed, the issue of truth becomes secondary." This position of Rav Kook, as Kaplan immediately goes on to observe, "rests upon a strikingly non-Maimonidean premise. For in Maimonides view truth is all important."[4] Kaplan's point is so obviously correct that it hardly needs any corroboration. Yet it might be useful simply to remember Maimonides' own statement on the subject. He says that with careful reflection on his teachings concerning prophecy, one may be saved from serious error. "And then only intelligible beliefs will remain with you, beliefs that are well ordered and that are pleasing to God. For only truth pleases Him, may He be exalted, and only that which is false angers Him. Your opinions and thoughts should not become confused so that you believe in incorrect opinions that are very remote from truth and you regard them as Law. For the Laws are absolute truth if they are understood in the way they ought to be."[5]

As a philosopher, Maimonides is necessarily concerned with the truth of his doctrines, not simply their legitimacy within the Jewish tradition. This is why he regularly presents carefully constructed arguments that are aimed at establishing the truth of his views. In considering, for example, the question whether the world is eternal or created, he gives us a meticulous analysis of the arguments on both sides of the question. In this case he concludes that there are no demonstrative arguments on either side, and that there is no satisfactory way even to establish relative probabilities. However, when he admittedly takes his stand on purely religious rather than philosophic grounds, he makes it clear that if a demonstration could be provided for the eternity of the world, he would be constrained to affirm that doctrine since truth is for him a controlling consideration.[6] Kook, not being constrained by considerations of philosophic rigor and demonstrative truth, can properly put the stress on the "legitimacy" of Maimonides' doctrines. For him their Jewish authenticity is what matters, not their independently established claims to truth. For Maimonides, in contrast, it is demonstrated truth that becomes the determinant of correct Jewish doctrine.

Kook praises Maimonides for having finally and definitively purified the Jewish idea of God of all vestiges of corporeality. What he fails to note, however, is that Maimonides first demonstrates that God must be absolutely incorporeal, and then argues that therefore all anthropomorphic references to God in Scripture should be read nonliterally. For the philosopher, it is the truth of his doctrine that is the controlling consideration, and it is truth alone that determines legitimacy in every case where demonstration can be called upon to establish the truth. It is easy to see in this regard why we should not consider Kook to be a philosopher.

Lawrence Fine, in his paper in this volume, presents us with another striking instance of a problem that concerns Kook and the philosophers, a case in which we can again see how different are their methods and their aims. Kook often takes up the problem of human cognition, what Fine labels "the problem of epistemology." What is most instructive in this case is just the fact that while Kook has much to say about human cognition, he is, in fact, not dealing with the problem of epistemology as philosophers understand it. The epistemologist is concerned not only with the nature and contents of human knowledge, but no less with the grounds of human knowledge. The question "How do we know?" is for him as important, perhaps more important, than the question "What do we know?" The former question appears not really to have concerned Kook at all, and with respect to the latter question he makes his case by way of assertions, not arguments based on a careful examination and analysis of the evidence.

Kook holds that all reality is organically interconnected and that all true knowledge must, therefore, also be organismic in character.[7] This is a view that has also been held by some philosophers. To see the nonphilosophic way in which Kook deals with this topic, one need simply contrast his bald and undefended assertions with the elaborate arguments and explications to be found in Hegel and the late Hegelians. The very ambiance of Kook's treatment of such a subject makes one feel that it is pointless, not to say improper, to raise the question "How do you know?" A philosopher must be prepared to answer such a question or his work is of no serious philosophical interest. A mystical visionary can allow himself to assert without offering any further evidence.

Fine also points out that Kook was convinced that the problem of human cognition is aggravated by the fact that we tend to be satisfied with a knowledge of the outer reality of things while we fail to penetrate into their inner reality that is their true essence. One hears echoes here of Kant's distinction between phenomenal and noumenal knowledge. However, when Kant claims that we can know only phenomena and never noumena, he bases himself on a most elaborate analysis of the knowledge situation and on a set of philosophic arguments that are exquisite in their detail and in their thoroughness. Kook, in effect, challenges the basic thesis of the Kantian theory of knowledge (consciously or not), but his challenge is unsupported by anything that even remotely resembles the philosophic work that Kant did in order to arrive at his position.

A striking instance of Kook's nonphilosophic stance is brought to our attention in Kaplan's comments on his preference for the imagination over the intellect. The major philosophic tradition of the West has rested for the most part on the conviction that there is a parallelism between the order of reason and the order of reality, that, as Hegel expressed it, the real is the rational and the rational is the real. This doctrine goes back at least as far as Parmenides. It receives its classical formulation in the divided-line image in Book 6 of Plato's *Republic,* in which the order of knowing and the order of being are exactly parallel, with true knowledge culminating in rational apprehension of the forms. Knowing and being are conceived here as fixed and stable, permanent rather than passing, unchanging rather than changing. It is the character of reason that its objects are just these fixed and universal aspects of being as over against the changing and particular objects of sense experience.

For this kind of philosophy, which is the dominant rationalism of our tradition, imagination poses a special problem. Since imagination is not in any way confined by the fixed order of reason or nature, we need to ask if the objects of imagination are reflective of reality. Maimonides fought against the doctrine of the Kalam that affirmed that whatever is present in imagination may be the case in reality. This is applied to the order of nature itself, all of whose fixed patterns are now treated as contingent rather than necessary. Thus, since we can imagine, for example, the sun rising in the west, it follows that this is as likely as that it should rise in the east. The net effect of this is to make all of nature dependent on God's will at each moment not only for its very existence but for each detail of its structure. In this case, it follows that no science is possible, since all facts are contingent rather than necessary.

It is possible to go even further in this direction and to assert that even that which may not be accessible to our imagination at this moment, may yet be possible because it may be grasped by a more highly developed imagination. Thus, there are even those who go so far as to hold that logical truths are not necessarily the case and that they too are contingent. In this case one could then even assert that the principle of noncontradiction is not a necessary description of the real world, but that it is possible that a thing should be both p and not-p in the same sense and at the same time. This, of course, represents the final destruction not only of all philosophy but of all intelligible discourse. It is not clear just how far Rav Kook would go in his defense of imagination against the claims of the intellect. However, any move in this direction must be construed as an attempt to destabilize the very foundations on which philosophy and science rest. Even David Hume was ready to admit, after all of his attacks on the rationalist claims about the world, that the rejection of their views runs counter to our own natural needs. If Rav Kook could say, as cited by Kaplan, "Whatever may be imagined exists in truth," then he certainly could not claim to have cast his lot with the philosophers of the great tradition.

Even in his mysticism, Rav Kook goes against the line that is concerned with providing the kabbalistic alternative to philosophical metaphysics. As Fine points out, Kook's mysticism focuses on the internal psychology of man, rather than on theosophy. Zoharic and Lurianic kabbalah are both concerned to provide us with an account of the processes within the divine being out of which the world emerges. Like the metaphysicians, although in their own special mode, they seek to make available to us an understanding of the ultimate nature of reality and of the way in which the chain of being extends from the Creator to the world of our experience. However esoteric their expositions may be, and however much they employ arcane symbolism, they nevertheless offer a genuine alternative to philosophic accounts of the world. When Kook abandons theosophy for concern with human inwardness, he reflects again his basically nonphilosophical stance.

In this regard he is, of course, influenced by certain types of Hasidism, but he tends in other regards to go even further than almost any usual Hasidic doctrine would take him. It is well known that many kabbalistic systems flirt with pantheism. In fact, this flirtation is itself part of the kabbalistic response to philosophy. As Scholem puts it,

Authoritative Jewish theology, both mediaeval and modern.
In representatives like Saadia, Maimonides and Hermann Cohen, has
taken upon itself the task of formulating an antithesis to pantheism and
mythical theology, i.e. to prove them wrong... What is really required,
however, is an understanding of these phenomena which yet does not
lead away from monotheism; and once their significance is grasped, that
elusive something in them which may be of value must be clearly defined.
To have posed this problem is the historic achievement of Kabbalism.[8]

Yet Scholem teaches us how cautious most works of kabbalah are
never to overstep the line and affirm pantheism openly and direct "The
author of the Zohar inclines towards pantheism, a fact made clearer by the
Hebrew writings of Moses de Leon, but one would look in vain for confession
of his faith beyond some vague formulae and hints at a fundamental unity of
all things, stages and worlds."[9] A similar restraint with respect to pantheism
is evident in most works of kabbalah. It is revealing to see how far Rav
Kook goes in the direction of pantheism, and more remarkably, the openness
with which he affirms his views. He is not restrained by any of the concerns
that animate the philosophic writers who see pantheism as the ultimate
defeat of Jewish teaching concerning God. Neither is he as cautious as the
kabbalistic writers usually are.

Kook in some passages of his writings seems openly to avow
pantheism, and, what is more, he uses the very term itself without hesitation
or apology. Thus he writes that the human heart "takes special delight in the
notion that all existence in its entirety is nothing but a matter of divinity and
nothing else exists outside of God."[10] He goes on to argue that the only
antidote to the feeling of worthlessness and inconsequentiality that often
besets man is a purified pantheism (he actually uses the term) that makes it
possible for man to perceive himself as an element in the divine reality. The
pantheistic doctrine that teaches that there is nothing outside of the
absoluteness of the divine is affirmed and defended openly by Rav Kook."
One is reluctant to think that he is prepared to take this doctrine in its full
literalness, yet there is no question that he not only follows in the line of
much kabbalistic and Hasidic teaching, but does so in a straightforward
way that is not typical of these movements. It may well be that Kook's
concern for the individual person was so great that he welcomed any doctrine
that he felt could elevate man and bring him closer to redemption. In this
case, the fact that the doctrine was anathema to the philosophers and a
source of some anxiety to the kabbalists did not seem to disturb him.

It should now be clear, even from this brief discussion, why we took the position that Rav Kook was neither philosopher nor kabbalist. This is not meant to detract from his greatness, but rather to call attention to his unique qualities as a thinker and an expounder of Judaism. It may well be that he can speak to the quest for Jewish spirituality in our time more effectively than those thinkers who follow a classical model. His vision of the supernal reality, his burning love of God, and his equal love for man are the animating forces in his thought. They may give us more than we can hope for from the great system builders, but this remains to be seen. What is clear, however, is that we must learn how to read Kook and sensitively. If we come to him looking for a twentieth-century Maimonides, we are bound to be sorely disappointed. If we allow him to engage our imagination and our intellect, to speak to us as poet rather than as philosopher, we may discover through him new visions and new worlds.

NOTES

[1] Both Lawrence Kaplan and Lawrence Fine, in their contributions to this volume, are fully aware of the unsystematic nature of Kook's thought as is clearly evident from their papers. I seek in this discussion only to expand the point and to explore more fully its significance.

[2] Cited in A. Haberman, "Shirat HaRav," *Zikkaron*, ed. J. L. Fishman (Jerusalem, 1945), 10.

[3] Ibid., 17-19. Translation is taken from Ben Zion Bokser, *Abraham Isaac Kook*, (New York, 1978), 379-80.

[4] Kaplan, 52 in this volume.

[5] *Guide of the Perplexed*, trans. Shlomo Pines (Chicago, 1963), II: 47, 409. (Fox's essay was based on an earlier version of Kaplan's paper that did not include notes. The version published here cites this passage in note 38.—eds.)

[6] Ibid. II: 25: 327-28.

[7] Kook's view about the world as an organic whole is also noted and discussed by Professor Kaplan in his essay.

[8] Gershom C. Scholem, *Major Trends in Jewish Mysticism* (New York, 1941), 38.

[9] Ibid., 222.

[10] *Orot Hakodesh* (Jerusalem, 1964), II:396.

[11] Ibid., 399-400.

20

NAHMANIDES ON THE STATUS OF AGGADOT: PERSPECTIVES ON THE DISPUTATION AT BARCELONA, 1263

Dedicated to the Memory of Professor Alexander Altmann,
Cherished Friend and Revered Colleague

Nahmanides' account of the disputation at Barcelona has evoked a considerable literature.[1] One of the themes which concerns many of the writers is the problem of the true attitude of Ramban to the aggadah. At a crucial point in the debate his chief antagonist cites a midrash which teaches that the Messiah was born at the moment that the Temple was destroyed. Ramban responds with the flat statement, 'I do not believe in this Aggadah... In truth, I do not believe that the Messiah was born on the day of the Destruction, and this Aggadah is either not true, or has some other interpretation derived from the secrets of the Sages.'[2] Ramban reports that on the following day he amplified his statement with an explanation of the types of canonical Jewish literature. These include the Bible, 'and we all believe in this with perfect faith'; the Talmud, whose explication of the commandments we fully accept; and finally, 'we have also a third book which is called the Midrash, which means "Sermons". This is just as if the bishop were to stand up and make a sermon and one of his hearers liked it so much that he wrote it down. And as for this book, the Midrash, if anyone wants to believe in it, well and good, but if someone does not believe it, there is no harm... Moreover we call Midrash a book of "Aggadah"... that is to say, merely things that a man relates to his fellow.'[3]

These statements of Ramban have generated an inordinate amount of confusion, concern, and in some cases even distress. Many of the scholars dealing with this text find it difficult, if not impossible, to believe that this great pillar of Jewish orthodoxy (as they perceive him) could possibly have seriously held such views. Generally, they take the position that his statement in the context of the disputation was only a ploy which he adopted in order to refute his adversary, but that it in no way represented his own position. Rabbi Mordecai Eliasberg, writing in Russia in the late nineteenth century, says that it is completely evident that 'while Nahmanides articulated these words with his mouth, he completely rejected them in his heart'.[4] It was only because of the very great pressure to which he was subjected in the disputation that he allowed himself to use this argument for polemical purposes. Presumably, no one of Ramban's piety could have seriously denied a belief in the teachings of the aggadot.

This same position is held by a considerable number of modern critical scholars and essentially on the same ground. It is rooted in their conception of the nature of orthodox belief and in their understanding of the specific stance of Nahmanides with respect to the elements of faith. In their view, Nahmanides is an anti-rationalist whose position must be that all aggadot are true. This is how they interpret his position in the anti-Maimonidean controversy where, despite his mediating role, they are convinced that on this particular point he stood with the attackers of Maimonides. The most prominent authority associated with this view is Yitzhak Baer, who asserts that in the disputation, Ramban 'argued-against his own convictions that belief in the Aggada is not obligatory'.[5] H. H. Ben-Sasson takes a similar position. He points to the danger in Ramban's statement, since he could easily enough have been condemned even by his Christian adversaries as a Jewish heretic. He adds, however: 'It is clear that this was a response which Ramban, nevertheless, considered appropriate to make to Christians in the polemical setting. However, Ben-Sasson adds, Ramban, the kabbalist believed in the aggadah and considered such belief to be obligatory. In a disputation with the Christians even a sage of his stature was forced to say things in defense of his position which were not a true representation of his internal [Jewish] position.'[6] Martin A. Cohen argues the case more elaborately. He holds that in the anti-Maimonidean controversy, Nahmanides 'belonged to the camp of the fundamentalists, to those who condemned "anyone expounding the words of our rabbis and their Aggadahs not according to Rashi's words".[7] Going on to discuss the statement of

Ramban concerning the authority of the aggadot, Cohen notes that this has 'mystified scholars who could not deny his belief in the Aggadah. It can best be explained as a move of desperation to undermine the foundation of Paul's entire argument[8] This view has dominated the discussions for a considerable time, to the point where, in many circles, it is taken as an established truth that Ramban did not mean what he said.

Some recent works express a rather more restrained position on this subject. Thus, Cecil Roth expresses the point with greater care when he says that, 'As a matter of fact, it is improbable that this rationalistic approach really represented the views of this pious mystic.'[9] Robert Chazan notes that it was not easy for Nahmanides to affirm the view that he expressed, since in his own writings we find 'deep reverence' for the aggadah. He could easily have demolished the very foundation of all the arguments of Friar Paul had he been prepared to 'espouse this view wholeheartedly and consistently... however, it was a ploy that was utilized sparingly and hesitantly'.[10] We have here not quite the vehemence and self-assurance that was present in the expressions of Baer and his school, but it is clear that these writers are also convinced that Ramban could not have meant seriously his statement that we are not obligated to believe in the aggadot.

I want to argue as strongly as I can against these interpretations of the views of our great medieval author. Happily, some recent works have seen the extent to which the position expressed rests on a misconception of the nature of Jewish orthodoxy and, in particular, the orthodoxy of Ramban, who is classified as a more or less anti-rationalist kabbalist. Chavel, in his note citing Eliasberg which we quoted above, goes on to make his own wise and sound evaluation. He notes that it is pointless to debate the question as to what Ramban was really thinking when he made these statements since, as he puts it, 'only God sees into a man's heart'.[11] He cites important, if familiar, sources that leave no doubt that Ramban was in line with a well-established internal Jewish tradition in his views about the Aggadah. His conclusion is that we should not dare to ascribe even the slightest degree of possible heresy to the teaching of the Ramban on this subject, since his words have 'their foundation in the highest holiness' *(devarim sheyesodam beharerei kodesh)*. Yet it must be noted that Chavel, after all his vigorous defense of Ramban, is not absolutely firm in his own conclusion with respect to the actual views of Nahmanides. Despite all the evidence that he himself cites, he appears to be hesitant to assert straightforwardly that Nahmanides denied that all aggadot, without exception, are authoritative and command belief. One has the feeling that Chavel was reluctant to ascribe to Ramban a position which might offend certain types of orthodoxy. However, two recent writers on the subject have made the point clearly and effectively, although in a somewhat muted and nuanced style.

Hyam Maccoby responds to Baer, Cohen, and all who follow in their footsteps, simply by showing that they have a misconception not only of Ramban, but of the very nature of the aggadah itself. What Chavel had already called to our attention is perfectly clear to Maccoby. There is ample authority in the earlier rabbinic literature to support the position espoused by Ramban. Moreover, the very nature of aggadah and midrash is such that there is something intrinsically unintelligible in the claim that we are obligated, as a matter of religious duty, to believe all aggadot. The literature of midrash and aggadah is vast and heterogeneous. It often contains not only differing, but directly contradictory, views. There is hardly any matter about which one will find in this literature a single unified monochromatic treatment. What then could it possibly mean to say that we must believe the aggadot? Anyone who approaches this body of rabbinic exegesis and elaboration will have no choice but to pick and choose. Otherwise, he will find himself in the unenviable position of having to affirm simultaneously views that are opposed and even contradictory. Ramban was merely reflecting a long-established teaching of the sages concerning the status and nature of aggadah within the system of Jewish faith.[12] Septimus makes the argument even stronger by virtue of the fact that he cites in his notes numerous sources which sustain the point that has just been made. His views are summarized with caution and clarity, when he says, 'I would venture to say that anyone who reads Nahmanides' commentary will find ample evidence that he did not accept the absolute authority of all aggadah.'[13]

What makes this entire discussion puzzling is the fact that anyone who would take the trouble even to read casually in Nahmanides' work, particularly, as Septimus points out, his commentary on the Torah, would see immediately how strange it is to assert as a truth beyond all question that his actual view was that we are obligated to believe all aggadot. There is hardly a page in that commentary where Ramban does not reject openly a midrash or a talmudic aggadah. This approach to aggadah does not imply, as some of the commentators on this subject supposed, irreverence or impiety. Neither does it imply a lack of appreciation for the importance and value of aggadah. It simply indicates an understanding that, in contrast with our relation to halakhah, we have here the option, nay, the need, to be selective. We have a revealing parallel in the way that Ramban relates to the commentaries of his two great predecessors, Rashi and Ibn-Ezra, and to the works of Maimonides. He is unsparing in criticism when it is called for in his judgment, even to the point of seemingly unrestrained acerbity. Yet it is immediately evident that he has the highest regard for these earlier commentators, learns a great deal from them, often expresses agreement and appreciation, while allowing himself the right to react to their work with careful selectivity. When he thinks they are relatively superficial or when he thinks they are wrong, he says so without hesitation. This does not diminish his respect for them or his recognition of their importance or that of other scholars and commentators who preceded him. No one who has studied the works of Nahmanides can doubt for one moment that he held Maimonides in very high regard. Yet, in one of the most extreme cases of opposition to the views of Maimonides, he attacks his teaching with remarkable lack of restraint, concluding his attack with the statement that the account which is given by Maimonides 'contradicts Scripture so that it is forbidden even to hear these words, to say nothing of believing them'.[14] Even so, there is no possible question about the deep regard in which Ramban held Rambam. Yet Ramban is totally confident that he knows how to be selective and which criteria to apply in particular cases. This same attitude is evident throughout his treatment of aggadot. Respect and appreciation do not imply that one is obligated to abandon all independent judgment. The interpreters who find it difficult to believe that Nahmanides could have meant what he said in his report of the disputation have not paid close enough attention to his statement in its context. Ramban is saying that we do not have to believe in the truth or correctness of any given midrash. This does not mean that he approaches the whole of rabbinic aggadah with an initial attitude of disbelief, irreverence or outright rejection, but that we are permitted, even mandated, to exercise our intelligence and our learning in order to determine when to accept and when to reject a particular midrash. Those who are shocked by Nahmanides' stance have paid insufficient attention to the nature and status of aggadic literature within the complex of the Judaic canon. They are equally lacking in an understanding of the style and mentality of one of the greatest Jews of the Middle Ages.

What is particularly revealing is the extent to which these interpreters are dominated by their preconceptions of the nature of Jewish orthodoxy. Since, as is clear from their writings, they identify orthodoxy with literalist fundamentalism, they reach the understandable conclusion that Ramban could not both be a voice of orthodoxy and question the authority of, 'canonized' aggadic texts. Had they taken the trouble to look at the sources with an unprejudiced eye, they could easily enough have discovered that very early authorities had already expressed doubts and antagonisms toward aggadah in general. In the view of R. Zeira, the very unstructured character of aggadah makes it dangerous. He asserts that one cannot readily extract sound doctrine from it since it tends to turn things upside down.[15] He thus advises his son to have nothing to do with the study of aggadah, but to devote himself exclusively to halakhah. In another well-known passage it is stated that a divine curse and other dire consequences await those who occupy themselves with aggadah.[16] These statements do not represent, by any means, the only opinion expressed on this subject in the rabbinic sources, but it is certainly not a view which is unique or totally idiosyncratic. Why then should Ramban be considered to have uttered heretical statements when he simply propounded the far milder position that we are not obligated to believe every aggadah?

The specific point at issue in our discussion is dealt with most explicitly by a major tenth-century authority, Hai Gaon, in a passage which has been so widely quoted that it surely must be known to any student of this subject. He gives preferred status to aggadot which are contained in the Talmud, but only so long as they are clear and intelligible. In this context he articulates the principle that we need not consider any aggadah as totally authoritative because 'we do not rely on aggadah' *(ein somkhin al aggadah)*. He lays down the rule that when we deal with aggadot in the Talmud we should made every effort to penetrate their meaning and to remove from them confusions or distortions to which they may have been subject. In the case of non-talmudic aggadot, we need not expend such efforts. Rather, if they strike us as correct and well formed, we may use them as subject matter for teaching. If not, then we need pay no attention to them *(ein mashgihin bahem)*.[17] To this seemingly incontrovertible evidence we should add the support provided by S. Lieberman who addressed directly the question of the honesty of Ramban in his statement at the disputation. Lieberman cites a variety of sources in support of the view that Ramban should be construed as having meant exactly what he said. He concludes with near certainty, as he puts it, 'that also in this case, the holy mouth of our master did not speak a lie, even if it would have been a permissible one'.[18] Lieberman makes the argument decisive when he cites a passage from

Ramban's *Torat Haadam* where he reacted to an elaborate aggadah that sets forth detailed dimensions of the nether world. Ramban says: 'These and similar teachings should not be construed as merely allegorical since they give a specific account of a particular place, its measurements, its length and its breadth. [Our sages] based specific halakhic rulings concerning the permissible and the forbidden on this account and cite it as a basis for legal decisions."[19] Lieberman points out that Ramban has insisted that we must accept this aggadah literally only because it has been used by the sages as the basis for halakhic decisions. It follows, he argues, 'that among the other aggadot, which are not sources for halakhic rulings, there must be some which it is appropriate to understand as allegorical'. Nahmanides seems here to have established a clear criterion for the relatively small number of cases in which we are required, in his view, to affirm the literal truth of aggadot. There is apparently no such obligation in other cases. One final example of this attitude toward aggadot should be noted. Rabad, in his gloss on a controversial passage in the Mishneh Torah, clearly accepts the correctness of Maimonides' doctrine concerning the incorporeality of God, but he questions the soundness of his halakhic judgment in designating as heretics those who hold that God has corporeal properties. Rabad observes that 'greater and better men than Maimonides have affirmed this view, basing themselves on their [literal] reading of verses in Scripture and, even more, on what they saw in the words of the aggadot which pervert sound doctrines' (*mimmah shera'u bedivrei ha'aggadot hameshabbeshot et hade'ot*).[20] When one of the most eminent sages of the medieval world allows himself to use such language concerning aggadot, we can hardly conclude that religious orthodoxy requires one to accept all aggadot as authoritative.

   Despite this overwhelming evidence that there was no special audacity, and certainly no heresy, in the views expressed by Ramban, the scholars have persisted in affirming the contrary. It may be, as some have thought, that it was particularly hazardous to express such an opinion in the context of a disputation before a largely hostile Christian audience, but it certainly was not an unusual view to be heard within the Jewish community. Even in the framework of the anti-Maimonidean controversy, Ramban did not have to fear that the expression of these views would expose him to charges of heresy or heterodoxy.

   An additional point should be noted. Some weight has been placed, quite properly, on the exact wording of the first statement in the disputation in which Nahmanides says that he does not believe an aggadah which was cited by his adversary. He adds that 'either this aggadah is not true or it has a different interpretation whose source is the secret teachings of the sages'.[21] The suggestion has been made that Ramban is here directing attention to a kabbalistic interpretation of this text. There is surely no possible doubt that he did devote much of his intellectual energy to understanding many aggadot and midrashim in accordance with kabbalistic interpretations. It does not follow, however, that he interpreted all aggadot this way, or that when he said that he did not believe particular aggadot that he necessarily meant that he did not understand them literally but instead construed them mystically. We have too many cases in his Torah commentary where he rejects a midrash or aggadah without even hinting that he has a kabbalistic interpretation to substitute for the literal or symbolic reading which is then under discussion. Moreover, as we have seen, there is no reason for us to go this route only to save Ramban from the charge of heresy. He is more than amply protected by the sources and authorities that we have cited.

In order to have a full appreciation of the almost bizarre quality of the views of Baer, Cohen and some of the other scholars whose views we have considered, it is useful to look with brevity, but care, at how Ramban actually deals with aggadot and midrashim in his Torah commentary. There is much to be learned about the meaning of what he said in the Barcelona disputation from a study of his practice as a Bible commentator. We find in his commentary to the Torah a richly textured tapestry in which he develops a variety of different types of response to the literature of midrash and aggadah. What follows does not claim to be an exhaustive typology by any means, but it does select characteristic instances of types of response which are directly relevant to our topic.[22] We shall see some of the diverse ways in which Ramban exemplifies the truth of his statement in the disputation that he does not believe in particular aggadot and that they have no absolutely authoritative standing or interpretation which is for all time binding on the faithful. For the purposes of this discussion, I shall restrict myself largely to examples from Genesis, but anyone who takes the trouble to study all of Nahmanides' commentary will discover easily enough that these examples are typical of the method which he uses throughout the entire work. What can be found with such ease in the commentary on the first book of the Torah is characteristic of all the other parts of the commentary.

We begin with a statement which can be taken as a general guide as to how Ramban relates to Midrash. In commenting on Gen. 8:4, he rejects the interpretation of Rashi which is itself taken from Genesis Rabbah. He makes the following preliminary observation: 'Since Rashi himself in various places scrutinizes the *midreshei aggadot* very closely and [finding them not in accordance with the *peshat*] expends special effort to explain the text according to the plain meaning of the verse, he has, by his example, authorized us to do the same. For the Torah has seventy aspects [i.e. it can be understood at many different levels and in many different ways] and furthermore many midrashim are understood by the sages in diverse ways.' Having made his point, Ramban goes on with a complete sense of freedom to offer his own account of the verse at issue. This is hardly the method or style of a literalist fundamentalist.

We can see in his specific point of interpretation of this verse one type of response to midrash. The midrash which Rashi cites asserts that, during the period of its voyage, Noah's ark was submerged to a depth of eleven cubits. Ramban argues in accordance with what he calls *derekh hasevara* that from the standpoint of the principles of naval engineering this is impossible. Given the size, shape and weight of the ark, if it had been, at any point, submerged to a depth of eleven cubits, it would have sunk. He explains briefly the principles involved, and draws his conclusion with complete confidence in its correctness. Here he rejects a midrashic teaching on behalf of the teaching of sound science on the subject.

Another example of his insistence on the legitimacy of scientific evidence is found in his comment to Gen. 9:12. Ramban notes that there are those who conclude from their reading of the text that the rainbow had not been created at the time of the original creation of the world, but was a new divine creation after the flood, which was designated to serve as the sign of the covenant with Noah and all future generations. To this he responds with a straightforward statement: 'We have no choice but to believe the teachings of the Greeks' that the rainbow is caused by the refraction of the sun's rays through the moisture in the air, that is to say, that it is part of the original creation set into the order of nature, and is not a special creation at the time of this covenant. Rather, the rainbow which was already present in the world is now designated as a sign of the covenant. He thus reads the verse, 'I have set my rainbow in the cloud', to mean, 'the rainbow which I set in the cloud at the beginning of creation will, from this day on, serve as a sign of the covenant between us'. It is instructive to see with how much more caution Ibn-Ezra, in his comment on these verses, approaches the same issue. Despite his reputation as somewhat radical and open to heretical opinions, Ibn-Ezra invokes Greek science here in a tentative and conditional way. He says: 'If we were to believe the teachings of the Greek scientists that the rainbow is caused by the refraction of the sun's rays, we could answer [the implicit objection] by arguing that after the flood God intensified the light of the sun, and this is the correct way for one who understands.' Ramban, who is generally thought of as far more pious than Ibn-Ezra, was unafraid to say directly what Ibn-Ezra only hinted at. Yet there are those who believe that he could not have meant what he said with respect to the status of aggadot!

Some midrashim are rejected by Nahmanides in favor of the halakhic understanding of the biblical text in question. Gen. 9:7 commands us to be fruitful and multiply. It follows immediately after a verse which condemns shedding the blood of a human being. Rashi cites the midrash which notes the juxtaposition of the verses and infers that a person who does not produce children is comparable to one who has taken a human life. Rashi also cites the straight halakhic understanding 'of this verse as making it a duty to have children. In his rendition both interpretations seem to have equal standing and both are correct. Not so Ramban. He cites the midrash only to reject it and restricts himself to the plain meaning of the text as it is understood in the halakhic sources. After quoting the midrash, he says: 'This midrash rests only on the juxtaposition of the verses [i.e. not on sound exegesis], but the verse was, in fact, written only for the purpose of transmitting a commandment.' This type recurs in other places where the trust is to deny a midrashic reading a coequal status with the halakhic use of the verse.

We have a type in which one midrash, even if cited approvingly, is labeled inferior to another. In the commentary to Gen. 6:4 which speaks of the Nefilim who were on the earth, Ramban cites at great length an elaborate midrashic explanation of who these creatures were and how they related to the other humans on earth. He concludes this section with the statement that this is a *peshat hagun,* a sound and worthy explanation. He goes on, however, to add the observation that the midrash of R. Eliezer Haggadol on this text is far deeper and far more in accord with the meaning of the language of Scripture. In making this judgment, he is not rejecting either midrash outright, but he does choose between them and evaluate them. This would hardly be permitted to him if he operated with the premise that we are obligated to believe in the authority and truth of every midrash and every aggadah.

Another type is the midrash which he deals with by way of kabbalistic interpretation. Here the treatment is almost always allusive, proceeding by way of hints without ever becoming explicit. It is intended for initiates who should be able to fill in on their own the full meaning at which Ramban is pointing. In these cases, he does not reject as incorrect the non-mystical interpretations, but he does make clear that he does not believe that they penetrate to the true inner meaning of the verse under discussion. One of the longest direct discussions of a kabbalistic interpretation is to Gen. 24:1 in the comment to the scriptural statement that God blessed Abraham with everything (*bakol*). The meaning of the term *bakol* is in question. Ramban first offers a straightforward interpretation which would appear to be pure *peshat,* namely, that God granted Abraham all those things that ordinary people normally aspire to have, i.e. 'wealth, property, honor, long life, children—and this is all that man desires'. All that he lacked now was grandchildren, and this is why his great concern is to find a wife for Isaac.. It should be noted that the quoted statement is found almost verbatim in Ibn-Ezra, but Ramban does not cite him as his source. Perhaps it is his way of saying that this first level of meaning is so obvious that one need not acknowledge in this case dependence on another commentator. While he allows this surface-level interpretation to stand, it is clear from what follows that he does not consider it to be an adequate account of the true meaning of the verse. He goes on to cite an aggadic interpretation from the Talmud which he introduces with the label '*inyan nifla,* which undoubtedly means here that it has a hidden meaning. Still he gives an account of this aggadah which is purely esoteric in character, that is to say a normal, careful and precise reading of the text. Now, however, he rejects this interpretation in strong words, condemning it as inadequate and unworthy of the depth of mind of our sages. It is at that point that he introduces in an unusually extensive and elaborate form his own kabbalistic account of the meaning of the verse. Despite its length, it is still accessible only to those who understand the symbolism and can follow the allusions. Apparently, Ramban saw this particular comment of his as an acid test for those who presumed to be able to follow the kabbalistic elements in his commentary. He concludes with the statement: 'If you understand correctly what I have written here, you will understand the meaning of Jer. 44:18 and you will also be able to penetrate the inner meaning of many hidden dimensions of the Torah and the rest of Scripture.' Here we have the kabbalistic interpretation side by side with simple *peshat,* but there is no doubt that he considers the *peshat* level only a surface understanding which does not succeed at all in expounding the true meaning of the verse. In turn, the *peshat* account of the rabbinic aggadah is similarly deficient. In the many other cases where Ramban introduces a kabbalistic interpretation, he is either offering it as a much deeper and much preferred alternative to the standard aggadic interpretations, or he is even rejecting the latter outright in favor of the kabbalistic understanding. In his gloss on Ex. 19:13, for example, he cites Rashi, who has cited a midrash, announces that he finds this midrash unintelligible, and then proceeds to offer a concise kabbalistic interpretation as the correct way to understand the verse.

This rejection of a midrash because it is unintelligible is a type of response to the aggadic teachings which we find with some frequency in Ramban's commentary. We mentioned just above the instance of his comment on Ex. 19:13, which is one of a number of such cases in his commentary. It should be noted that the assertion that he finds a particular aggadah unintelligible is not necessarily a prelude to his offering a kabbalistic account in its place.

In commenting, for example, on Gen. 14:7, he cites Rashi, who has given us the aggadic midrash as an explanation of the place-name, Ein-Mishpat. Ramban says flatly, 'I do not understand this.' He goes on to explain why he finds the midrash beyond all intelligibility, and adds that he fails also to comprehend the comment of Onkelos. He then makes a tentative attempt to make some sense out of it, but seems to be dissatisfied with his own solution and just leaves the matter there. To evaluate soundly the full force of Ramban's statement that he finds a particular midrash or aggadah unintelligible, we should remember his statement concerning the doctrine of the trinity at the end of the Barcelona disputation. Although Paul is unable to provide an explanation of even the elements of the doctrine, he defends himself on the ground that the matter is so deep that even the angels and other supernal beings are not able to understand it. To this Ramban replies, 'It is perfectly clear that one cannot believe what one does not know.'[23] What he said about others would also apply to himself, and we can conclude that when Ramban announces that he finds a midrash unintelligible he can hardly be supposed to be saying that he nevertheless believes it.

One should distinguish between cases where Ramban says that he himself is unable to understand something and those cases where his kabbalistic interpretations are certain to transcend the understanding of all but those few who are fully initiated into esoteric lore. In the latter instances he refuses to say anything, or else restricts himself so severely that his words convey almost nothing to his ordinary readers. This is not a case of not believing or of rejecting an interpretation, but rather one which sees the interpretation as too esoteric even to record. In his extended comments on Gen. 1:1, he apologizes for the seeming inadequacy of his exposition in the following way: 'It is impossible to expound the interpretation of this matter in writing at great length, but allusions alone are very dangerous, since the readers will interpret them in ways which are far from the truth.'[24] In such a case one must say as little as possible. In commenting on Gen. 6:6 he makes the same point very tersely: 'There is a profound esoteric meaning to this which cannot be reduced to writing.' He adds that anyone who already knows this esoteric teaching would do well to give particular attention to certain specific points. The kabbalistic interpretations are in all these cases being affirmed by him as the true way of understanding the meaning of the text, but they are withheld from the general readers for good reasons.

There is another type in which Ramban rejects midrashic explanations on purely philological grounds or simply as a matter of a more accurate and sensitive reading of the text in order to determine its plain meaning. Gen. 3:8 reads: 'They heard the sound of the Lord God moving about in the garden at the breezy time of the day.' This verse poses a problem since it is ambiguous. It is not clear whether the sound is moving about in the garden, or the Lord is moving about in the garden, or Adam and Eve are moving about in the garden. Ramban cites a midrash on this point, followed by a number of other commentators. He rejects the midrashic reading and that of the commentators who were influenced by the midrash in favor of his own reading which construes the verb *mithalekh* as referring to God, meaning, as in other cases of this usage of *halakh,* that God revealed himself to man. Based on the evidence which he marshals, he does not hesitate to conclude that the midrash is wrong. He then cites a second midrash which understands the key terms in the same way as himself, except that it gets the meaning reversed. This midrash reads the phrase 'moving about in the garden' to mean that God took leave of them, while Ramban holds that it means that God came to them, i.e. revealed Himself. He concludes by affirming that his own explanation is 'correct and fits best the meaning of the verse'. In Gen. 4:13 he cites Rashi, who quotes a midrash explaining Cain's statement, 'My sin is too great *mi-neso'*. In this explanation the term *nasa* is understood to mean 'carry' or 'bear'. Moreover, as the midrash and Rashi read the text, it is not a declaration by Cain about himself, but rather a challenge by Cain to God. He says to Him, 'Can You the bearer of the upper and the lower worlds not also bear my sin?' Ramban, however, understands *nasa* here to mean 'forgiving', as it does in certain other contexts. He construes Cain's statement to be in the form of a confession in which he says that God is justified since his sin is too great to be forgiven. This type occurs frequently and it is a common move for Ramban to reject a midrash on the ground that its reading of the text is inferior to that which he then proposes.

In all these cases we have seen types of commentary in which Nahmanides, with little hesitation, rejects midrashim and aggadot in favor of other interpretations. He feels no compunction about this and certainly sees no heresy in his refusal to believe the teaching of every midrash contained in the literature. We should also be clear about another supposed 'orthodoxy' which was ascribed to Ramban. Earlier we cited a statement of Martin Cohen that Ramban 'belonged to the camp of the fundamentalists, to those who condemned "anyone expounding the words of our rabbis and their Aggadahs not according to Rashi's words"'[25] One is tempted to observe that if this is the case, then Ramban must have condemned himself frequently and without restraint, since one of the most common features of his commentary is the regularity with which he cites Rashi only to disagree with him. There is no question about the great respect he felt for Rashi. One need only read his poetic introduction to his commentary to see how reverently Ramban speaks of him. Yet he also indicates that he will carry on debate with Rashi and will not simply accept his teachings in every case as being the final and authoritative commentary. This he does regularly and it constitutes one of the most illuminating features of his commentary, since it helps us to see the same verse from a variety of perspectives. The point is well made by Septimus when he observes: 'Nahmanides' *Commentary* is, among other things, a sustained critique of Rashi's more midrashic interpretations of Scripture.'[26] The language of the criticisms is for the most part restrained and rarely *ad hominem*. There are, however, occasions when Ramban allows his polemical enthusiasm to push him to quite extreme expressions. The most familiar of these cases, in all probability, is his critique at Gen. 6:3, where he cites Rashi and concludes: *V'ein beferush ha-zeh ta'am 'o re'ayah.* This is hardly the language of one who condemns any deviation from Rashi's teachings.

We should note one final type of commentary. We have tried to make the point that Ramban revered the tradition and took rabbinic aggadah and midrash with the highest seriousness. Furthermore, he related to the sages of Talmud and Midrash with great respect for their special eminence in the Jewish tradition. Despite this he did not feel that he was constrained to accept all of their teachings. Yet when he felt that these sages were being dealt with in a cavalier fashion he could rise to their defense with a fierce attack on their detractors. We see this particularly in the case of his responses to Ibn-Ezra, for whom he had high regard and from whom he learned a great deal.[27] When, however, he perceives in Ibn-Ezra the suggestion of disrespect for the sages or for the tradition, or interpretations which may be an active danger to the foundations of Jewish faith, Ramban responds with anger, derision, even contempt. The same holds for cases in which Ibn-Ezra presumes, wrongly in Ramban's view, to understand the esoteric meanings of Scripture, or, even worse, to take a position which would undermine or distort the teachings of kabbalah. Typical of such reactions is his comment at the end of his gloss to Gen. 24: 1. He does not name Ibn-Ezra, but the object of his attack is evident to all who understand these matters. He says: 'If all this [that has been set forth in the gloss] were known to him who arrogantly claims knowledge of esoteric lore, his lips would be stilled and he would stop his derisive attacks on the teachings of our sages. I have written this in order to stop up the mouths of those who speak about the righteous with contemptuous haughtiness.' At Gen. 46:15 he cites a midrash which strains credulity, but which he is determined to support. He then notes the attack of Ibn-Ezra on this midrash, after which he adds the observation: 'Lest he be excessively wise in his own eyes as he seeks to refute the teachings of our sages, I find it necessary to respond to him.' Clearly, Nahmanides knew how to be an effective combatant in defense of traditional teachings, just as he knew how to select from among those teachings the interpretations which he found to be sound and persuasive.

We have tried to present in this study strong evidence that there is no ground for the view that Nahmanides was dissembling when he announced at the disputation in Barcelona that we are not obligated to believe in all rabbinic aggadot. Those who have taken this position have an incorrect understanding of the nature and process of internal Jewish thought. They imagine the existence of an official fundamentalism which has no foundation in fact. They have, moreover, failed to give to Ramban's most readily available works the consideration that they deserve in determining what were his true views about the status of midrash and aggadah in Judaism.[28]

I want to express here my gratitude to my friends and colleagues, Professor Nahum M. Sarna and Professor Lester A. Segal, who were kind enough to read this paper and give me the benefit of their comments.

NOTES

[1] For the earlier literature see Cecil Roth, 'The Disputation at Barcelona (1263)', Harvard *Theological Review* 43 (2) (1950), 117-18. Subsequent literature is listed in Robert Chazan, 'The Barcelona Disputation of 1263: Christian Missionizing and Jewish Response', *Speculum* 52 (4) (1977); and in Bernard Septimus, "Open Rebuke and Concealed Love": Nahmanides and the Andalusian Tradition', in Isadore Twersky (ed.), *Rabbi Moses Nahmanides (Ramban): Explorations in His Religious and Literary Virtuosity* (Cambridge, 1983), 11-34. To the literature listed in these sources add the recent valuable study by Hyam Maccoby, *Judaism on Trial: Jewish-Christian Disputations in the Middle Ages,* Littman Library of Jewish Civilization London, 1982), and the large bibliography listed there, as well as Hans-Georg von Mutius, *Die Christlich-Jüdische Zwangsdisputation zu Barcelona* (Frankfurt am Main, 1982), where in addition to text and commentary there is an extensive bibliography.

[2] Cited from Maccoby's translation, 110.

[3] Ibid. 115-16.

[4] Rabbi Mordecai Eliasberg, *Shevil Hazahav,* 27, as cited in Chavel, *Kilvei HaRamban,* 1, 308, fn.

[5] Yitzhak Baer, *A History of the Jews in Christian Spain* (Philadelphia, 1961), 1, 153. See also his statement that 'It is not correct that Ramban did not believe in aggadot, but on the contrary, he considered them to have profoundly esoteric significance, which it is forbidden to reveal to Christians', *Tarbiz* 2 (2), 184. H. Beinart repeats the identical view in his article on the Barcelona disputation in *EJ* 4, 214.

[6] H. H. Ben-Sasson, *Perakim Betoldot Hayehudim Biyemei Habeinayyim* (Tel-Aviv, 1969), 251.

[7] Martin A. Cohen, 'Reflections on the Text and Context of the Disputation of Barcelona', *HUCA* 35 (1964), 169. The statement concerning Rashi is quoted by him from Samuel Saporta. Cohen fails to note that the statement of Saporta is contained in-his letter to the rabbis of France. This letter is a strong defense of Maimonides and a strong condemnation of the French rabbis. In the course of his argument he condemns them bitterly for the curse which they pronounced on anyone 'who interprets the words of our rabbis and their aggadot not in accordance with the interpretation of Rashi'. (The letter is contained in *Ginzei Nistarot,* IV, 37-67. The quoted passage is on p. 64.) Cohen ignores the context of the letter and, above all, the fact that it makes no reference whatsoever to Nahmanides' views on this point. As we shall show subsequently, it is nothing short of ludicrous to attribute such a view to Ramban who disagrees with Rashi frequently and openly in his own commentary on the Torah.

[8] Ibid. 171.

[9] Cecil Roth, 'The Disputation at Barcelona (1263)', *HTR* 43 (2) (1950), 128.

[10] Robert Chazan, 'The Barcelona Disputation of 1263: Christian Missionizing and Jewish Response', *Speculum* 52 (1977), 835-6.

[11] This expression is based on I Sam. 16:7.

[12] Hyam Maccoby, *Judaism on Trial,* 44-7, 58-66, 68-74. In my summary I have gone beyond the exact arguments of Maccoby, but have remained faithful to their spirit and their major thrust.

[13] Bernard Septimus, "'Open Rebuke and Concealed Love": Nahmanides and the Andalusian Tradition', 20, and passim.

[14] See Commentary on the Torah to Gen. 18: 1.

[15] P. T. Ma'aserot, III: 10, 51a.

[16] P. T. Shabbat, XVI: 1, 15c. This passage may well be concerned primarily with the ban on committing aggadot to writing. Nevertheless, there can hardly be any question about the attitude of antagonism that is expressed here to aggadah as a danger to sound faith. For a brief discussion see my 'Judaism, Secularism, and Textual Interpretation', in M. Fox, *Modern Jewish Ethics: Theory and Practice* (Ohio State University Press, 1974),.16-18.

[17] Cited in B. M. Levin, *Otzar Hageonim,* Hagigah, 14a, 60. Note that a few lines earlier Rav Hai records the opinion that aggadic teachings do not have the standing of those teachings for which we have a fixed tradition, 'but each individual can construe them in whatever way occurs to him as correct' *(kol ehad doresh mah she'alah al libo).* See also *Otzar Hageonim to* Berakhot, 58b, 91. See also the discussion in S. W. Baron, *A Social and Religious History of the Jews* VI, 176 ff.

[18] Saul Lieberman, *Sheki'in* (Jerusalem, 1939), 81 – 3.

[19] Nahmanides, *Torat Ha'adam, Sha'ar Haggemul, Kitvey Haramban,* Chavel edition, 11,285.

[20] Rabad to H. Teshuvah, 3:7. It should be noted that Nahmanides recognized Rabad as one of the great figures of the previous generation, and, although he often took issue with him in matters of halakhah, certainly would not have questioned he orthodoxy or propriety of the view concerning aggadah which he expresses here.

[21] Chavel edition, 306.

[22] For a different approach to the problem of typology in Nahmanides' commentary on the Torah, see Ámos Funkenstein, *'Parshanuto Hatipologit shel HaRamban', Zion* 45 (1980).

[23] Chavel edition, 320; Maccoby edition, 146.

[24] Chavel edition, to Gen. 1:1, II.

[25] See above, endnote 7.

[26] Septimus, op. cit. 16, n. 2 1. See there a selected list of instances in which Ramban offers critical reviews of Rashi's commentaries.

[27] On this point see the Septimus article cited above.

[28] It is well known that the debate concerning the status of aggadot and midrashim went on through the centuries and, in some ways, continues down to our own day. There are always those who insist that orthodox religious teachings require belief in the authoritative status of all aggadot, and always those who take the counterposition. It is rare to find the so-called orthodox' position internal to the community of believers except among those who are convinced that literalist fundamentalism is the only correct stance. Serious scholars and true *talmidei hakhamim* do not normally affirm such a view. What they reject is an attitude of irreverence toward rabbinic aggadah, an attitude which scorns these aggadot, rather than making the effort to understand them and to see their significance. This is what underlies, for example, the bitter attack of Maharál of Prague on Azariah dei Rossi (see *Be'er Haggolah,* Ch. 6, 126 ff. in the Jerusalem, 1960 edition). It is simply wrong, however, to conclude that Maharal 'defended the absolute truth of the talmudic legends and traditions' *(EJ* 14, 318). As in the case of Nahmanides, one need only study the actual way in which Maharal deals with aggadot to see how far he is from insisting on a literalist reading. Once we open up the option of non-literal readings, which he certainly did, we can no longer speak about a defense of the 'absolute truth' of aggadot, since the term has lost all sense. What Maharal finds offensive in dei Rossi is not that he does not read all aggadot with a kind of simple-minded literalness or that he fails to affirm that every aggadah is to be understood as absolutely true. He is offended rather by what he construes to be his attitude of disrespect for the teachers of earlier generations and his unwillingness to make the intellectual effort which is required in order to understand their teachings in a serious way.

21

THE RAV [RABBI SOLOVEITCHIK] AS MASPID

Among the variety of forms which Rav Soloveitchik z"tl chose for his writings, one of the most striking and instructive is the *hesped*, a eulogy given in memory of a recently departed figure of outstanding stature in the world of Jewish life, learning, or leadership. The corpus of his published works includes six such eulogistic essays, each one a carefully crafted study which is a source of illumination and instruction.[1] I shall try to show that an analysis of these eulogies opens up dimensions of the Rav's thought and method which have not been sufficiently noted in the literature about his work. Each of them is of intrinsic interest and importance, making them eminently worthy of careful study. These *hespedim* should not be confused with the annual *yahrzeit* shiurim which the Rav gave in memory of his father, or with lectures that he gave on similar memorial occasions. The eulogies which we shall study are of a quite different genre. In this essay we can do no more than make a first attempt to open up this fascinating area of Rav Soloveitchik's thought.

Although each of the six eulogies has its own distinctive character, there are certain common qualities which they share. First, they are an informed by the Rav's understanding of what the halakha defines as the nature and function of every true *hesped*. As he puts it, a *hesped* must fulfill two separate, but related functions. It must cause us to feel deep sorrow over the loss we have sustained, and it must make us aware intellectually of the depth and significance of that loss. A *hesped* "seeks, first of all, to make people weep... The Halakhah did not like to see the dead interred in silent indifference. It wanted to hear the shriek of despair..." But in its other dimension "the *hesped* turns into *kilus*, eulogy, informative and instructional. Instead of addressing ourselves to the heart... we try now to contact the mind. We no longer try to arouse emotions. We seek to stimulate thoughts by telling a story... the life story of the deceased."[2] The Rav introduces this same distinction in the opening of his eulogy for R. Hayyim Heller. The *maspid* must cause the sounds of agony to be heard and tears to flow as he makes his audience aware of their loss. At the same time, he must serve as a pedagogue, using calm reason to teach the people the full significance of the personality whom he eulogizes.[3]

Yet, there is a near insoluble problem, which is the second feature held in common by all these eulogies. Rarely do we manage during the lifetime of a person to come to know him or her thoroughly and deeply. Even when we are in frequent contact with an individual, we tend to have only a superficial sense of the complex and subtle elements which constitute a human personality. This is true of our efforts to understand ordinary individuals, how much more so of the attempt to grasp the inner reality of great figures, scholars, teachers, moral guides and leaders. Only when they have left us do we begin to realize how little we really knew them. How then can we eulogize them? As a paradigm of this dilemma the Rav cites a talmudic episode in which the disciples of a great sage discovered, to their distress, how little of his teaching they had mastered. Returning from his funeral, they sat down to eat, and could not resolve a seemingly simple problem about the laws of grace after meals. With all they had learned from their teacher, they were now aware that they had barely scratched the surface of his vast scholarship. Usually it is only after we sustain the loss of a loved one or a great teacher, that we become painfully aware that there is so much we now want to know that we failed to learn. During life we maintain a distance even from those to whom we are closest, which leaves us, after their death, ignorant of what they knew and of what constituted their true inner being.

This imposes on the *maspid* a very heavy burden, for he must uncover the secret recesses of the inner life of his subject, and he must do so with full responsibility for the accuracy and the perceptiveness of the picture which he paints. The Rav cites an extended talmudic passage concerning the last rites for Rav Huna (Moed Katan, 25a) from which he draws the sharp conclusion that we may only eulogize if we are able to depict the deceased accurately and perceptively as he truly was, in his full reality. Under no circumstance should we eulogize if we diminish in any way the stature and personality of the deceased. We must not reduce great men to our limited conceptions and understanding. We must rather elevate ourselves and the people to the point where we are capable of some sound understanding of the nature of the departed.[4] With characteristic modesty, the Rav repeatedly expresses his sense of his own inadequacy to create a full and accurate picture of his subject. Yet, he is so aware of the failures of others that he is driven to try. One thing is certain. In his depictions of his subjects he avoids the trite language, the cliché-laden rhetoric, which he finds so offensive in ordinary eulogies. In an expression of frustration with the limits of all language, Nietzsche somewhere observes that, "The word dilutes and blunts; the word depersonalizes; the word makes the uncommon common." Struggling against this problem, the Rav understands that he must use language to overcome language, that as a *maspid* he must be not only a rational teacher, but a creative artist. With rare skill, his artistry makes itself manifest in each of his *hespedim* as he penetrates, intellectually and emotionally, into the depths of the individual personalities. His rational discourse goes beyond itself to become poetry, poetry which teaches us by stimulating the imagination while arousing the intellect. If it is possible to use language effectively to portray a human personality in its hidden inner reality, then the Rav has achieved rare success in his efforts.

A third feature common to these eulogies is the Rav's familiar practice of dealing with a problem by formulating archetypes which provide the architectural framework within which he then carries on his eulogistic work. It is well known that such typology is a central feature of very much of the Rav's teaching. We see it in these eulogies in its full flowering. Let us consider some examples. He illuminates the personality of R. Yitzhak Zev, his uncle, through the distinction between the Rosh ha-Shana and Yom Kippur personality types. Rosh ha-Shana is associated with public divine revelation, while Yom Kippur is characterized by private divine revelation. The Rosh ha-Shana prototype is Aaron, while the Yom Kippur prototype is Moses. The Brisker Rav is then described as a Moses type, and it is from this perspective that we are helped to understand him.

Similarly, the account of R. Zev Gold is located within the distinction between the kedusha, the holiness, of the Sabbath and Festivals and the *kedusha* of Rosh-Hodesh. The former is public and the latter is hidden and private. Rabbi Gold is then described as a Rosh-Hodesh type. The personality and the leadership of R. Hayyim Ozer is explicated by way of the distinction between two of the vestments of the high priest, the *tzitz* and the *hoshen*. The former was worn on the front of the elaborate headdress of the high priest, while the latter was worn as a breastplate. The *tzitz* is located on the forehead of the *kohen gadol*, a location which associates it with the center of intelligence and knowledge. The hoshen is worn over the heart, the center of love and devotion to the people of Israel whose tribal names are engraved upon it.[5] The role of R. Hayyim Ozer as Jewish leader is then explicated through these archetypes. Unlike conventional leaders he represents a unique combination of head and heart, of learning and love of Israel. This combination determines his decision making process so as to assure that it flows from the teachings of the Torah and is simultaneously determined by an overflowing love of the Jewish people.

As we noted, this method of understanding various phenomena through the delineation of archetypes is a central feature of the Rav's work. It is present not only in his eulogies, but also in his philosophical-theological essays, and, with certain variations, also in his purely halakhic discourses. If we reflect on the way in which this method is used in the *hespedim*, we can gain insight into its meaning and purpose in the other genres of the Rav's writings.

There are two features of the Rav's thought which come into play at this point. As is well known, the Rav consistently insisted that the halakha is the only sound source of authentic Jewish ideas. Thus, we must always seek for the halakhic foundations of any doctrine which he sets forth. Furthermore, central to all of his methodology in the analysis and exposition of Jewish texts is conceptual formulation and clarification. These features are immediately recognizable by anyone who ever attended a *shiur* which he gave, no matter what the subject or what texts were being studied. We must ask ourselves what is the relationship of articulating typological distinctions to the process of formulating and clarifying basic concepts. My contention is that we can come to an understanding of this method and its significance if we pay close attention to what the Rav did in his *hespedim*.

We begin from a premise that I believe is basic to the Rav's thinking, although it has not been widely noted in the literature. Early in 1959, Dr. Hillel Seidman published a very important and rich account of a discourse which the Rav had recently given. His text was based on his careful notes of the Rav's presentation, and he assures his readers that the final text was "reviewed and authorized by the Rav."[6] In this discourse the Rav argued that to achieve a proper halakhic understanding of the question, "what is a Jew," we must focus on the fact that in the halakha the individual Jew is regularly treated on the model of a Sefer Torah. A few examples will make the point clear. The rule is that when one is present at the time of the death of a fellow-Jew, he is required to rend his garments. As the *gemara* explains, this is comparable to being present when a Sefer Torah is destroyed by fire.[7] A second example: A Sefer Torah which disintegrates from age or use is to be buried next to a *talmid hakham*.[8] The two are perceived as sharing certain common qualities. We rise in respect for a Sefer Torah as we do for the scholars who devote themselves to the study of Torah.[9] The point of these halakhic examples is to establish that in halakhic-conceptual terms, a Jew is to be understood as analogous to a Sefer Torah. It then follows that the concept, "Jew," receives its clarification and formulation from the concept, "Sefer Torah." The Rav further supports this contention by citing aggadic passages in which the same analogy is drawn. When R. Eliezer's pupils visited him during his illness, R. Akiba found them crying bitterly. When he asked why they were crying, they answered that if one sees a Sefer Torah suffering, it is impossible not to cry.[10] He finally, sets forth a whole series of the halakhic effects of this analogy. From the halakhot of preparing the parchment, writing a Sefer Torah, and giving it the sanctity which it requires, the Rav teaches us a series of halakhot that pertain to the life of the Jew as if he were himself a Sefer Torah. This is not the place to elaborate further on this essay, but we should stress that it is eminently worthy of careful study.

We can now begin to understand the significance of the Rav's stress on the law of *hesped* which requires the *maspid* to give a full account of the personality of the deceased. If a Jew is a Sefer Torah, then to know an individual Jew requires the same kind of intellectual effort, the same kind of conceptual formulation and elucidation, as does every other topic in the study of Torah. The more eminent the person, the greater and deeper his learning, the more exemplary his virtue, the more creative and sound his leadership, the more sensitive his piety, the greater the intellectual challenge to understanding the departed personality. To give an accurate and adequate account of that person the *maspid* must employ the same processes of analysis and exposition that he uses in explicating any passage in the halakha. Moreover, understanding the person is a step toward the knowledge of God. Every man is created in the image of God, but that divine image is present in a unique way in the personalities of *gedolei yisrael*. "The attributes of the Holy One, blessed be He, descend to the lower realm and are concretized in *gedolei yisrael*, the Sages of the sacred tradition... They serve as a dwelling-place for the Shekhina... A great man becomes the instrument through which one of the divine attributes is actualized [here on earth]."[11] Thus, the study and exposition of the essence of a particular human personality constitutes a major step in the study of Torah, which is, in turn, a necessary condition for the knowledge of God. The acquisition of that knowledge is the first positive commandment in Maimonides' listing of the mitzvot. Study of the Rav's method in formulating a *hesped*, provides us with a model for understanding his method in straightforward halakhic analysis.

A striking example of this method is found in his characterization of the mode of Torah knowledge of R. Yitzhak Zev, the Brisker Rav, and of his father, the Rav's grandfather, the incomparable R. Hayyim Brisker. I have discussed this in more extended form elsewhere,[12] and shall simply summarize briefly here. The Rav begins from the halakhic distinction between *erusin*, betrothal, and *nissu'in*, marriage. In the former state, the couple constitute two separate entities, closely related, with intimate knowledge of each other, but still separate. In the latter state, all the barriers have been broken. In a true halakhic marriage, the couple are as one. They share a common essence; their hearts beat with a common rhythm; their knowledge of each other is not simply discursive, but immediate, intuitive, and deeply perceptive. Providing us with prooftexts from the classical sources, the Rav analogizes the relationship of a *talmid hakham* to Torah to the relationships of erusin and nissu'in. The former represents a great achievement, but is still purely discursive. It relies on all the tools of the highly developed intellect to grasp and give structure to each topic in Torah learning. A few rare individuals may be said to be married to the Torah, not just betrothed. Blessed with the highest qualities of intellectual depth and acuity, they transcend the limits of intellect to understand Torah by way of direct intimacy. Their knowledge is intuitive. Their intuitive formulations will subsequently be verified by discursive analysis, but they could never be achieved by such analysis alone. If we perceive R. Yitzhak Zev as married to the Torah, then we have the indispensable key not only to his way of Torah learning, but to his entire personality.

There is in these eulogies a dialectical movement back and forth between pure halakhic categories and the elucidation of the individual personality that has been taken from us by death. The distinction between Rosha ha-Shana as public revelation and Yom Kippur as private revelation provides the general halakhic-conceptual framework. This, in turn generates a way of understanding Moses and Aaron. The Priest is the open man of the people, and the Prophet is the withdrawn figure, his face covered by a veil that hides his shining brilliance. The priest is mourned by all the people, while the prophet only by the limited number who have some sense of who he truly was.[13] R. Yitzhak Zev is now characterized as a Moses /Yom Kippur figure, and the Rav sees more than symbolic significance in the fact that he died on Yom Kippur. He was a hidden personality, living, like Moses, behind a cloud that kept him from being accessible to the general public. The people "sensed intuitively that this was a holy man who walked among them, however, only a very small number of select individuals knew and understood him."[14]

Having placed his uncle appropriately in the typological framework, the Rav now confronts the question of what this characterization teaches us about R. Yitzhak Zev as student and teacher of Torah. This is the essential question, since it was Torah learning which was the chief defining force of his life. Here the Rav introduces us to a second typology which we have already discussed, namely, the distinction between being betrothed to the Torah and married to the Torah. Having set out the halakhic grounds and implications of this distinction, he turns first to his grandfather, who presents us with the ideal model of one who is married to the Torah, and then helps us to see how this characterization helps us to gain insight into the personality of R. Yitzhak Zev. In the course of this extended presentation, there are a number of intricate and technical discussions of complex halakhic topics. This is not the place to expound these discussions, but it must be said that any reader who is at home in the literature of halakha will have no difficulty in seeing how all of these discussions connect to the central theme of the *hesped*. In turn, these discussions illuminate for us the connection between forming basic concepts in halakha and forming conceptual structures for understanding a great Jewish personality.

In the *hesped* for R. Hayyim Heller we find a similar methodology. I shall mention only one common characteristic, the description of R. Hayyim's way in Torah learning. Here we are introduced to the familiar halakhic categories of long and short forms of benedictions, *berakha aruka* and *berakha ketzara*. These categories are then applied to other areas of halakhic practice, in particular, to the procedures of the priests in the Temple service. There is a setting in which the ritual involves a long extended procedure, and another in which the procedure is short and direct. This is then applied to styles of learning, and finally to the method of R. Hayyim which was direct, concise, compressed, immediate and intuitive. Although this may sound very much like the *erusin/nissu'in* distinction that was used to illuminate R. Yitzhak Zev, it is not fully identical. While the Rav had unlimited admiration for both of these great luminaries, he saw that each had his own defining characteristics. It would be presumptuous to try to spell out the full and exact nature of their differences and how these are implicit in the different typologies, since the Rav did not choose to do so himself.

There are, however, three striking differences that come to the fore as we study these eulogies. One is that R. Hayyim, unlike most classical *talmidei hakhamim*, was a great and creative master of the Bible, as well as rabbinic literature. Second, he was unique among such figures in his knowledge of semitic and classical languages and in his application of this knowledge to a defense of the integrity of the Tanakh. Third, the Rav stresses the special importance of R. Hayyim as a last living link between the earlier generations of Torah learning and the generations that followed him. In this discussion the Rav introduces historical concerns into the mix of halakhic typology with which he illuminates the personality of R. Hayyim. He does so by giving us other examples from Jewish history of figures, such as Serah bat Asher and Ahiya ha-Shiloni, who were indispensable links between earlier and later generations.

Even this historical perspective emerges from a quasi-halakhic description of R. Hayyim Heller by Dr. Samuel Belkin. Using the language of the liturgy, Dr. Belkin speaks of R. Hayyim as belonging to a special group known as "*peleitat sofereiham*", the remnants of the Scribes of Jewish antiquity. The Rav gives a historical account of the meaning of the term "remnant." No matter how many great Torah scholars adorn any given generation, they can not be truly connected to the great chain of tradition, unless there is among them at least one figure who is a remnant of the past, who alone is able to bridge the abyss which separates the later generations from the earlier. In this sense, we have in R. Hayyim Heller the necessary connecting link which authenticates and authorizes the present generation of scholars by joining them with their past. R. Hayyim, by the Rav's reckoning, had intimate connections with three generations of the greatest Torah scholars that preceded him, and he transmitted not only their formal teaching, but their inner reality, to the generations which followed him.

The *hesped* for the Talner Rebbe reveals essentially the same characteristic methodology as well as a certain commonality of themes with those that we have already discussed. Yet, what should occupy the attention of the careful reader is what is distinctive in each case. We saw how, despite similarities, R. Hayyim Heller is carefully delineated in ways which distinguish him from R. Yitzhak Zev so that he emerges as the unique Torah personality that he was. Both are differentiated from R. Hayyim Ozer who shares their learning, but also assumes a role of public leadership which was alien to the others.

In his learning, in his piety, and in his love of Israel, the Talner Rebbe is similar to the other great figures whom the Rav eulogized. The most obvious distinction is that while the others represent the great tradition of *mitnagdim*, the Talner Rebbe was the scion of one of the great hasidic dynasties. Superficially, it would seem that the Rav does little more than follow a by now familiar pattern in his *hesped*, but closer reading shows us that this is not a sound conclusion. There is the usual expression of regret over the failure to know the person in sufficient depth during his lifetime, and the gnawing, agonizing questions, "Who was He? Whom did we lose?".

This is preceded by an extended halakhic discourse in which two types of mourning are carefully defined and distinguished. The first stage is *aninut*, which is the initial "spontaneous human reaction to death. It is an outcry, a shout, or a howl of grisly horror and disgust. Man responds to his defeat at the hands of death with total resignation... Beaten by the fiend... man begins to question his own human singular reality... He starts downgrading himself. He dehumanizes himself. He arrives at the conclusion that man is not human, that he is just a living creature like the beast of the field."[15] In this state, the halakha freed man of all mitzvot. The reason, as the Rav explains, is that "our commitment to God is rooted in the awareness of human dignity and sanctity." When a despairing individual questions all that makes us distinctively human, there is no longer any ground of human dignity and no foundation on which to view man as uniquely bound by God's commandments.[16] If we are merely animals, then we have no more obligation, no more divinely imposed duty, than do animals. Following the burial, the stage of *avelut* begins. Here the halakha requires man to overcome his self-rejection, to reaffirm his own humanity and to grieve without allowing his distinctive humanity to disintegrate. Thus, we begin with an illuminating halakhic typology from which we learn much not only about the formal laws of mourning, but even more about the conceptual world, the world of religious ideas, which underlies these halakhot.

There is here another motivation which is more explicit than in some of the other eulogies. The Rav had already eulogized the Talner Rebbe at his funeral. There he raised the question, "who was he?", but failed, in his own judgment, to answer it properly. "Of course, due to the fact that I was in a state of total confusion and despair, I could not pursue the analysis in an orderly manner."[17] In other words, in the condition of *aninut* it was not possible to supply the mode of discourse which could answer the question adequately. Now that *aninut* has yielded to *avelut*, it is not only emotionally and intellectually possible, but obligatory, to answer the unanswered question through a proper *hesped*. Here the halakhic analysis serves as a direct mandate for practical fulfillment of an obligation.

At this point, the Rav is able to turn to an account of the qualities which made up the personality of the Talner Rabbe. "All our great leaders, both hasidic and mitnagdic, were preoccupied with and committed to one task—teaching. The teacher, the rebbe, has been throughout the generations the central figure within the covenantal community. The teacher towered above any other figure—king, warlord, or high priest."[18] In this respect the Talner Rebbe was similar to the other great Jewish leaders whom the Rav has eulogized. The task of the maspid, however, is to help us understand what is distinctive about his subject, what constituted the essential nature and contribution of the person whose death we are mourning.

To achieve this end, the Rav introduces us to a new typology, the distinction between the "king-teacher" and the "priest-teacher" or "saint-teacher." The king-teacher "addresses himself to the mind. He teaches both pure halakha and applied halakha. He teaches disciples how to conceptualize, how to classify, how to reconcile texts and opinions, how to systematize, to infer, and to analyze." This king-teacher is concerned, above all, with the use of the tools of the intellect, and with forming the capacity of his students to use their own intellectual powers creatively to understand and systematize every topic in the study of Torah. He is concerned with what the Zohar describes as the outer garments of the Torah. This study is of vital importance for the religious life of the Jews. It is indispensable, not only as a *sine qua non* for the fulfillment of our obligation of *limmud ha-Torah*, but also as a central element in Jewish spiritual life. The great models of this king-teacher type are the Rambam, the Gaon of Vilna, and Rav's own ancestors.[19]

The saint-teacher, in contrast, "focuses his attention upon the invisible, intangible letters, the soul of the Torah... the saint-teacher speaks to the heart, communes with the heart and tells the heart how to attune its own excited accelerated beat to that of the Torah. The saint-teacher teaches man the art of catharsis, how to cleanse and purge the heart of vulgarity and inhumanity, of unworthy sentiments, uncouth emotions and selfish desires. How can a man merge his soul with the soul of the Torah if his inner life is unclean?"[20]

In making this typological distinction, the Rav has succeeded in teaching us who the Talner Rebbe really was. In fact, he teaches us what constitutes the nature of the life and service of the true hasidic rebbe, in contrast to that of the classical mitnagdic *talmid hakham*. His learning may be no less than that of his king-teacher colleagues, but there is an added dimension which defines him as saint-teacher. He is concerned not only with transmitting intellectual understanding of the Torah to his disciples, but even more with forming their characters. He guides them so that they hear not only the words of the Torah, not only the intense rational discourse of Talmud study, but shows them how to penetrate to the non-verbal, perhaps super-verbal, soul of the Torah. He creates not just great Talmudic virtuosos, but virtuosos of the spirit who are so fully purified, so refined in character, so delicate in sensitivity, that the soul of the Torah expresses itself through them and in them. To achieve this end he directs himself, not only to a highly select intellectual elite, but to every Jew, however humble. "Hence, the teaching of the saint-teacher is exoteric, democratic, understandable and accessible both to the simpleton and to the philosopher." While other hasidic dynasties came so to intellectualize their teaching that they lost their democratic touch, the Talner Rebbe and the Tchernobil dynasty of which he was such a glorious representative remained faithful to the original charge of teaching every Jew and uncovering the spiritual capabilities of even the most ordinary disciple.[21] The *maspid* places his subject into the general framework of understanding which is part of the apparatus for knowing the essential reality of any great Jewish leader. He then brings to our attention those special characteristics which define the uniqueness of the particular person whom he is eulogizing. In this process, he never abandons that part of the art of *hesped* which requires him to serve as the poet who arouses our deep sense of loss, even while he is serving as the rational teacher who illuminates for us in intellectual categories the nature of the person whom we have lost.

In the eulogy for R. Zev Gold we find the stress on another distinctive characteristic. The opening moves seem to be one more variation on the themes to which we have already been introduce. A distinction is drawn between the kedusha of two types of holy days, Shabbat and Yom Tov, on the one hand, and Rosh-Hodesh, on the other. The former is holiness which is open, public, evident to everybody, while the latter is holiness which is hidden, not immediately apparent. This general description is based on halakhic sources which are rigorously examined and carefully illuminated. Following his principle, which we discussed earlier, that the Jewish personality is to be understood on the halakhic and theological model of the essence of a Sefer Torah, the Rav uses the typology of the holy days, which he has set forth, as a paradigm for a typology of human holiness. "In the holiness of man there are also two types: publicly revealed holiness and hidden holiness... Both of them flow from the deepest recesses of the human soul and from the spiritual dimension of the personality."[22]

Those great figures who embody the Sabbath/Festival type of holiness are fortunate in being immediately recognized and revered. Their holiness is evident in their life-style, in every aspect and dimension of their being. As a result, they need not struggle for public regard, since they have an immediate and indelible effect on every person with whom they come into contact. All grasp their special distinction and deal with them in humble submission. "אשרי האדם שקודשתו משוועת מתוכו ומזעזעת את הזולת" Even the coarsest and the least learned are profoundly affected by the holy light which shines forth from them.[23]

The Rosh-Hodesh types, those whose kedusha is hidden, are far less fortunate when it comes to public recognition and reverence. Like Rosh-Hodesh, they give little direct evidence of the holiness which permeates every fiber of their being and which makes them persons of unique spiritual worth and importance. Their outer garb is so seemingly ordinary that it hides from public view the luminous inner reality of their sanctity. R. Zev Gold is represented by the Rav as such a personality type whose holiness was generally hidden from public view. The Rav confesses that these Rosh-Hodesh types have a special attraction for him. He grew up among such types in his own family, particularly his father the sainted Rabbi Moshe. It is hard to imagine a higher tribute from the Rav, than to identify Rabbi Gold as belonging, in this respect, in the category of his own immediate forebears.

A *hesped* for a great Jew whose holiness was hidden and not widely noted presents a special challenge. The *maspid* must open up that which was suppressed. He must bring to the consciousness of his audience the holy reality of the deceased person, a reality of which they had almost no awareness during his lifetime. "My task is to dig up the coffin of R. Gold, who was buried in such unseemly haste, to open it up and to examine carefully the image of the person hidden there... to penetrate to the interior of his hidden holiness, and to find, beyond the external cloud of obscure darkness, the Rosh-Hodesh man."[24] The description which follows is based on a three-fold distinction. R. Gold is described as a man of three great loves, one in whom there burned with high intensity three flaming fires: the fire of his love for Abraham, the fire of his love for Eretz Yisrael, and the fire of his love for the people of Israel.

There is no need to set forth here the details of this description. They are readily available to any reader of the text. We shall concentrate on the exposition of one of these three loves, because it is here that we see what the Rav understood to be the distinctiveness of R. Gold. The love of Abraham implies a thorough knowledge of the tradition which derives from Abraham and forms the spiritual reality of the Jewish people, for without knowledge love is empty and meaningless. This brings the Rav to raise a startling question: Was Rabbi Gold a genuine master of Torah learning, that is was he truly a master of the classical sources? It is inconceivable that he should have raised such a question about any of the other figures whom we have discussed. Each was a great *talmid hakham*, known and acknowledged as such in all circles. Why then raise such an unseemly question about R. Gold? And why find it necessary to answer it publicly and positively? The reason is easy to come by. R. Gold was quite different from the other *gedolim* whom the Rav eulogized. He was a world leader of Religious Zionism which was in itself enough to cast suspicion on him in certain religious circles. He was a superb orator whose appearances drew large and enthusiastic crowds of fascinated listeners. He was an incomparable master of the interpretation and exegesis of midrash and aggadah. In all these regards, he was different from the types of great Jewish figures to whom the Rav was usually drawn. In his *hesped* he both explicates for us who this unusual figure really was and explains his personal admiration and affection for him.

After assuring us that R. Gold had deep mastery of classical talmudic learning, the Rav draws our attention to the full significance of his area of special achievement, the mastery of midrash and aggadah. Anyone who ever learned in a typical yeshiva is aware that mastery of the aggadic portions of the Talmud was not required. In fact, excessive preoccupation with this material served to call into question one's intellectual seriousness. It is then not surprising that Rabbi Gold was not recognized as a member in good standing of the elite fraternity of great and creative Torah scholars. The Rav sees it as his task to teach us how mistaken this attitude is.

He makes the point by telling us that as a youngster he once heard an address by R. Gold and was overwhelmed by the experience, not simply by the powerful oratory, but by the intellectual force of the presentation. "On that night this American rabbi opened up for me the gates of the hidden inner meaning of the aggadah. Suddenly I understood that "*drush*" is not only a matter of "*maggidut*," of preaching... that we must present the words of the Sages in accordance with their exact structure; that we must stress the central motif in their text and explicate their words just as we explicate a verse in the written Torah. Proper stress on a single word can shed new light on the entire pericope."[25]

If we are to take the Rav at his word, and there is every reason why we should, this experience of hearing R. Gold interpret a rabbinic aggadah was a transforming moment in his own life. To appreciate the full significance of this moment, we must remember that the youngster who was so affected that night by his newly won insight into aggadah, emerged in later life as one of the greatest masters of the exposition of midrashic and aggadic texts. Who better than the Rav could, on mature reflection, appreciate the significance of R. Gold as a *ba'al aggadah*? Who better than he could appreciate the extent to which this aspect of R. Gold's life accounted for at least part of the hidden *kedusha* of this paradigmatic Rosh-Hodesh man?

There is an important lesson to be learned from this discussion. In the *hespedim* which we have been studying, as in very much of his own public teaching, the Rav gave a prominent place to reflection on midrashic and aggadic texts. This great master of halakha was an equally great master of aggadah. In general, when he dealt with a topic he joined together in a kind of inseparable unity halakhic and aggadic analysis. This is true of the *hespedim* that are before us, but it is no less true of almost all his published work. It was certainly the case in most of his public discourses, with the possible exception of his regular Talmud shiurim. My contention is that he wanted to teach us that proper understanding of aggadic materials requires the same kind of intense intellectual effort that is required by halakhic materials. When he learned in his youth from Rabbi Gold that expounding a midrash is not just a matter of "maggidut," he became aware of the seriousness of aggadah as a branch of the Torah. I believe that he assigned to aggadah a place of critical significance in the whole body of Torah literature. This by itself may be a conventional enough attitude. What is distinctive is that, as I understand him, the Rav wanted us to learn that we need to bring to the exposition of aggadah the same intellectual tools that are required in the study of halakha. Conceptual formulation and analysis, systematic structuring, proper classification, exact understanding of language and terminology, are demanded by the study of aggadah as they are by the study of halakha. These must be informed by a feeling for the poetic, by literary imagination, by artistic sensitivity. They do not, however, take the place of the intellectual/analytic tools which are so characteristic of the Rav's treatment of a talmudic *sugya*.

Basically, I am arguing that in the *hespedim*, but not only there, the Rav has taught us one more aspect of the meaning of his regular affirmation that the halakha is the only authentic source of Jewish ideas and doctrines. This is not a rejection of aggadah, nor is it a denial of its importance in the formulation of Jewish doctrine. On the contrary, his own practice provides the strongest evidence of the high value that the Rav assigned to aggadah. What he tried to teach us is how to treat aggadah with the same intellectual seriousness as halakha, a methodology which transforms discussions of aggadah from pretentious sermonics to intensely serious explorations of fundamental Jewish doctrines and values. We might say that in this way the aggadah is absorbed into the world of halakha, that the boundaries which separate them are diminished, if not eliminated. In eulogizing R. Gold, the Rav made it clear that, in his view, there cannot be a responsible expounder of aggadah who is not, at the same time, a master of halakha. Midrash and aggadah are inseparable parts of Torah, not separate realms of Torah discourse. In these eulogies, as in much of his other work, the Rav showed us how to integrate aggadah into halakha, how to give to aggadah the rigorous structure which entitles it to be treated with the highest seriousness as a source of Jewish self-understanding.

Finally, we must take note of the Rav's *hesped* for the Talner Rebbitzen. Here we seem to have a very different model before us. The deceased was not a world-class rabbinic scholar or Jewish leader, although she was certainly a woman of great piety and unusual learning. Because of his family relationship to her and because for many years he saw her almost every day, the Rav had a special understanding of the character of this remarkable woman. As we might expect, he approaches the task of eulogizing her with the same tools and the same sense of great responsibility that he does in all the other cases. He sets forth a halakhic account of the obligation of *hesped*, followed by the familiar question, "Who was this woman?". As the Rav says, "We were always under the impression that we knew her well. Apparently, this assumption on our part was just an illusion, a mirage... the woman we met and greeted every morning—'gut morgen rebbitzen'—was a cryptic figure, kind of a mystery... Now we ask ourselves who was the woman who never omitted *tefillah be-tsibbur* [participation in communal worship], who never could catch up with the congregation, and who continued to recite her prayers long after the worshippers had left the synagogue?"[26] We see that the same problem which we face in knowing *gedolei Torah* of the first rank, confront us when we reflect on the personality of a woman of no such public standing and recognition, but of no less piety and perhaps of no less intellectual attainment. One suspects that the Rav would face this problem with any person. Rarely, can we be confident that we truly know any individual, even one with whom we have been in close contact. The problem is intensified when the individual is a person of rare stature, of great depth, of profound spirituality, and of serious learning, such as the Talner Rebbitzen.

To meet the double obligation of causing us to sorrow over our loss and to teach us to understand whom we have lost, the Rav uses here the same devices that we saw in the other eulogies. He establishes formal classifications into which he then fits the Talner Rebbitzen. He makes an important distinction between the Torah we learn from our fathers and that which we learn from our mothers. He calls upon his own experience to clarify that distinction, and then calls upon his personal knowledge of his subject to show us how effectively she lived her life as a transmitter of the tradition, and specifically of *torat imekha*, that which can be taught with unique understanding and effectiveness only by mothers.

The final step is to set forth a threefold account of the character and essential nature of the Talner Rebbitzen. She was a wise woman, a great woman, a dignified woman. The first two characterizations are based on biblical verses, and the third on a talmudic expression. Each is expounded with examples and anecdotes from her life. Through them the Rav paints a striking portrait of the Talner Rebbitzen, and in the process gives us a careful exposition of the meaning of the three traits which he ascribes to her. The same deep learning, the same penetrating insight, the same sense of loss, which moved the Rav in his *hespedim* for the great figures whom he eulogized earlier, are fully present in this eulogy for the Talner Rebbitzen.

There is also an even more intimate personal dimension than in the other eulogies. In his admiration for her, the Rav saw in the Talner Rebbitzen more than just the rare individual that she was. He saw her also, as we might expect, as an archetype of the essential Jewish woman, the true Jewish mother, the ideal Jewish woman. "Quite often when I extended 'gut shabbos' greetings to her, I used to think of the great women through the ages who represented with wisdom, greatness, and dignity the torat imekha. Consciously or unconsciously, I greeted not only her, but her mother and her mother's mother, the entire community of mothers who kept our tradition alive. I felt as if all of them had been assembled in the dining room of the Rebbitzen, as if Shabbat ha-Malka herself had been present there. The room looked the way I imagined Sarah's tent must have looked. It was enveloped in a cloud, and there was a burning candle; there was the shekhinah." Thus, he perceived the Talner Rebbitzen simultaneously as an individual whom he knew well and whom he saw daily, and as an embodiment of the archetype of the ideal Jewish woman/mother first embodied in the matriarch Sarah.

Our preliminary examination of the Rav's printed *hespedim* should serve to make us aware that a rich body of material awaits further serious study. These eulogies are not simply wonderful personal tributes. They are, at the same time, treasure houses of Jewish learning, of methodological sophistication, of poetic creativity, and of human sensitivity. In the hands of this incomparable master of halakha and aggada, these eulogies are important creative treatises of Jewish learning, and models of how to approach the understanding and evaluation of a human personality. Reasoned analysis and poetic portrayal are held in tight balance. A tearful sense of loss is fully integrated into brilliant halakhic exposition. The intersection between halakha and aggada is established, explored and exploited for the purposes of the eulogy. Even though the subjects were almost all people whom the Rav knew well and for whom he felt deep attachment, there is never a moment of false or excessive sentimentality. With this body of material, the Rav put us further into his debt, leaving us an added legacy of precious texts to study and models to imitate.

NOTES

[1] The six eulogies to which reference will be made in the course of this essay are as follows: "מה דודך מדוד" contained in Pinchas H. Peli, ed., "בסוד היחיד והיחיד" (Jerusalem, 1976), pp. 189-254: this is a eulogy for the Rav's uncle, R. Yitzhak Zev Soloveitchik, the Brisker Rav; "פליטת סופריהם"*ibid.*, pp. 255-294; this is a eulogy for R. Hayyim Heller; "בסתר" "ובנלוי" *ibid.*, pp. 295-330; this is a eulogy for R. Zev Gold; "נושאי הציץ והחושן", contained in essays of the Rav under the title, "דברי הגות והרכה" (Jerusalem, 198 1), pp. 187-194; this is all that was published of an apparently longer eulogy for R. Hayyim Ozer Grodzenski; "A Eulogy for the Talner Rebbe", in Joseph Epstein, ed., *Shiurei HaRav*, (New York, 1994, reprinted from edition of 1974), pp. 66-81; "A Tribute to the Rebbitzen of Talne", *Tradition*, 17(2), Spring, 1978, pp. 73-83. Most of these eulogies have been reprinted in other collections of the Rav's writings. A bibliography containing many of these references may be found in Zanvel E. Klein, "*Benei Yosef Dovrim:* Rabbi Joseph B. Soloveitchik, zzl: A Bibliography," *The Torah U-Madda Journal*, Vol. 4, 1993, pp. 84-133. All references in this essay are to the editions listed above.

[2] "A Tribute to the Rebbitzen of Talne," pp. 73-74.

[3] "פליטת סופריהם", 259-260.

[4] "נושאי הציץ והחושן", pp. 188-190.

[5] *Ibid.*, pp. 191-192.

[6] "יאידישע פערזענליבקייט איז געגליבען צו א ספר תורה" *Die Yiddishe Vokh*, Jan. 30, 1959-March 20, 1959, seven installments.

[7] b. Shabbat, 105b.

[8] b. Megillah, 26b.

[9] b. Kiddushin, 33b.

[10] b. Sanhedrin, IO la.

[11] "ימה דודך מדוד" pp. 199-200.

[12] M. Fox, "The Unity and Structure of Rabbi Joseph B. Soloveitchik's Thought," *Tradition*, 24(2), Winter, 1989, pp. 56-58.

[13] In a brilliant insight, the Rav calls attention to the difference of one word between Num. 20:29 and Deut. 34:8. The former reports that *all* the people mourned the death of Aaron, while the latter reports only that the people mourned the death of Moses. Aaron is the revealed personality, known and mourned by the entire nation. Moses is the hidden personality, known and mourned by the small elite that was capable of gaining some understanding of his essence and Ws greatness.

[14] "מה דודך מדוד" pp. 209-2 1 0.

[15] "A Eulogy for the Talner Rebbe," p.66.

[16] *Ibid.*, p.68.

[17] *Ibid.*, p.74.

[18] *Ibid.*

[19] *Ibid.*, pp. 75-76.

[20] *Ibid.*, p. 76.

[21] *Ibid.*, pp. 77-78.

[22] "בסתר ובנלוי", p. 305; for the previous discussion, see *Ibid.*, pp. 297-304.

[23] *Ibid.*, p. 306.

[24] *Ibid.*, P. 317.

[25] *Ibid.*, p. 320.

[26] "A Tribute to the Rebbitzen of Talne," p. 75.

Jacob Neusner

The Aggadic Role in Halakhic Discourses. Lanham. February 2001. University Press of America. Academic Studies in Ancient Judaism series. Volume I

The Aggadic Role in Halakhic Discourses. Lanham. February 2001. University Press of America. Academic Studies in Ancient Judaism series. Volume II

The Aggadic Role in Halakhic Discourses. Lanham. February 2001. University Press of America. Academic Studies in Ancient Judaism series. Volume III

A Theological Commentary to the Midrash. Lanham. April 2001. University Press of America. Academic Studies in Ancient Judaism series. Volume I. *Pesiqta deRab Kahana.*

A Theological Commentary to the Midrash. Lanham. March 2001. University Press of America. Academic Studies in Ancient Judaism series. - Volume II. *Genesis Raba.*

A Theological Commentary to the Midrash. Lanham. April 2001. University Press of America. Academic Studies in Ancient Judaism series. Volume III. *Song of Songs Rabbah*

A Theological Commentary to the Midrash. Lanham. April 2001. University Press of America. Academic Studies in Ancient Judaism series. Volume IV. *Leviticus Rabbah*

A Theological Commentary to the Midrash. Lanham. June 2001. University Press of America. Academic Studies in Ancient Judaism series. Volume V *Lamentations Rabbati*

A Theological Commentary to the Midrash. June 2001. University Press of America. Academic Studies in Ancient Judaism series. Volume VI. *Ruth Rabbah and Esther Rabbah I*

A Theological Commentary to the Midrash. June 2001. University Press of America. Academic Studies in Ancient Judaism series. Volume VII. *Sifra*

A Theological Commentary to the Midrash. July 2001. University Press of America. Academic Studies in Ancient Judaism series. Volume VIII. *Sifré to Numbers and Sifré to Deuteronomy*

A Theological Commentary to the Midrash. August 2001. University Press of America. Academic Studies in Ancient Judaism series. Volume IX. *Mekhilta Attributed to Rabbi Ishmael*

The Unity of Rabbinic Discourse. January 2001. University Press of America. Academic Studies in Ancient Judaism series. Volume I: *Aggadah in the Halakhah*

The Unity of Rabbinic Discourse. February 2001. University Press of America. Academic Studies in Ancient Judaism series. Volume II: *Halakhah in the Aggadah*

The Unity of Rabbinic Discourse. February 2001. University Press of America. Academic Studies in Ancient Judaism series. Volume III: *Halakhah and Aggadah in Concert*

www.ingramcontent.com/pod-product-compliance
Lightning Source LLC
Chambersburg PA
CBHW020632110726
47899CB00002B/742